Security and Terror

The publisher and the University of California Press Foundation gratefully acknowledge the generous support of the Ahmanson Foundation Endowment Fund in Humanities.

Security and Terror

AMERICAN CULTURE AND THE LONG HISTORY OF COLONIAL MODERNITY

Eli Jelly-Schapiro

UNIVERSITY OF CALIFORNIA PRESS

University of California Press, one of the most distinguished university presses in the United States, enriches lives around the world by advancing scholarship in the humanities, social sciences, and natural sciences. Its activities are supported by the UC Press Foundation and by philanthropic contributions from individuals and institutions. For more information, visit www.ucpress.edu.

University of California Press
Oakland, California

© 2018 by The Regents of the University of California

Chapter 1 was originally published in slightly different form as "Security: The Long History," *Journal of American Studies*, vol. 47, no. 1 (2013): 801–26, © 2013 by Cambridge University Press. All rights reserved. Reprinted with permission.

Chapter 5 was originally published in slightly different form as "'This Is Our Threnody': Roberto Bolaño and the History of the Present," *Critique: Studies in Contemporary Fiction*, vol. 56, no. 1 (2015): 77–93, © 2015 by Taylor and Francis Ltd. (tandfonline.com). All rights reserved. Reprinted with permission.

Brief portions of the Epilogue were originally published in slightly different form in "The Crazy: Writing the Iraq War," *The Nation*, October 29, 2012: 44–45, © 2012 by *The Nation*. All rights reserved. Reprinted with permission.

Library of Congress Cataloging-in-Publication Data

Names: Jelly-Schapiro, Eli, author.
Title: Security and terror : American culture and the long history of colonial modernity / Eli Jelly-Schapiro.
Description: Oakland, California : University of California Press, [2018] | Includes bibliographical references and index. |
Identifiers: LCCN 2017053887 (print) | LCCN 2017059017 (ebook) | ISBN 9780520968158 (ebook) | ISBN 9780520295377 (cloth : alk. paper) | ISBN 9780520295384 (pbk. : alk. paper)
Subjects: LCSH: War on Terrorism, 2001-2009. | War on Terrorism, 2001-2009, in literature. | Terrorism–United States. | National security–United States. | International relations and terrorism–United States. | Imperialism.
Classification: LCC HV6432 (ebook) | LCC HV6432 .J445 2018 (print) | DDC 363.3250973–dc23
LC record available at https://lccn.loc.gov/2017053887

27 26 25 24 23 22 21 20 19 18
10 9 8 7 6 5 4 3 2 1

For my parents

CONTENTS

Acknowledgments ix

Introduction: History, Narrative, and the War on Terror 1

1 · "All the World Was America":
The Long History of Homeland Security 20

2 · "A General Principle of Democracy":
Terror and Colonial Modernity 44

3 · "Choc en Retour": Security, Terror, Theory 74

4 · "Vanishing Points": Postcolonial America 105

5 · "This Is Our Threnody": Writing History as Catastrophe 140

Epilogue: Rupture and Colonial Modernity 163
Notes 179
Bibliography 203
Index 209

ACKNOWLEDGMENTS

Profound gratitude: To Hazel Carby, for opening up this project—and the worlds it addresses—so many times, with a few precise and luminous words. To Michael Denning, for countless clarifying readings of my work, and for demonstrating—through his indomitable capacities for collaborative inquiry—that intellectual labor can itself be a form of political praxis. To Alicia Schmidt Camacho, for reminding me what's at stake, and for showing me what's possible, in the classroom and on the page.

To Jean-Christophe Agnew, a wonderful teacher. To Lisa Lowe, whose urgent pedagogy provoked some of the questions at the core of this book. To Paul Gilroy, for support and inspiration. To You-Me Park and Henry Schwarz, for planting a seed. To Garnette Cadogan, interlocutor sui generis. To Colin Apple, Philip Bell, Goodloe Byron, Erik Lamb, Elizabeth Manekin, Nikki Smirl, Scott Statland, and Cody Upton—dear friends and guides. To Ed Krcma and Boris Pennington, for rigorous tea times, from Brooke Road to Osbaldeston. To my students, whose moral and imaginative thinking pushes my own, and restores my faith in what is to come. To my Yale comrades—among them Sigma Colón, Rossen Djagalov, Amina El-Annan, Daniel Gilbert, Joshua Glick, Tao Leigh Goffe, Sarah Haley, Andrew Hannon, Edward King, Monica Muñoz Martinez, David Minto, A. Naomi Paik, Ariana Paulson, J. Jesse Ramírez, Yenisey Rodriguez, Andrew Seal, Van Truong, and Gabriel Winant—for solidarities intellectual and otherwise. To Susan Amussen, Katherine Brokaw, Nigel Hatton, David Torres-Rouff, and the University of California, Merced Center for the Humanities, for providing me with a nurturing home in which to think and write at just the right time. To Samuel Amadon, David Bajo, Elise Blackwell, Liz Countryman, Susan Courtney, Holly Crocker, Michael Dowdy, Brian Glavey, Anne Gulick,

Anthony Jarrells, Catherine Keyser, Seulghee Lee, Nina Levine, Evren Ozselcuk, and Gretchen Woertendyke, and to all of my colleagues in the English Department at the University of South Carolina, for creating such an extraordinary community, and for welcoming me into it with kindness and warmth. To one of those colleagues, Greg Forter, for reading two iterations of this book, and for responding each time with vital and brilliant insight. To its anonymous reviewers, whose trenchant readings improved it immeasurably. To its editor, Niels Hooper, for listening to and hearing my ideas with acuity. To Bradley Depew, Jolene Torr, and Jessica Adams, for their crucial and consummate interventions.

To Krisztina Harsanyi, Tamas Jilling, and Andrea Jilling, for embracing me in their beautiful family. To Zsofia Jilling, whose grace and love touched every word. To Amália. To Joshua Jelly-Schapiro, who has taught me so much about writing and being in the world. And finally, to Katherine Jelly and Steven Schapiro, my first and greatest teachers; this book is for you.

Introduction

HISTORY, NARRATIVE, AND THE WAR ON TERROR

ON SEPTEMBER 11, 2001, General Mahmud Ahmed, director of Pakistan's Inter-Services Intelligence, was visiting Washington, D.C., as a guest of George Tenet, director of the CIA. Following that morning's attacks, the general's itinerary changed; he was summoned not to the office of his host but to that of Richard Armitage, George W. Bush's Deputy Secretary of State. As Armitage recalled the meeting, "I literally took [Ahmed] privately to my room and said: 'No American will want to have anything to do with Pakistan in our moment of peril if you're not with us. It's black or white.' And [Ahmed] wanted to tell me about history. He says, 'You have to understand the history.'" One can speculate as to the histories Ahmed had in mind: the British Raj, Partition, civil war in Pakistan, war between India and Pakistan, the role of Pakistan as a proxy for U.S. power in the region—the braided stories, in other words, of empire and its aftermaths in South Asia. But Armitage's focus was already fixed on the military project that would come to be known as the "War on Terror." He was firm in his response. "No," he insisted to his guest, "history begins today."[1]

In the days and weeks following September 11, the refusal of history became a central trope of George W. Bush's fast-building case for war. But the notion that history began on "9/11" was more than just a calculated neoconservative mantra. The idea was echoed, that autumn and thereafter, by columnists, critics, and cultural producers from across the political spectrum. In an essay published in the *Guardian* on September 14, 2001, the writer Jay McInerney foreshadowed the founding conceit of his own "9/11 novel" and so many others: "I have a feeling," he wrote, "that everything will be 'before' and 'after' now. As I walked through the streets at midnight, I thought of

Frank O'Connor's line at the end of *Guest of the Nation*: 'And anything that ever happened to me after I never felt the same about again.'"[2] In accord with the "before and after" frame signaled by McInerney, the scholarly response to the War on Terror has accented radical newness above continuity or genealogy. Since the opening stages of the wars in Afghanistan and Iraq, for example, countless critics have highlighted the emergence of a new "state of exception"—a diagnosis that reinforces the notion of the post–September 11 world as a time apart.

This book aims to resist and redress this assumption of historical rupture. It endeavors to show how the central political forms and ideas of the War on Terror both derive from, and reveal the persistence of, what I term the "long history of colonial modernity": the five-hundred-year history of European empire and its afterlives. Comprising a history of the present, this book also examines how our present's history is registered and reckoned with in contemporary culture. I begin by developing parallel genealogies of security and terror. I then turn to the question of how these conjoined paradigms—and the colonial rationalities and processes with which they intersect—are historicized in, and denaturalized by, works of theory and fiction.

In one such novel, Teju Cole's *Open City*, the narrator Julius, pausing from his contemplative walks around New York City, visits often with his friend and mentor Professor Saito, a Japanese-American veteran of an Idaho internment camp. Professor Saito is dying, and during one of their last conversations, the elderly man, looking back on the tumults of his lifetime, reflects on the confusion of war, the struggle to grasp the immensity of the suffering as it happens and the struggle to preserve it in memory: "There are towns," he observes, "whose names evoke a real horror in you because you have learned to link those names with atrocities, but, for the generation that follows yours, those names will mean nothing. Forgetting doesn't take long. Fallujah will be as meaningless to them as Daejon is to you."[3] The prosecution of imperial violence in the present, Professor Saito's words intimate, is conditioned by the elision or disavowal of imperial pasts. This is a truism of which Armitage was keenly aware when he eagerly declared the advent of history in 2001. And this is the cycle of imperial erasure and reproduction that this book labors to counter—by tracing the imperial origins of contemporary political and cultural forms, and by reflecting upon the strategies of representation that bring those origins into relief.

SECURITY, TERROR, AND COLONIAL MODERNITY

When in 1492 Christopher Columbus set out for Asia but instead happened upon the Bahamas, Cuba, and Hispaniola, his error inaugurated a specifically colonial modernity. Columbus's "discovery" of the New World helped precipitate the capitalist mode of production, the liberal state, new typologies of racial difference, and the discursive construction of Europe—and later "the West"—as the center of the world, the source and vanguard of historical progress.[4] Today, in the moment of imperialism's putative aftermath, the fundamental material and symbolic architecture of colonial modernity endures. The routes of continuity between the colonial past and postcolonial present are evidenced with an especial clarity, I want to argue, by the conjoined conceptual paradigms of security and terror.

"Security" is the keyword of contemporary governance. Economic security, financial security, national security, food security, social security, border security, job security, human security, environmental security, energy security, homeland security, and so on—security pervades political discourse. A basic human want, a normative social good, security is also a mode of power. Provoked by the advent of Homeland Security in 2001, scholars have in recent years offered an extensive critique of the violence done by and in the name of security. This critique, however, has centered on the political forms of the present, and has—with few exceptions—left unexamined the relationship between contemporary security formations and the longer history of the modern security project.

The security project emerged in the context of the settler-colonization of the New World and the innovation of capitalist social relations within Europe. One fundamental imperative of the nascent modern state, as John Locke affirmed, was to secure the processes of primitive accumulation—the extraction of resources, traffic in slavery, and enclosure of the commons—in both Old World and New. In accordance with Locke, Thomas Hobbes foresaw that the bourgeois logic of perpetual accumulation would require a corresponding, and likewise perpetual, expansion of political power—the limitless growth, in other words, of the security state. Writing in the mid-twentieth century, Hannah Arendt observed that the early modern vision of Locke and Hobbes still obtained. "Lest the motor of accumulation suddenly die down," she wrote, "the original sin of simple robbery" must be constantly repeated;[5] and the endless accumulation of capital, Arendt saw, necessitates the endless acquisition of political power. This truism is again brought into relief by the forms of "accumulation by dispossession," to borrow David Harvey's phrase, that prevail in the neoliberal moment—the forcing open of markets, the privatization of everything, the deliberate devaluation of assets and labor, the creation and manipulation of crises, the redistribution of wealth upward.[6] All of these strategies of dispossession, which engender ever more pervasive social and economic insecurity, are made possible by the threat and actuality of state violence. In one definition, neoliberalism signifies the extension of market rationality to all spheres of human social life. Relatedly, neoliberalism describes the invention and intensification of methods of "securitization"— the seizure or fabrication of non-capitalized space, and the transmutation of non-colonized entities and geographies into a concern of the security state.

The contradictions generated by processes of capitalist securitization are legitimated by, and deepen the effects of, racial thinking and practice. In its colonial origins, as David Theo Goldberg has observed, modern racial thought combined "naturalist" and "historicist" theories of difference.[7] The Spanish theologian—and humanist—Juan Ginés de Sepúlveda insisted, in the sixteenth century, that the indigenous people of the Americas were incapable of civilization. His compatriot Bartolomé de las Casas—an historian and Dominican friar—countered that the Indian, if lagging behind culturally and spiritually, could, in time, attain membership in universalisms both secular and theological. The debate between Sepúlveda and las Casas has been rehearsed repeatedly in the centuries since, as colonial methods of exclusion and extermination have coincided with narratives of development, modernization, and assimilation. In the context of the War on Terror, the ostensibly discordant but frequently symbiotic interrelation of naturalist and historicist racisms is on stark display. The "clash of civilizations" thesis, first enunciated by Samuel Huntington in 1992 but recited with new volume at the onset of the War on Terror, condemns the other to eternal confinement in a space outside of history. What Mahmood Mamdani has described as the "good Muslim, bad Muslim" thesis, meanwhile, suggests that privileged subjects from the "backward" regions of the world are capable of modernity. Today as in the past, these two racial imaginaries work together to mark the line between inside and outside and condition the uneven distribution of social and economic security within the realm of political belonging.

Both the securing of capitalist accumulation and the racial clarification of political order are enabled by the imagination and enactment of "emergency"— the politics of exception. Modern sovereignty emerged in response to the emergency of the "state of nature." The savages who inhabited this constitutive outside—what would become the colonized world, the "zone of exception par excellence," in Achille Mbembe's words—could be killed with impunity. The extralegal violence honed in the colony was subsequently sublimated in the legal apparatus of the modern state. The United States, for example, has been governed under one emergency or another since 1933, when President Roosevelt declared a national emergency to shore up the banking system. The conditions that might provoke the declaration of emergency today are multiple, ranging from financial crisis, to social unrest, to natural disaster, to foreign or domestic war. In each case, it is "security"—the security of the body politic, or the security of capitalist order—that permits the suspension of the law, by the law, in the name of the law. In the context of the War on Terror, the politics of exception operates in the name of security and under the euphemistic guise of terms such as "battlefield detainee" and "extraordinary rendition." As in the early modern era, the terror inherent in and expressed by civilization's others provokes the perpetual interventions of the security state, the violent conduct of which is compelled and concealed by the invocation of "emergency."

Chapter 1 examines these intersecting modalities of the modern security project—capital, race, and emergency—in turn. More specifically, I locate these political forms within two imbricated genealogies—the long history of colonial modernity, and the recent, twentieth-century, history of the U.S. security state. Though my emphasis here is on the latter-day and longue-durée continuities of the security project, I do not aim to deny the uniqueness of Homeland Security. My intention rather is to demonstrate that the particularities of the Homeland Security moment are elucidated when their contiguity with the long history of security thinking and governance—as with the more recent formations of Social Security and National Security—is brought into the analytic foreground. And inversely, I am concerned to convey how those same particularities clarify the essential and enduring rationalities of the modern security project.

The trope of "security" has long been joined to the trope of "terror."[8] In Immanuel Kant's formulation, the sublime terror of the non-civilized world demands a countermovement of Enlightenment reason and rationality, which will secure the European subject against the corporeal and metaphysical threat of barbarism. Terror, in other words, is a pretext for the security state. Terror is also a method of state power, as the history of Europe's modern empires reveals with a particular clarity. In 1919, at the highpoint of the British Empire, Winston Churchill argued for the use of poisonous gas in "[spreading] a lively terror" amongst "uncivilized tribes" (specifically, in this case, the Kurds).[9] In 1936, during the war waged by Italian fascism on Ethiopia, Benito Mussolini advised his military commander to "pursue a systematic policy of terror and extermination against the rebels and all accomplice populations."[10] Though not meant for public reception, the words of Churchill and Mussolini nonetheless represent unusually open acknowledgments of an otherwise unspoken truth: terror—terror as a method and effect of violence—is fundamental to the practice of colonial governance, and to the modern state more broadly. The centrality of terror to the modern state was brought into especially stark relief by the events of the French Revolution. In that moment—the moment of the liberal state's emergence—the dialectic of security and terror was articulated in the vocabulary of necessary intimacy rather than essential opposition. The Jacobin Reign of Terror was carried out by the Committee of General Security (along with the Committee of General Safety). Terror, Maximilien Robespierre put it, "is nothing other than prompt, severe, inflexible justice; it is therefore an emanation of virtue; it is less a particular principle than a general principle of democracy, applied to the most pressing needs of the nation."[11] In the period of the Thermidorian Reaction, when Robespierre himself met a prompt and severe end, terror was recast as the enemy of the state rather than a central element of its constitution—as the antithesis of security rather than its guarantor. The *narrative* of the War on Terror conforms to the latter paradigm; but the *conduct* of the War on Terror again reveals the ways in which terror is a fundamental technology of the modern security state, its imperial form in particular.

One basic argument of this book is that the intersecting genealogies of security and terror are obscured by the assumption that September 11 constituted a historical rupture. Chapter 2 demonstrates that the history and contemporary articulation of terror in particular—and the dialectic of security and terror more broadly—are concealed as well by cultures of erasure that are fundamental to modernity itself. As the conjoined concepts of fetishism and reification clarify, the commodity form renders invisible its own social history. The state likewise labors to elide its violent origins—to make its existence appear natural and fixed rather than historically produced and contingent. The critical historicization of capital and the modern state uncovers instead the terror that founds modernity's essential political and economic forms. But the latter critical revisions often reproduce aspects of the historiographic omissions they work to resist. Karl Marx, for example, imagines the terror of capital's birth as eventually giving way to the "silent compulsion" of economic relations. And meditations on the centrality of terror to the invention of the modern state—from Kant and G. W. F. Hegel to Hannah Arendt—tend to cast to the historiographic margins both the colonial conditions of that terror and its endurance beyond the moment of putative foundation. Chapter 2 counters these conjoined tendencies by highlighting the continuing centrality of state terror to extant processes of primitive accumulation.

Focusing on terror as a pretext for and method of the imperial security state, my inquiry is additionally guided by a third primary modality of terror—terror as a form of resistance to imperial power. The slaves that authored the Haitian Revolution intimated, in the act of violent revolt, that the seeds of a radical—anticolonial and universal—humanism would necessarily be sown in soil nurtured by the ashes of the plantation and the blood of its masters. In the mid-twentieth century, Frantz Fanon and other anticolonial thinkers avowed, in a kindred vocabulary, that the terror of colonial order would only yield when confronted with a counter-assertion of revolutionary violence. And today, the figure of the suicide bomber distills into subjective form the objective necropolitical logic of contemporary imperial power. The imperial state explains these instances of violent resistance as the expression of an essential native savagery rather than as a rational political response to, or reflection of, the terrors of empire. This is as true in the moment of the War on Terror, when terms such as "Islamic barbarism" enjoy a mainstream political currency, as it was in the sixteenth century.

During the course of the twentieth century, rightist parties across the world met the emergence of socialist and anticolonial internationalisms with a fluid synthesis of fascism, authoritarianism, and market fundamentalism. The ascent of the latter in particular coincided with the increasing prominence of "security," and correlatively "terror," in state discourse. With the imposition, proliferation, and intensification of neoliberal forms of accumulation, governments around the world today acknowledge and present security as the primary reason of state. The global disorder occasioned and exploited by neoliberal processes—characterized by profound *insecurity* for the bulk of the world, recurring economic crises, and endless war—demands the regulatory and punitive powers of the security state. Since the later stages of the Cold War but especially in its aftermath, any violent resistance—occasionally even nonviolent resistance—to neoliberalism is labeled by the state as "terror" and met with the securing "counterterror" interventions of the police or military. This logic is clarified by the declaration of a so-called War on Terror. The War on Terror, I argue, represents the latest iteration of a paradigm fundamental not simply to the neoliberal moment but to colonial modernity itself—a paradigm in which the imperial state, in the name of security, posits, generates, and violently responds to the terror resident in and emanating from its internal and external others.

Locating the moment of the War on Terror within deeper historical time, this book critically converges with an expanding field of contemporary historiography. In the early years of the wars in Afghanistan and Iraq—a high point for neoconservative ideology—a series of academic and popular books affirmatively tied America's existential struggle against terror to a tradition of confrontation between Western civilization and its others. Rightist intellectuals such as Niall Ferguson, Philip Bobbitt, and John Gaddis—seeking to defend both the War on Terror in particular and empire in general—highlighted the legal, philosophic, and military threads that connect the contemporary security apparatus with the longue-durée history of European and American imperialism.[12] Gaddis's *Surprise, Security, and the American Experience* (2004), for example, traces the Bush doctrine of preemptive war—according to which "security" is achieved through imperial expansion—back to the Indian wars of the nineteenth century. Another constellation of works offers a more critical historicization of the present. In *Cultures of War* (2010), the historian John Dower elaborates a series of analogies between the War on Terror and the Pacific Theatre of the Second World War, reflecting on the destructive consequence of imperial hubris in either historical moment. Writers such as Chalmers Johnson—in his *Blowback* series (*Blowback*, 2000; *The Sorrows of Empire*, 2004; *Nemesis*, 2008)—place the War on Terror on a single line of geopolitical cause and effect, examining the relationship between the late twentieth-century assertion of U.S. power abroad and the resistance to which it has given rise. My own approach shares with Dower and Johnson a basic insistence on the urgency of historical explanation. I am principally concerned, though, with genealogy above analogy or causality. The genealogical method, as theorized by Michel Foucault, avoids the search for causation and labors instead to apprehend and understand the present through an analysis of the complex, multiple, and contingent—never inevitable—historical contexts and processes from which it emerged. Thinking genealogically, this book situates the conceptual paradigms and political forms of the War on Terror within the long, planetary history of colonial modernity.

THEORIZING THE COLONIAL PRESENT

For the guardians of established political order, the terror of revolution is defined not simply by physical or corporeal destruction but by the capacities it contains for *abstraction*—the totality that is revealed within and by the collective self-consciousness forged in the moment of struggle. Edmund Burke condemned the revolution in France because of the blood it shed but also because of the "doctrine and theoretick dogma" it projected toward the world. Though the histories of "terror" and "theory" are inextricably bound, terror has been under-theorized. So too has security. In contemporary theory, the tropes of security and terror are—with important exceptions—approached obliquely. Their theorization is less a discrete analytic pursuit than an adjunctive product of three intersecting critical strands: the critique of spectacle; the critique of the politics of exception; and the critique of empire qua global capita.

Chapters 1 and 2 forground the continuity across time of colonial rationality, as expressed by the dialectic of security and terror. Considering how the critiques of spectacle, exception, and empire illuminate the longer history of the colonial present, chapter 3 persists in this basic route of inquiry. But I am simultaneously concerned here to emphasize and reflect upon the *geographic* implications of the contemporary reproduction of colonial political and economic forms. In a basic and important sense, the processes of combined and uneven development unfolding in the postcolonial moment are contiguous with the colonial era. Now as then, the imperial state enables the violent application of commodity rationality in the global South, thereby reproducing the geographic asymmetry between metropole and postcolony.[13] I also want to highlight, though, the inverse trajectory, the boomerang return—"choc en retour," in Aimé Césaire's phrasing—of colonial rationality to the advanced capitalist world. In his *Discourse on Colonialism* (1950), Césaire sought to shed light upon the colonial origins of intra-European genocide, a genealogy also identified by Arendt. More broadly, Césaire accented how the prosecution of colonial power disfigured the humanity of the European subject and deepened the terminal sickness in European civilization. My use of the concept is yet more expansive. Choc en retour, as invoked herein, signifies the reenactment in the postcolonial metropole—including the "Homeland" of the U.S. imperium—of various modes of governance and accumulation that were innovated or perfected in the space of the colony; it names, even more capaciously, the contemporary reverberation, in the global North and South alike, of intersecting, often unacknowledged imperial histories.

The critical theorizations of spectacle, exception, and empire, I contend, are conditioned by—and symptomatic of—this boomerang return. The critique of spectacle is responding to what Guy Debord termed the "colonization of everyday life," the turning inward of capital's imperial predations. The critique of exception is an effect of the enactment of "emergency" governance—ever the basic mode of colonial rule—within the juridical sphere of the liberal democratic state. And the critique of empire (qua global capital) is symptomatic of the return of colonial methods of accumulation to the economies of the advanced capital world. In more synthetic terms, these three instances of "return" evince the global normalization, in a moment marked by permanent war and perpetual neoliberal crisis, of emergency governance and economic insecurity.

If conditioned by this choc en retour, however, the intersecting critiques of spectacle, exception, and empire are unevenly revelatory of the colonial origins and essence of contemporary political and economic forms. This unevenness, I argue, is owed in part to theory's symptomatic tendencies—the ways in which certain works or premises of critique reprise not simply the vocabulary but the formal logics of their object. The contributions on which I focus in chapter 3 exemplify this formal echo. As authored by Jean Baudrillard and Slavoj Žižek, the critique of spectacle mirrors the ahistoricity of the image. In his 2002 essay "Welcome to the Desert of the Real," Žižek observes that the attacks of September 11, 2001, entered the world as narrative, as symbol—not as event and later as image, but as an "image-event."[14] In Baudrillard's reading, the event is taken hostage, consumed, by its image—and thus cleansed of any historical content.[15] In highlighting this evacuation, the critique of 9/11-as-spectacle itself struggles to look off screen—away from the "unforgettable incandescence of the images"[16]—and toward the concrete historical forces from which the event emerged. Similarly, the critique of exception—for which the work of Giorgio Agamben acts as a touchstone—often reinforces the assumption of rupture, the exceptionalism of the "post-9/11" state of exception. In *Precarious Life* (2004), Judith Butler reflects, in a largely ahistorical manner, on the "new war prison" and new juridical concept of "indefinite detention." Agamben's work, by contrast, is profoundly genealogical. In *Homo Sacer* (1998), for example, Agamben identifies the Nazi concentration camp as the space wherein the *conditio inhumana* is most absolute.[17] But in the context of "a new kind of war," Agamben's *State of*

Exception (2004) describes the U.S. military prison at Guantánamo Bay as the space wherein "bare life reaches its maximum indeterminacy."[18] This appeal to the exceptionalism of the "post-9/11" moment, however subtle, compounds the absence, in Agamben's historical framework, of a sustained engagement with the colonial origins of the politics of exception. The tendency of theory to mimic the form of its object is likewise evidenced by the third intervention I examine in chapter 3, Michael Hardt and Antonio Negri's *Empire* trilogy. Hardt and Negri's theorization of the new global imperial order emulates key tropes of the triumphalist enunciation of "globalization"—the idea that there is no longer a constitutive outside, to capital or to the space and subject of sovereignty, and the related assumption that the political and economic forms of this achieved globalism originate within and emanate from the advanced capitalist world. The universality of contemporary imperial order is evinced, in Hardt and Negri's account, by the "qualitative hegemony" of biopolitical production—forms of immaterial and affective labor that are ascendant in the post-Fordist economies of the global North but shape the cultural logics of production everywhere—and by the planetary projection of U.S. constitutionalism. My own argument in this chapter foregrounds the inverse trajectory—the return to the global North of colonial modes of governance, methods of accumulation, and conditions of social life—and accents more broadly the contemporary iteration of a colonial rationality that Hardt and Negri consign to the past.[19]

*

The tendency of left critique to conform to the logics of its object was observed by Walter Benjamin, in his "Theses on the Philosophy of History" (1940). In that enduringly resonant text, Benjamin highlighted the pitfalls of social-democratic historicism—a quasi-religious belief in the idea of history as progress, and an impulse to array unique moments of the past on a single chain of cause and effect, like the "beads of a rosary." Benjamin argued instead for an understanding of history as catastrophe, and a concomitant apprehension of the "constellation" that connects one's present to other epochs across time. This conceptualization of history's substance and shape is clarified by what Benjamin termed the "tradition of the oppressed," which teaches us—upon its own return—that the state of emergency within which we live has long been the rule in the colonized world. The postcolonial reverberations of Benjamin's interlocking insights will be audible, I hope, throughout this book.

RUPTURE AND THE PROBLEM OF REPRESENTATION

The conjoined political formations of the War on Terror and Homeland Security sanction a multitude of social processes—from war and occupation in Iraq and Afghanistan, to extrajudicial incarceration in Guantánamo Bay, to the militarization of the U.S.-Mexico border, to an assault on civil liberties and democratic culture within the United States. These formations also represent the state's attempt to discursively frame the world, and U.S. power in the world, at the dawn of the twenty-first century. Following the denouement of the Cold War two decades ago, the United States struggled to devise and impose an interpretive schema that equaled, in its binary simplicity and ideological force, the opposition of the capitalist "free world" to its unfree communist antithesis. Indeed, the ascendant post-1989 idea of the "end of history"—or "New World Order," as George H. W. Bush had it—announced an era beyond ideology. (And if history is over, narrative becomes somewhat redundant too.) The administration of George W. Bush and its enablers saw in the rupture of September 11 an opportunity not only to institute particular policies, but to compose a vocabulary and narrative that would guide U.S. global supremacy in the coming decades—that would herald not the end of history, but its urgent beginning (or resumption). The basic structure of this narrative predated the moment that conditioned its application. In 2000, the neoconservative think tank Project for the New American Century (PNAC) published an influential—and subsequently infamous—report entitled *Rebuilding America's Defenses: Strategy, Forces and Resources for a New Century*. This document outlined the necessity of an emboldened U.S. military apparatus, which would secure the "American homeland," wage "multiple, simultaneous major theatre wars," and perform "'constabulary' duties associated with shaping the security environment" in strategic regions across the world.[20] Technocratic language about defense spending dovetailed with more grandiose, and manifestly imperial, appeals to the righteousness of a "global security order" shaped in the image of "American principles and prosperity." The report regretfully acknowledged that the transformations in U.S. military infrastructure and attitude it called for would not be realized in the immediate term—"absent," that is, "some catastrophic and catalyzing event—like a new Pearl Harbor."[21] Not simply in the aftermath of, but indeed *during*, the "catastrophic and catalyzing" event of September 11, 2001, neoconservative officials and pundits imposed a narrative of imminent and interminable war.

They fashioned this narrative out of materials already on hand—the strategic and ideological substance of documents such as *Rebuilding America's Defenses*—and abiding colonial tropes of absolute civilizational difference and the white man's burden.

Across the aesthetic disciplines, the indistinction of the event and its narrativization provoked an acute crisis of representation. How to resist the calcification of the event into ideology? How to undo the fixity of the meaning attached to it by the security state? The early and still emblematic instances of the 9/11 novel responded to these questions by refusing any political or historical emplotment of the attacks. Works such as Jay McInerney's *The Good Life* (2006), Lynn Sharon Schwartz's *The Writing on the Wall* (2005), Helen Schulman's *A Day at the Beach* (2007), and Don DeLillo's *Falling Man* (2007) revolve around the intimate lives of bourgeois citizens of New York City struggling, in the days and weeks following September 11, with the intersections of collective trauma and interpersonal—often specifically sexual—discord. Dust from the Twin Towers in a downtown loft or actual fragments of a victim's body lodged underneath the skin of a survivor symbolize the sense that a certain security—the private, the corporeal—has been violated. These transgressions serve as metaphor for a greater violation—of the seemingly stable boundary between inside and outside, oneself and the world. The standard reaction to this violation is, in these fictions, to look and move inward—to retreat into the layered domestic spheres of self, home, city, homeland. This inward turning is joined to a corresponding temporal myopia, an unwillingness to look beyond the moment of putative rupture toward the histories to which it belongs.[22]

The title of DeLillo's *Falling Man* refers to an artist who haunts the city, and enacts its collective trauma, with his unannounced restagings of a body arrested in flight—a performance that evokes the bodies that fell to their deaths from the upper floors of the World Trade Center towers on September 11, captured in iconic photographs against the buildings' austere geometry, or beheld in person. Like the spectacle of the attacks, the falling body is suspended outside of time. Just as each televisual repetition of the towers falling reinforces the event's historical dislocation, the Falling Man keeps our vision fixed on the moment of rupture, away from both past and future.[23] DeLillo's novel has a similar effect. Encountering the same aporia as Žižek and Baudrillard, fictions such as *Falling Man* both evince and struggle to evade the ahistoricity of the image-event.

Escaping assimilation by the conjoined logics of historical erasure and geographic myopia requires a different framing of, less than a different answer to, the problem of representation. It requires, more specifically, reckoning with the ways in which it is not only the terror of the singular spectacular event that incites the crisis of representation, but the terror of the society of the spectacle, or indeed capitalist modernity, broadly conceived—not only the towers coming down, in other words, but their existence in the first place.

How to articulate unique moments of catastrophe with the catastrophe of history itself? How to grasp, in Benjamin's words, "the constellation which [our] own era has formed with a definite earlier one"? These questions are posed and engaged by an emerging formation of postcolonial American novels, which locate the colonial content of the contemporary United States within hemispheric and global imperial histories. Chapter 4 focuses on three such works. Traveling across space and time, from post–September 11 New York to postcolonial Nigeria to Germany during the Second World War, Teju Cole's *Open City* (2011) excavates buried histories of violence and reveals their imbrication, aboveground and below. Articulating the long global history of uneven development with militarized neoliberalism, Mohsin Hamid's *The Reluctant Fundamentalist* (2007) highlights the "atavistic and newfangled" nature of contemporary imperial forms—the concurrence of retrograde racial imaginaries and crude methods of accumulation with hyper-modern information technologies and financial instruments.[24] The eponymous narrator of Junot Díaz's *The Brief Wondrous Life of Oscar Wao* (2007) describes his native Santo Domingo as the "Ground Zero of the New World"—the site of modernity's foundational terror, the reverberations of which remain, to borrow Édouard Glissant's phrase, "obsessively present."[25] Tracing the routes of contiguity between the fifteenth century and the twenty-first, the Dominican Republic and New Jersey, Díaz's novel reflects upon the modes of collection and transmission—the fable or the rumor; the body; the written word—through which the long history of empire and its afterlives might be made visible.

The term "postcolonial," read literally, denotes the time beyond modern colonialism. In a different interpretation, however, the postcolonial names the resumption or rearticulation of colonial culture, in the metropole and the colony, after the moment of formal independence. As Simon Gikandi defines it, "postcolonialism is a code for the state of undecidability in which the culture of colonialism continues to resonate in what was supposed to be its negation."[26] This definition describes precisely the (post)coloniality of the United States, which is at once the first postcolonial nation and the first neocolonial nation—an "infant empire" in the moment of independence and a fully mature, even declining, empire today. But as Jenny Sharpe has observed, when applied to the contemporary United States, the term postcolonial usually has a more limited resonance: "postcolonial," she writes, "does not name [the United States'] past as a white settler colony or its emergence as a neocolonial power; rather, it designates the presence of racial minorities and Third World immigrants."[27] In dialogue with writers such as Cole, Hamid, and Díaz, this book does not simply *designate presence*, but *excavates the past in the present*. I endeavor, that is, to illuminate how overlapping imperial histories—the settler-colonization of the New World, European colonialism in Africa and Asia, and more recent projections of U.S. power across the formerly colonized world—imbue and shape the cultural formations and social relations of the present, within and beyond the boundaries of the United States.

Demonstrating the possibilities of historical recovery, Cole, Hamid, and Díaz possess a concomitant sensitivity to enduring modes of concealment and forgetting. *Open City* meditates on the ways in which the coloniality of the War on Terror is both obscured and enabled by the elision of imperial histories. *The Reluctant Fundamentalist* reveals how the futurism of finance capital and nostalgia of militaristic nationalism disable critical reckoning with the history of the present. *Oscar Wao* implies that the silencing of the past makes possible its eternal return. This attention to cultures of archival erasure is expressed, moreover, by the form and not merely the content of each novel. All three texts self-reflexively perform their own inability to completely transcend—or indeed their own complicity in—the silencing of the past and its presence. In *Open City*, Julius's narrative voice is affectively deadened, performing the repression that the intellectual substance of his historical insights aims to undo. The monologic form of *The Reluctant Fundamentalist* stages an attempt at historical edification—as the Pakistani narrator Changez labors to educate his American companion on the extant history of Euro-American imperialism—that is not met, in the novel itself, with any gesture of empathetic recognition. And the unilateral narrative voice of *Oscar Wao*'s Yunior calls attention to those voices that remain silent, that do not possess the power of self-narration and can only be made audible through the extrinsic act of fictive imagination.

In my readings of fiction, I am especially concerned with how novels betray and, often, self-critically address their own capacity as one origin and repository of historical narrative—one site, among the manifold formal and informal venues of historical production, wherein both archival presences and absences are created. Reflecting upon and dramatizing the politics of narrative form, self-reflexive novels in particular can help us think about the dialogue between two moments of representation: the naturalization and deconstruction of various structures of dominance. Through what narrative strategies, for example, is colonial rationality—the ideological frameworks that order the peoples and places of the world within hierarchies of race, culture, and time, and that guide imperial methods of governance and accumulation—established and normalized? And through what narrative strategies might colonial modes of reading and writing the world be exposed, undone, and countered? The novels that I consider are engaged, in specific ways and to varying degrees, with these essential questions. But in the broadest sense, I am interested in their close attention to the production of "history" as narrative—an attention, crucially, that includes a fundamental concern with those archival silences that either evade or are an effect of the act of representation.

Both the potentialities and pitfalls of literary witness are confronted with a particular urgency by the writer whose work I examine in chapter 5, Roberto Bolaño. In accord with the fictions of Cole, Hamid, and Díaz, Bolaño's work—which was ecstatically received across the Anglophone world upon its translation, beginning in 2003—defies the trope of rupture.[28] Bolaño's counterpoint to the historical myopia of the "post-9/11" lens, though, is found in his rendering of another epochal September 11—September 11, 1973, the date on which a military coup overthrew the elected president of Chile, Salvador Allende, and installed in his place the rightist dictatorship of Augusto Pinochet. Using September 11, 1973—in conjunction with an allied moment of rightist reaction, the brutal state response to student demonstrators in Mexico City in 1968—as a prism that refracts the planetary history of modernity, novels such as *Amulet* (1999) and *The Savage Detectives* (1998) imagine the space of ostensive rupture not as a wall that blocks off the past and the world but as an opening that brings deeper histories into view. Confined to a bathroom stall during the army's occupation of the National Autonomous University of Mexico (UNAM), accompanied only by a book of poems, the narrator of *Amulet*, Auxilio, perceives the imbrication of past, present, and future. "The year 1968 became the year 1964 and the year 1960 became the year 1956. But it also became the years 1970 and 1973 and the years 1975 and 1976."[29] In *The Savage Detectives* this trans-temporal recognition is joined to a de-territorial consciousness and desire; Arturo Belano (Bolaño's fictional alter ego) and his comrades move from the space and time of catastrophe in Mexico and Chile in 1968 and 1973, to postcolonial Africa, post-Franco Catalonia, and Sandinista Nicaragua (among other places). This global imagination is realized with especial scope and depth in Bolaño's magnum opus *2666* (2004)—a novel that traces two intersecting genealogies of the present: the late twentieth-century history of neoliberal transformation in Latin America, which leads from Chile in 1973 to the U.S.-Mexico frontier at the turn of the millennium, and the longer history of permanent global war, which unites colonialism, fascism, and militarized neoliberalism on one spatial and temporal map. *2666*'s rendering of these histories highlights the mutual inherency of civilization and barbarism, security and terror. One correlate of Bolaño's expansive historical and geographic consciousness, in other words, is a heightened sensitivity to the affiliation of security and terror—the terror, and the insecurity, that accompanies the modern security project. This abiding theoretical concern is central as well to *By Night in Chile* (2000) and *Distant Star* (1996), two novels set in Chile, in the era and aftermath of Pinochet, that meditate on the complicity of literature and state violence. The latter intimacy is defined by a kind of formal mimicry. Like the novels of Cole, Hamid, and Díaz I discuss in chapter 4, Bolaño's fiction self-reflexively dramatizes the problem of reprisal—the ways in which the technologies of erasure or "semblance" intrinsic to capital and the state are reproduced by the apparatuses of representation, literary and otherwise. But literature, Bolaño's work demonstrates, is also capable of formal transcendence—the blasting open of, rather than confinement by, the trope of historical rupture.

*

Just as the War on Terror's prehistory was elided by the mantra "post-9/11," the continuance of its narrative frameworks and political forms was obscured by a conjuncture of putative endpoints. First, the 2008 election of Barack Obama communicated, among many other political feelings, popular discontentment with the Bush administration's military adventurism. In the months following his inauguration, Obama oversaw the drawdown of the U.S. military presence in Iraq, and outlined a more protracted schedule for eventual withdrawal from Afghanistan. The Obama White House made a point of retiring the phrase "War on Terror," tacitly replacing it with the more technocratic heading "Overseas Contingency Operations." Second, the "Arab Spring" of 2011 demonstrated to a global audience that progressive political transformations in the Middle East and North Africa would be brought about not via aerial bombardment by U.S. warplanes, but from below, through popular struggle. The critique emanating from Cairo's Tahrir Square and indeed across the region voiced a rejection of both the War on Terror and the neoliberal imposition with which it is bound. Third, in May 2011, U.S. Special Forces assassinated Osama bin Laden, an extrajudicial killing that was consumed by much of the U.S. public as a cathartic conclusion to the decade of militarism occasioned by the terrorist attacks of September 11, 2001. Though the killing of bin Laden was not the primary goal of the wars in Afghanistan and Iraq, the achievement of the former nonetheless served to signal the redundancy of those conflicts.

Mirroring and magnifying the false rupture of September 11, the "sense of an ending" implied by this series of events encouraged the concealment of imperial histories and obfuscation of extant imperial processes. In texts such as Kathryn Bigelow's acclaimed but controversial 2012 film *Zero Dark Thirty*, which chronicles the pursuit and assassination of Osama bin Laden, we can perceive the outlines of a narrative framework that will displace the ongoing disasters of Iraq and Afghanistan—the brutality that unfolded and continues to unfold therein—with the ultimate triumph of bin Laden's assassination. We can discern, in other words, the techniques of historical distortion that will work to absolve the War on Terror of its own manifestly imperial substance, thereby creating the conditions for future reenactments of colonial rationality.

There do, however, exist myriad examples of cultural texts that counter the cycle of historical erasure and imperial reproduction, by excavating buried histories and by reminding us that the War on Terror is a present-tense phenomenon. Notably, a growing body of War on Terror veterans' narratives illuminates the lingering effects of war's traumas, summoning a tragedy we have learned to forget. Ben Fountain's novel *Billy Lynn's Long Halftime Walk* (2012)—unfolding over one day, and centering on the jingoistic pageantry of the Dallas Cowboys' Thanksgiving Day game—chronicles the surreal immersion of Bravo Company in the commercial spectacle of the War on Terror's domestic production. And Atticus Lish's novel *Preparation for the Next Life* (2014) follows Skinner, a veteran of the Iraq War, and Zou Lei, an undocumented immigrant from China's remote northwest, as they fall in tragic love, wander the far reaches of New York's outer boroughs, and struggle to survive in a Homeland defined by pervasive insecurity and quotidian terror. In conversation with these two texts, I offer in the epilogue a summary reflection on the false beginning and false endings of the War on Terror—the ways in which the assumption of rupture enables the resumption of colonial culture and process.

There is one moment of historical rupture that I am concerned to avow—the "discovery" of what would become the Americas, an event that founded the colonial modernity within which we still live. The political and ontological forms born of or conditioned by that moment continue to shape the world in profound ways. The articulation of capital and state terror, which was clarified by the plunder of the New World and institution of chattel slavery, and which was accelerated by later manifestations of European imperialism in Africa and the Indian sub-continent, endures. And today as in the early modern era, the terrors of the security state are justified and obscured by a particular way of imagining the world and its inhabitants—one that assumes "the West" is a synonym for, or privileged exponent of, the universal; and one that marks political boundaries, and polices their internal contents, via appeal to the idea of race and other modes of difference. Confronting the presence of these colonial forms, this book submits, requires that we register and reckon with their long history.

ONE

"All the World Was America"

THE LONG HISTORY OF HOMELAND SECURITY

The dialectic of security and insecurity, like that of security and terror, is central to the philosophy and form of the modern state. For John Locke and Thomas Hobbes, the insecurity—or terror—of the state of nature necessitates the ascent of the sovereign and constitution of the social contract; the state arises to delineate what is secured from what is not, civilization from savagery, inside from outside, citizen from non, the bearer of rights from the rightless. Despite the reciprocal emergence of security thinking and the modern state, the absolute saturation of social and political discourse with security rhetoric is a twentieth-century phenomenon. In the United States, Social Security acquired its rhetorical power and bureaucratic form in the 1930s. The postwar years witnessed the emergence of National Security as an organizing principle of governance. And in the aftermath of September 11, 2001, Homeland Security has attained discursive prominence, giving name to a new state form. In this chapter, I argue for the efficacy of conceptualizing the above-mentioned security paradigms together—shedding light upon the ways in which, for instance, Social and Homeland Security are bound up in one another, sharing both a genealogy and a political rationality. This common genealogy and rationality, I contend, can be traced to the advent of colonial modernity, and to the settler-colonization of the New World in particular. Countering ahistorical accounts of post-9/11 political-economic order, this chapter situates the contemporary manifestation and twentieth-century evolution of security discourse and practice within the long history of modernity at large.

This expansive historical framework, I contend here, as throughout this book, is essential to any critical reckoning with the political forms and narratives of the imperial present. My objective is not to deny the transformations embodied in the Homeland Security state, but to demonstrate the ways in which those transformations are contiguous with—rather than a departure from—the long and recent histories of the modern security project. Essayed in this chapter, to borrow from Fredric Jameson (for his "capitalism" I substitute "security"), "is a dialectical view of [security] ... in place of the latter's breaks and discontinuities: for it is the continuity of the deeper structure that imposes the experiential differences generated as that structure convulsively enlarges with each new phase."[1] Newness, in other words, is both a consequence and expression of continuity.

My analysis proceeds through an examination of three elemental relations: security and capital, security and race, and security and emergency. Each of these relations works with and through the others, and all are fundamental to the constitution of a specifically colonial modernity. The security state emerges to guarantee the process and outcome of capitalist accumulation, in the colony as in the metropole. The securing of private property is enabled by and in turn reinforces race thinking and practice, which also functions to structure internally, and mark the external boundaries of, the political community. The capitalist and racial logics of the security state dovetail with the politics of emergency. The enactment of emergency or exception legitimates the preemptive and punitive violence of the security state; sanctions extra-legal forms of accumulation by dispossession; and clarifies the racial distinction between the bearer of rights and the rightless, human and infrahuman.

SECURITY AND CAPITAL

Though the lexiconic proliferation of security thinking is a relatively recent phenomenon, the security project was manifold in its inception. The state was founded to secure the sovereign, "the People," and the identity, personhood, and liberty of the individual subjects that composed the body politic. All of these principles, meanwhile, were underlain by the security of property. Here Enlightenment philosophers of government and political economy were in agreement. Security was central to the rise of the modern state and, as Mark Neocleous has observed, to the ascendance of the bourgeois property rights enshrined therein.[2] The meaning and object of the term "security" is always contested; the vocabulary of security animates movements of resistance as well as processes of dispossession and domination. In its ascendant form, though, the modern security project is constructed and deployed by and in the service of the state and capital—to justify discursively and provide structural mechanisms for the accumulation, uneven distribution, and maintenance of political and economic power.

"In the beginning," Locke wrote, "all the world was America." In the beginning, in other words, all the world—untamed and uncultivated—invited the virtuous procedures of primitive accumulation. In the opening paragraphs of "Of Property," the fifth chapter of his *Second Treatise of Government* (1689), Locke introduces what is often termed his "labor theory of property." Because "every man has property in his own person," he is rightfully entitled to whatever he extracts or derives from nature: "For this labour being the unquestionable property of the labourer, no man but he can have a right to what that is once joined to."[3] Crucially, in claiming land and laboring upon it, thereby increasing the bounty derived from that land, man is in fact increasing, or "improving," the "common stock" of humanity: "he that encloses land, and has a greater plenty of the conveniences of life from ten acres than he could have had from a hundred left to nature, may truly be said to give ninety acres to mankind." The dispossession of common lands for the purpose of industrious cultivation is, Locke insisted, in effect a gift to the dispossessed, the Yorkshire peasant and indigenous American alike. "I ask," Locke wrote, "whether in the wild woods and uncultivated waste of America, left to nature, without any improvement, tillage, or husbandry, a thousand acres yield the needy and wretched inhabitants as many conveniences of life as ten acres of equally fertile land in Devonshire, where they are well cultivated."[4] North American land, lying fallow due to the indolence of its native inhabitants, invites the intervention of the European settler, who through his labor will increase the product of the land and thus the stock of mankind in general.

In a telling passage in "Of Property," Locke writes that "the grass my horse has bit, the turfs my servant has cut, and the ore I have digged . . . become my property without the assignation or consent of anybody."[5] The phrase "the turfs my servant has cut" intimates that the property owner is entitled to the produce of the labor of anyone he hires or forces to work upon his land. Though "every man has property in his own person," the product of labor ultimately belongs, in Locke's formulation, not to the laborer but to the owner of the property upon which the laborer works. "Improvement," then, might be achieved not just through the enterprising individual whose industry animates the dormant commons, but through the institutions of wage labor and chattel slavery. It is the purpose of government to facilitate, and to *secure*, this process of expropriation and improvement.

Contrary to Locke, Hobbes argues that property is not intrinsic to the state of nature but is the invention of political authority, of the sovereign who can secure the possession of goods and land and oversee their improvement through industry. Property, in other words, only emerges as a concept when conjoined with security. Hobbes is close to Locke, though, when, in an oft-cited passage from *Leviathan*, he holds forth on the necessity of labor discipline. While the unable should receive the charity of the sovereign, he writes, "for such as have strong bodies . . . they are to be forced to work; and to avoyd the excuse of not finding employment, there ought to be such Lawes, as may encourage all manner of arts; as Navigation, Agriculture, Fishing, and all manner of Manifacture that requires labor."[6] The duty of the sovereign is to provide security for private property, and to compel through law the labor of those who hold no title to the means of production.

Securing the Social

One lineage of Social Security can be traced to 1834, when the Poor Law Amendment Act was passed in England and Wales. Systems of localized poor relief had existed since at least the mid-sixteenth century in England, but not until the 1834 Act was the administration of poor law centralized and codified at the level of the state. The 1834 Act created a network of workhouses, which absorbed the unemployed into institutions of disciplined and disciplinary labor. The Act sought a solution to the problem of the general insecurity and "superfluous" populations created by early industrial capitalism. Dispossessed of the means of their own subsistence, the proletariat is forced to enter the market to sell their labor for a wage. But there is of course never a guarantee of employment and thus the state must intervene, in a biopolitical manner, to ensure the reproduction of the working classes. In one sense, the poor law provided a measure of security—miserable, horrid security, in the case of the workhouses: "houses of terror," Marx called them in *Capital*—to a population defined by its insecure existence, its naked subjection to the basically inhuman laws of the market.[7] In another sense, though, poor laws protected the bourgeoisie from the threat of large-scale social unrest and helped ensure the maintenance of capitalist property relations.[8] This dual purpose—securing the individual (and the hetero-familial unit to which *he* belongs) and securing the larger capitalist order—characterized the Social Security provisions inaugurated a century later on the other side of the Atlantic.

Contemporary social insurance programs, though, differ from earlier "poor laws" in important ways. If in eighteenth-century England the poor laws provided a "charity" to the unemployed, Social Security is allocated only to those who contribute to its funding. The Poor Law Act of 1834 demanded labor from its beneficiaries, while Social Security limits its benefits—with few exceptions—to those who labor. The insurance component of Social Security, Jennifer Klein has argued, inspired the rapid proliferation of non-state, for-profit insurance providers[9]—a moment of entrepreneurial ingenuity in which a capitalist industry arose to protect people against the ravages of capitalism. The market is the solution to the market: a refrain that would echo loudly in the latter part of the century, and indeed one that continues to reverberate in the neoliberal moment, in the context of recurring economic crises.

The securitization of the social went hand in hand with its capitalization. Security became not simply something provided by the government, but something purchased on the market. The biocapitalist industries of life and health insurance emerged in concert with the biopolitical functions of the Social Security state. One object of security for both state and business, in other words, became *life itself*—an evolution that enabled the broadening and deepening of security governance, the intensification of its effect upon the individual and social body.[10] The tripartite pact between state, business, and labor—consolidated to an even greater degree following the Second World War—blunted the class contradictions at the heart of the security/insecurity binary and contributed to the hegemonic reach of the security project. The ultimate effect was the continuation of capitalist social relations, the reproduction of a social order based on the security of private property and accumulation in perpetuity.

Security in the Shadow of War

From its inception, but with a particular intensity following the Second World War, the Social Security project dovetailed with the rhetoric and policy of National Security. During both the Truman and Eisenhower administrations, arguments made for the expansion of Social Security deployed the vocabulary of National Security. Major public infrastructure projects such as the Interstate Highway System—inaugurated by the Federal Aid Highway Act of 1956—and Saint Lawrence Seaway reconstruction—a project undertaken jointly with Canada, which enabled the development of massive hydroelectric power works, and which significantly expanded commercial shipping routes from the Atlantic to the Great Lakes—were likewise justified on National Security terms. Sputnik and the Soviet threat it embodied, meanwhile, occasioned sharp increases in math and science funding, initially allocated for in the National Defense Education Act of 1957—another instance of a major federal investment in domestic public infrastructure made in the name of National Security.[11] Generally speaking, the welfare state and the warfare state emerged from the war closely entwined, and would remain conjoined for the next two decades.

Expanding and deepening its social infrastructure at home, during the early stages of the Cold War the United States worked to construct a "Keynesian empire" abroad. This National Security paradigm was founded on a developmentalist logic that cohered with domestic policy, specifically Social Security. In the immediate aftermath of the war, the United States asserted itself as a world power intent on creating and dictating a new international political and economic order—the initial manifestations of which were the European Economic Recovery Program (the Marshall Plan) and the financial framework conceived at Bretton Woods, New Hampshire, in 1944. The intellectual rationale for the Bretton Woods system was capitalist security—the belief that peace amongst nations depended upon a liberal system of international trade, one that would be regulated by select governments and supported by international financial institutions (created at Bretton Woods) such as the International Monetary Fund (IMF) and World Bank (known in 1945 as the International Bank for Reconstruction and Development, or IBRD). Though a departure from the explicitly territorialized logic of the modern colonial system, the international economic order devised at Bretton Woods and instituted in the decades to come maintained the stark divide between the overdeveloped global North and underdeveloped global South. It maintained, moreover, a commitment to the ethos of "free enterprise." The architects and authors of U.S. policy during the Cold War imagined the freedom of enterprise as that freedom which conditions the possibility of all others. Here we find a more modern version of the Enlightenment axiom that there can be no liberty and security prior to the liberty and security of private property.

Neoliberal Security

In the late 1960s and 1970s, the particular economic expression of U.S. foreign policy underwent a dramatic change. Before the close of the 1960s, "embedded liberalism"—the economic order, based on a market sphere subject to extensive social constraints, that facilitated high levels of economic growth in the advanced capitalist world throughout the 1950s and 1960s—had begun to show signs of distress. In the early 1970s, a conjunction of factors—notably energy crises, high unemployment, and inflation—resulted in fiscal crises across the global North, and the Bretton Woods system of international financial regulation broke down. Embedded liberalism no longer seemed capable of guaranteeing the conditions for capital accumulation. The alternative that established itself in the early 1970s, and that has remade the capitalist world in the years and decades since, is neoliberalism.

Broadly defined, neoliberalism signifies an economic order wherein markets are deregulated, trade is liberalized, industries and services are privatized, and market rationality is imposed upon all facets of social life. Whereas in classical liberalism the state is thought to confer legitimacy upon the market, in the neoliberal order this relationship is reversed: the market legitimates the state. And whereas in classical liberalism the social and the economic are imagined as separate spheres, each conforming to its own rationality, under neoliberal governance the distinction between the social and the economic, society and the market, is blurred or dissolved completely. American neoliberalism in particular, Foucault observed, "involves ... the generalization of the economic form of the market ... throughout the social body and including the whole of the social system."[12]

Friedrich Hayek, one of neoliberalism's intellectual founders, argued—in Foucault's paraphrasing—that "the general form taken by the institutional framework in a renewed capitalism should be a game of enterprises regulated internally by a juridical-institutional framework guaranteed by the state."[13] The mechanism of competition between individuals or between (personified) enterprises, which founds the state and is guaranteed by it, and which is "regulated internally" by the formal dictums of the rule of law, is the economic rationality formulated by the original neoliberals, and their argument for the possibility of capitalist renewal. The juridical foundation that allows for and secures free enterprise was affectionately described, by Hayek, as the "science of liberty."[14] This is not a condition of laissez-faire, but of a pure market space deliberately created through government intervention (though as Karl Polanyi noted, laissez-faire itself was planned). Free enterprise, in other words, is imagined in neoliberal thinking as the one true purpose of government. Any curtailment of the free exercise of market competition is a violation of the most essential and highest human liberty. The introduction of this fundamentalist ideology into the Cold War milieu, at a time of economic crisis—when the discovery of new sources of surplus value was an urgent imperative of both class and state—provided the intellectual impetus for new assertations of U.S. imperialist power. It also provided a policy prescription and structural framework for the re-catalyzing of capitalist accumulation. The forcing open of markets; the privatization of everything, including social services and public welfare programs; the deliberate devaluation of assets and labor (so as to enable their later seizure by currently idle, overaccumulated capital)—these latter-day methods of dispossession are sanctioned by the institutional mechanisms of the IMF, World Bank, and World Trade Organization (WTO), and enforced by both national militaries and private security forces.[15]

If starkly opposed in certain respects, New Deal liberalism and neoliberalism both belong to the modern security project. "Securitization," as the term is used herein, signifies the transformation of an issue, concept, asset, or geography into a security concern. Though the New Deal names the largest expansion of public assistance programs in the nation's history, one of its consequences was the securitization of the social, the implication of social welfare within the process and logic of capitalist accumulation. Paradoxically, then, the New Deal moment—the private insurance industries that emerged therein, and the appropriation by corporate entities of Social Security rhetoric—prefigured one defining aspect of neoliberal order: the subjection of the social sphere to market rationality, market calculation. In the late twentieth century, new mechanisms of securitization arose, most notably within private financial institutions in New York and London, and in the context of a dramatic increase in the importance of financial speculation to the engine of accumulation. In the latter instance, the now more explicit invocation of "securitization" refers to the amalgamation and packaging of financial assets, shares of which are then sold as securities. The avowed intention is to distribute risk amongst a wider pool of investors. In practice, though, the engineering and proliferation of ever more opaque securities—particularly those backed with sub-prime mortgages—contributed to the onset of the financial crisis in 2008.

But the larger point is this: "securitization" is a euphemism for the occupation—or fabrication, in the most recent case—of previously non-capitalized space. It is a euphemism, that is, for the continuance of primitive accumulation—the same processes of capital generation the modern security project was conceived to protect.

Securitizing the Homeland

In the nascent stages of the War on Terror, the Bush administration set out to accelerate the privatization of government. Beginning with the onset of neoliberal policy prescriptions in the 1970s and with increasing intensity in the decades since, governmental bodies in the United States—at the federal, state, and municipal levels—have sought to outsource many of their traditional responsibilities. The partial or complete privatization of prisons, airports, hospitals, waste removal, public utilities, war, etc., has proceeded apace under the guise of "public-private partnerships," a term that names a new culture of governance wherein corporations exert an ever-greater influence over policy decisions. The Bush administration's commitment to extending these transformations was symbolized most readily by the advent in 2002 of the Department of Homeland Security (DHS), a major reorganization of the federal government—one enabled most immediately by the attacks of September 11, 2001, and the heightened culture of counterterrorism they provoked, but one that brought into relief already existing currents of public retrenchment.

"Homeland security state," Naomi Klein observes, quickly became synonymous with "homeland security industry"—today a booming $200 billion (per annum) global economic sector.[16] Though the Department of Homeland Security (DHS) has occasioned the expansion of government bureaucracy, the tax dollars allocated to DHS are just as likely to end up in the coffers of private entities. Between September 11, 2001, and 2006, Klein notes, DHS spent $130 billion on private contractors.[17] The outsourcing of government operations has been undertaken with diligence abroad as well, as private companies have received untold billions in public money to construct, secure, and carry out the war apparatus in Afghanistan and Iraq. The ever-more privatized military, meanwhile, is fighting not merely for "democracy," but for neoliberal revolution. Upon the U.S. takeover of Iraq in 2003, Klein details, the head of the Coalition Provisional Authority (CPA), L. Paul Bremer, declared the privatization of over 200 state-owned companies, fired over 500,000 state employees, and lowered the corporate tax rate from 40 to 15 percent.[18]

Managing the Crisis?

The "homeland security" moment is defined by myriad contradictions—between imperial expansion and imperial decline; between the willful performance of state failure (Hurricane Katrina and Hurricane Maria) and spectacular performance of state power (the "shock and awe" conquest of Iraq); between the labor imperatives of business and anti-immigrant nativism; between the hyper-modern weapons of info-war and atavistic methods of (neo)colonial expropriation; between the universal aspirations of capital and territorial exigencies of the nation-state.[19] Perhaps one contradiction connects all the others; property and the state, if always allied, have never been identical. Potentially, the privatization of public space and of government itself will have the effect of rendering the capitalist security project unstable, less able to withstand—or capitalize on—the crises that naturally befall it. Marx observed in the nineteenth century that capital, left to its own devices, is sometimes its own worst enemy, prone to destroy the very mechanisms that exist for its self-protection. The historical role of the state in the modern security project is not only to protect property from its outside and its other, but to protect property from itself.

Following the economic crisis inaugurated by the bursting of the U.S. housing bubble in 2008, the most powerful national and supranational entities within the advanced capitalist world—for example, the United States, Germany, the European Union, the European Central Bank (ECB), the IMF—demonstrated little sign that they were capable of 1) regulating financial capital in a way that would obviate future cataclysms and 2) buttressing public infrastructure in a way that would prevent or temper widespread and recurring social protest. At the highpoint of the postwar social-democratic moment, the capitalist state provided its citizens a measure of social and economic security in exchange for mass participation in processes of expanded reproduction (production and consumption). In the neoliberal moment, the state is ever less capable of upholding its side of the social contract, and an ever-shrinking percentage of the population is able to secure its own existence through market participation. In other words, the dialectical underside of the modern security project—the insecurity it has always produced, particularly for populations in the formerly colonized world—is in the neoliberal context on uniquely stark display in both the global North and global South. The crisis today is not periodic, an anticipated trough in capital's undulating patterns of regeneration, but perpetual.

"The racial coding of the world," to borrow a phrase from Paul Gilroy, emerged concomitant with the European conquest and settler-colonization of the Americas. Race discourse configured the state form and helped make available the subjection and exploitation of people within and beyond the boundaries of the political community. In the latter half of the seventeenth century, the era in which Hobbes and Locke wrote, Europeans were waging war at home and abroad: enslaving and dominating peoples of Africa and the Americas, and prosecuting a race-inflected assault on the working poor—"the 'savages' of the civilized world"[20]—domestically. Drawing the boundary between inside and outside at the same time it articulated the social body into opposed classes, race was central to the formation and securing of emergent property relations and methods of accumulation in both Old World and New.[21]

The state arises to secure the *civis*, the space of law and reason, from the anarchy and infrahumanity of the state of nature. The distinction is a racial one. With the foundation of the state, the crisis of the state of nature is not left behind but delimited and counterposed, remaining that against which the inside is defined, the pretext for and antithesis of the secured body politic. The security project requires the perpetual and simultaneous production and repression of difference: "Race appears in this scheme of things," David Theo Goldberg writes, "as a mode of crisis management, as a mode . . . of managing manufactured threats, and curtailing while alienating the challenge of the unknown."[22] Race is both that against which society must be secured and the means of its securing.

From the inception of the state form, liberalist promises of progress and assimilation coexisted, uneasily but necessarily, with essentialist racial narratives that confined the other to an ahistorical emptiness from which there can be no escape. This two-fold racial imagination endures. *Naturalist* racisms ensure the reproduction of the imaginary of the state of nature, the outside that continues to occupy a central discursive role in Western political orders. *Historicist* racisms ensure the adaptability of racial thought, which must undergo perpetual transformation in response to evolutions in the mode of production and periodic crises of accumulation. The other who yesterday lacked the capacity for industry may tomorrow be required as a critical source of cheap wage labor.

Race, Gender, and Social Security

One effect of Social Security is to clearly define who counts as a properly laboring member of the citizenry, and who does not—who is a public concern and who has a marginal or subordinate place in the calculus of public good. Social Security, in other words, draws a line between the citizen and the non-citizen, and between different occupations, different forms or sectors of labor. From its inception in the United States, Social Security was highly gendered and highly racialized, reproducing the prevailing norms of the time, which confined women and racial minorities to unpaid—as in the case of household work—or lower-paid labor. Agricultural and domestic workers, of whom the vast majority were women and minorities, were not included in the original Social Security act; nearly two thirds of black workers and more than 70 percent of women workers were not covered by the 1935 legislation. And "illegal" immigrants and the non-working population were left out altogether. (This is not to paint the greatest innovation of public services in U.S. history as a reactionary development, but rather to highlight that the content of the original Act did little to challenge—and in important ways even reinforced—the gendered and racialized organization of labor in particular and society more broadly.)

In her study *Pitied but Not Entitled* (1994), Linda Gordon writes that the Social Security Act of 1935 "excluded the most needy groups from all its programs, even the inferior ones. These exclusions were deliberate and mainly racially motivated."[23] The Southern Democrats who controlled Congress were determined to limit the bill's provisions to the white industrial working class, thereby exacerbating already existing structural inequalities. The exclusion of women from the legislation, moreover, reinforced gendered power relations within and outside the home. As Gwendolyn Mink concludes, "Reflecting masculinist assumptions, gender conventions, and maternalist achievement, the New Deal reproduced social policies contingent on maternal dependence, tying women's economic security to men's wages."[24] Social Security legislation enacted processes of exclusion *through* incorporation; "by routing women and men toward economic security differently, the New Deal entrenched separate, gendered citizenships."[25] It also entrenched separate, racial citizenships. In addition to the marginal place of African Americans in Social Security legislation, the explicitly racialized immigration policy of the 1930s—one based on a national quota system that would prevail until

1965—ensured that white would remain the color of Social Security citizenship for some time to come.

The categorical exclusions contained within the original Social Security Act did not go uncontested, as the claims of African Americans and women to political recognition and a fuller citizenship translated into significant, if limited and limiting, changes in the form and content of Social Security policy. But the point remains: Social Security is one way of separating the citizen sphere from its outside, and one way of dividing the inside into racial and gender hierarchies both symbolic and real. Like the security project at large, Social Security is simultaneously about social inclusion and social exclusion.

The Cold War and Racial Security

During the Cold War, the security of identity existed alongside economic security and military security as an urgent National Security concern. Integral to the embryonic Cold War order was the discursive enunciation of U.S. exceptionalism, which strictly delineated what is "American" from what is "un-American," what is to be secured—freedom, capitalism, individualism —from what is a threat to "our" security—totalitarianism, communism, collectivism. Reworking enduring colonial binaries, the National Security narrative of the Cold War imagined the communist threat to global capitalist hegemony as irrational and degenerate—a retrograde recapitulation of barbaric tendencies.[26] The ownership of property in common, for example, was understood as a savage trait, in opposition to the free system of private property that undergirds U.S. civilization and is the prerequisite for all human progress.[27] The racial content of these oppositions is apparent. The "primitive" peoples that the United States must uplift through developmentalist programs or discipline through counterinsurgency warfare are cast in an explicitly racial nomenclature. The convergence of the "red scare" with the "yellow peril" in Korea, Vietnam, Cambodia, and elsewhere, for example, represented the synthesis of various racial tropes, each with its own unique history. But it represented as well the reproduction of the foundational binary between (Western) civilization and its outside. Domestically, moreover, the McCarthyite effort to purge communist contagion from within the national political community occasioned an attack on all manner of radical or alternative social identities and formations. Just as the line separating inside from out needed to be perpetually retraced and reinforced, so too did the composition and social structure of the interior body politic require perpetual definition and control.

That said, the racial *nomos* of the United States—its national and international dimensions—was throughout the Cold War subject to and altered by critiques emanating from within and without. The civil rights movement at home, and a combination of Soviet and anticolonial voices abroad, highlighted the contradiction—inherent to the domestic and foreign expression of U.S. state power—between the rhetoric of democracy, freedom, and equality and the endurance of racialized forms of social exclusion and political repression. The contours of this basic contradiction were already apparent during the Second World War, when the United States' claims of anti-imperialism and its corresponding affirmation of the right to "self-determination" clashed with its transparently expansionary geopolitical ambitions, with the realities of Jim Crow, and with the wartime policy of Japanese internment. "By framing their war propaganda as a struggle for democracy and against the Third Reich's racist tyranny," Thomas Borstelmann has observed, "the Western Allies opened themselves to intensive critiques of their own colonial and segregationist practices."[28] In the early stages of the Cold War, this critique was taken up by the Soviet Union, which highlighted the inequality and discrimination endemic to U.S. society. If failing to radically alter the dominant racial paradigms of the war, this line of criticism did have significant consequence, pressuring administrations from Truman to Johnson into a less tepid—if still profoundly qualified, and motivated as much by diplomatic as by moral concerns—embrace of civil rights transformations.

The conjoined critique of segregation at home and militaristic meddling abroad had less impact on U.S. conduct in the world—compelling not major foreign policy changes but the addition of further euphemistic cover for the proxy wars and counterinsurgency conflicts sanctioned by the containment doctrine. Moreover, as Mary Dudziak, Carol Anderson, and others have argued, McCarthyite repression blunted the anti-capitalist, internationalist potentialities of the civil rights movement.[29] In other words, Cold War concerns over image nudged the U.S. government in a slightly more progressive direction on civil rights issues but de-radicalized the civil rights movement itself—marginalizing its anticolonial voice and preventing the emergence of a more comprehensive struggle for social and economic change.

Broadly speaking, the securing of racial order in the moment of the Cold War involved the careful balancing of exclusionary and inclusionary narratives and policies—the line separating "us" from "them" was rigorously defined and policed while a measured politics of inclusion reshaped the United States' racial landscape. The dual nature of the modern security project's racial logic—the delineation of inside and outside and differentiation of the inside—was transformed but not transcended by the struggle for civil rights nationally and independence globally.

Race and Neoliberalism

The neoliberal transformations begun in the early 1970s and intensified in the 1980s were accompanied by evolutions in the way racial difference was thought about and acted upon—not the invention of a completely new conceptualization of race, but the subtle adaptation of extant racial narratives and practices to the changing imperatives of both capital and state. The "flexible," post-Fordist forms of accumulation heralded by neoliberal doctrine require more "flexible" racial imaginaries.

Theorists such as Michael Hardt, Antonio Negri, and Fredric Jameson argue that in the late capitalist moment there is no longer an outside. The process of modernization is complete; nature has been completely assimilated into the social order. For Hardt and Negri, the movement from "modern" to "imperial" sovereignty represents the movement beyond the "fixed and eternal boundaries" of modern colonial racism toward a racism defined by "the play of differences and the management of micro-conflictualities within [imperial order's] continually expanding domain."[30] While right to note the more "fluid and amorphous"—yet still "stable and brutal"—racial ideology deployed in neoliberal governance, they go too far in pronouncing the disappearance of the outside altogether.[31] "The central moment of modern racism ... the global antithesis between inside and outside"[32] persists, even if the precise delineation of that foundational boundary is subject to periodic redrawing. A racism that rests upon a "strategy of differential inclusion" can coexist with a racism that rests upon binary exclusion. Indeed, the modern security project has always maintained a balance between these two modes of racial practice. The newness of the neoliberal moment is evinced by the dexterity with which imperial order navigates between them—casting superfluous bodies or convenient enemies into the outside, while incorporating non-capitalized space and a multiplicity of others into its sphere of power and tribute. In the neoliberal moment, triumphalist narratives of an imminent "post-racialism" coincide with loud reassertions of absolute civilizational alterity. The premature universal and the retrograde particular stand side by side.

The Racial State after September 11

Within the discursive frames of the War on Terror, "homeland" evokes a bounded territorial space with a definitive outside that must be resisted and policed. This boundary, moreover, is understood to define not just geography but the limits of a distinct ethno-political or ethno-cultural community. It suggests, in other words, the enduring dream of the perfect imbrication of race, space, and nation. And it implies as well that abiding imperial anxiety: the specter of difference encountered in the world returning home to corrupt the essential cultural homogeneity and social or economic integrity of the nation-state. In this way, the term "homeland" is ideally suited to the security project in its postcolonial yet still manifestly imperialist incarnation. It describes the peculiar predicament of a fading imperial power reverting to blood-soil nativism as its military marches around the world under the banner of Enlightenment universals.

The racial logic of Homeland Security governance was laid bare by Katrina floodwaters. Following Hurricane Katrina, New Orleans's poorest residents, of whom the vast majority were African American, were left to fend for their own survival, or—as was the fate of nearly 2,000 people—to die. Tens of thousands crowded into stadiums, convention centers, or along elevated stretches of highway, without adequate food, water, or medical attention. Affecting images of government failure in New Orleans played across the television news, but so too did images of "out-of-control" black residents "looting" abandoned supermarkets. When the federal relief effort did arrive, its loyalties were ambivalent—divided between protecting the property of New Orleans's wealthier residents and aiding in the survival of its most marginal and most vulnerable. The security of the former seemed to take precedence, as the incessant media invocation of "looters" and marauding "armed gangs" served to criminalize the hurricane's victims and highlight the final sanctity of private property. Louisiana Governor Kathleen Blanco gave soldiers authorization to "shoot to kill" in the course of their order-restoring mission: "These troops are fresh back from Iraq, well trained, experienced, battle-tested and under my orders to restore order in the streets.... They have M-16s and they are locked and loaded.... These troops know how to shoot and kill and they are more than willing to do so if necessary and I expect they will."[33] Subsequently, those displaced by the hurricane were labeled "refugees" by the media: first criminalized, and then symbolically stripped of their citizenship.[34]

When Governor Blanco highlighted the Iraq War experience of the soldiers called upon to enforce order in post-Katrina New Orleans, she revealed the profound connections between racialized militarism in the homeland and in the world. This connection is further evidenced by the governance of and public discourse surrounding immigration. Dispossessed of economic self-determination by free-trade agreements, the legacies of colonial expropriation, and related geographic inequities, migrants from the global South arrive in the North as living reminders of imperial brutalities present and past. Their presence in the metropole, though, does not provoke a serious reckoning with either neoliberal governance—and the state failure and social death it engenders—or the living sediment of colonial histories. Instead, in the dominant media and governmental discourses the presence of immigrants is either affirmatively cited as proof of democratic tolerance and multicultural vitality or condemned as an attack on domestic labor, drain on public services, and threat to normative national identity—as a cause, in other words, of both cultural and economic crisis. This ambivalence should not disguise the central import of each racial narrative—the universalist and the nativist—to the Homeland Security project in particular and to the modern security project in general.

SECURITY AND EMERGENCY

As elaborated above, capital and race are two keywords of the modern security project. The triad of security terms "prerogative/emergency/exception"—all of which here refer to the political movement, by an executive power, beyond the normative constraints of legislative or juridical democratic process—is another crucial entry in the security lexicon. Executive prerogative is unsurprisingly central to the pre-liberal or "absolutist" philosophy of Thomas Hobbes. But as Mark Neocleous demonstrates, prerogative and exception are also of great import to the liberalism of John Locke.[35] There are moments of political exigency, Locke allows, when the legislature is incapable of acting with the required expediency; the executive power must in these instances arrest democratic deliberation and enact the power of decision. The "public good" (which is, as Neocleous observes, often merely a euphemism for the protection of private property), the "safety of the people," and the security of society more generally, periodically demand the exercise of prerogative power.[36] The prerogative power of decision is not in fact exceptional but rather a basic and permanent feature of the modern liberal state.

Before the procedural enactment of emergency powers, the particular threat that occasions the emergency must be identified or imagined. In the settler-colonial context, the emergency that required or sanctioned the exception was the (racialized) state of nature broadly conceived. Following September 11, 2001, the "terrorist threat" was quickly established as an emergency that demanded the invocation of emergency powers. In all cases, "security" is the reason of state that permits the invocation of emergency or enactment of prerogative *within* the normative body of the liberal state. When the "security" of the political community is under threat from the savage or the terrorist, exception is justified—indeed, is legally provided for. Perhaps it is more appropriate to think not of a power that moves beyond "the rule of law," but one that is sanctioned by it, that is essential to it. The instances in which a state of emergency might be invoked in the name of security today are various, ranging from economic crisis to natural disaster to foreign or domestic war. But in each case a fundamental contradiction is at work: the suspension of the law, by the law, in the name of the law.

As with race, the concept and practice of "emergency" were developed in concert with the exercise of colonial power. Locke imagined the "state of nature" as a space of pure exception. "In the State of Nature," he observed, "every one has the Executive Power of the Law of Nature."[37] One fundamental purpose of government, Locke contended, is not to do away with this natural exception, exactly, but to centralize and codify it. Exception (or "emergency") is both a reason for and core technology of the nascent security state, its imperial form in particular. In the British imperial imagination, the "rule of law" was upheld as a singular gift, bestowed by the colonizer upon the colonized. "The establishment of a system of law which regulates the most important parts of the daily life of the people," the political philosopher James Fitzjames Stephen put it in the 1870s, "constitutes in itself a moral conquest more striking, more durable, and far more solid, than the physical conquest which renders it possible."[38] Central to this colonial "system of law," though, was the fact of its recurrent suspension: the fluid definition of certain "acts of state"—including, in circumstances both exigent and everyday, murder—as beyond juridical oversight, and the indefinite detention of colonized subjects without charge or trial.[39] The colony, Achille Mbembe has argued, is the *zone of exception par excellence*—a space "where the violence of the state of exception is deemed to operate in the service of 'civilization.'"[40] "That colonies might be ruled over in absolute lawlessness," Mbembe writes, "stems from the racial denial of any common bond between the conqueror and the native. . . . *Savage life*," he continues, "is just another form of *animal life*."[41] Unrecognizably human, capable of neither political commonwealth nor industrious labor, the savage exists outside the moral and rational calculus of the modern state. The state of nature, the pure space of exception, is the laboratory within which colonial power synthesizes methods of dehumanization with processes of extra-juridical violence. The *extra*-legal violence honed there is later institutionalized in the *legal* apparatus of the modern state, and in the security project that is its raison d'être.[42]

Economic Emergency, Capitalist Security

In the United States, the invocation of emergency powers—usually expressed in the enactment of martial law—was until the late nineteenth century limited to moments of imminent physical threat or danger, due to invasion from without or rebellion or civil war within.[43] In the decades surrounding the turn of the century, however, martial law was in multiple instances imposed to suppress labor unrest.[44] Further, during the First World War but most profoundly in its aftermath, exceptional executive power was enacted in the economic realm, as a response not to violent disorder but to capitalist crisis. In continuance of this trend, the purview of emergency powers expanded throughout the twentieth century.

The economic recovery legislation that gave initial form to the New Deal was enacted by President Roosevelt under a legally declared state of emergency and was conditioned by the recurring invocation of "emergency" in public discourse—a rhetorical proliferation that coincided with the heightened discursive power of "security." The emergency of the Great Depression, Roosevelt held, required a countervailing exercise of emergency executive power. Roosevelt was responding to mass unemployment and a dramatic fall in national income, and to a wave of labor protest and intensifying culture of class struggle more broadly. Immediate and decisive intervention was an imperative if people were to be put back to work and economic growth were to resume; but intervention was also required to alleviate class fracture and obviate the possibility of socialist revolution. The emergency, that is, referred not only to the welfare—or security—of the citizenry but to the security of capitalist social relations.[45]

Cold War Emergency

The emergency declared by Roosevelt in 1933 marked the beginning of a continuous line of emergency governance that remains unbroken today.[46] The normalization of emergency has had profound political and social effects, occasioning the dramatic expansion of executive powers and contributing to the militarization of society.[47] President Truman's declaration of emergency in 1950, in response to China's invasion of Korea, represents one particularly important moment in this twentieth-century genealogy. Truman's proclamation consolidated the emergent but already hegemonic National Security state—a new political order founded on the specter of total and permanent war, which blurred the spatial and temporal distinctions between war and peace and incorporated all of society into the military sphere.[48]

Truman's declaration of emergency in 1950 concretized and escalated an extant policy program, one the president had famously articulated to a joint session of Congress in his 1947 "Truman Doctrine" speech. In that address, Truman outlined a new, more anticipatory and interventionist foreign policy based on "containment" rather than détente. The emergency declared by Truman in 1950—in the name of the nation's economic and military security, and in the defense of capitalist freedom against "communist imperialism"—was premised not just on the actuality of military conflict but on the "looming peril" of an existential threat to the nation. The infamous internal policy document NSC-68, drafted by the National Security Council and approved by President Truman just two days before his declaration of emergency in 1950, outlined the culture and rationale of Cold War emergency governance. The intellectual and spiritual antecedent of the Bush Doctrine, NSC-68—which warned of "the ever-present possibility of annihilation," and which argued that at stake was the survival "not only of this republic but of civilization itself"—argued for constant military and security mobilization in the face of the communist threat.[49] It argued, moreover, that the struggle against communism would necessarily be waged internal to the United States as well as in the world. NSC-68, that is, defined the ways in which National Security is more than a mode of U.S. global power—it is also a technique for policing individual citizens and structuring the national body politic.[50] In the Cold War emergency order, military buildup and McCarthyite repression went hand in hand, just as the War on Terror and Patriot Act exist in tandem today.

Neoliberal Emergency

In the neoliberal moment, the expanding scope of emergency powers—an expansion that has coincided with security's ever-greater purchase on human social life—is on full display. In the case of the New Deal, emergency was enacted to mitigate class contradiction and ensure the reproduction of capitalist social relations. Today, emergency powers have a different intent and effect: not the mollification of class contradiction but its intensification; not the preemptive management of economic insecurity and crisis, but the deliberate cultivation of a general culture of insecurity and crisis. If the security of capital has always been prior to and above the security of the person or the public—the latter only privileged when it acts as a conduit to the former—this enduring hierarchy is in neoliberalism utterly transparent. The neoliberal state of emergency demands the constant and militarized securing of capital, and the constant and militarized policing of the insecure spaces inhabited by the multitudes that fall through the chasms of the "ownership society." Capital, in neoliberal order, is always embattled, always in danger—because only the feeblest of attempts is made to assimilate its other into the realm of achieved security. In place of the social contract are the gated community and the private security force on the one side and the proliferating slum on the other.

The New Deal and the "embedded liberalism" it helped entrench is one example of the second phase of what Karl Polanyi called capitalism's "double movement": first, the movement toward the liberation of markets and universalization of the commodity form; and second, the countermovement—encouraged by labor primarily but at moments in the twentieth century by capital as well—toward the amelioration of capitalism's most alienating and destructive effects. Without the second movement, Polanyi contends, capital would completely destroy the "fictitious commodities" that are its foundation—land and human labor most of all—and thus destroy itself. The actual complete disembedding of the market—the dream of the market fundamentalists—is, Polanyi insists, an impossibility, as it would mean turning nature and people into *pure* commodities, and thus ultimately destroying nature and people.[51]

In embedded liberalism, the state recognizes this danger and responds by instituting various protective measures to guard against the violence and reach of the market. Neoliberalism, though, disregards the imperative of the second movement. According to neoliberal doctrine, the brutalities of the market are not to be counteracted. Indeed, neoliberal policy proceeds through the annihilation/privatization of the public institutions and services historically created in the moment of countermovement. In neoliberal order, emergency powers regulate not the stability of society at large—"there is no such thing as society," Margaret Thatcher intoned—but the security of private property, and the security of the ongoing processes of commoditization and privatization that make up the first movement described by Polanyi. Whether the economic crisis that began in 2008 will provoke a new and sustained countermovement remains unclear. In the immediate context of the crisis, the U.S. executive used its powers of emergency intervention—outsourced, in large part, to the Federal Reserve—to bail out precarious financial institutions and to stimulate dormant credit markets. But tellingly, it did not—with the tentative exception of 2010's healthcare reform legislation—"exploit the crisis" to buttress beleaguered social safety nets or establish new ones. And at the state level, the invocation and enactment of "emergency" enabled the imposition of anti-union legislation and other austerity measures. In Michigan, to cite just one example, Governor Rick Snyder oversaw in the spring of 2011 the passage of a law that gave him the power to remove elected officials, abrogate union contracts, and eliminate services in any municipality or school district declared by the state to be in a condition of "financial emergency."[52]

New and Old States of Exception

The War on Terror was imagined by its neoconservative authors as a "forever war." The interminable temporality of the conflict is implicit in the very idea of a struggle against terror, which is not a material entity that can be eradicated but an animating idea, a mode of representing a particular—if fluid in definition—form of violence or difference. The declaration of a War on Terror, in other words, explicitly posits the emergency as permanent. But as I discuss above, the emergency—and the war that it compels—has been a structural component of modern political order since its inception. And as Julian Reid and Michael Dillon put it, "when emergency becomes the generative principle of formation of community and rule" the political sphere is determined by the urgency, "the compelling political economy," of war.[53] This inherency is most visibly evidenced in the space of the colony and by colonial histories.[54] The colonial rationality of the War on Terror thus betrays—even as it strives to obscure—the other, deeper, permanent war with which it is continuous.

The principal policy documents and laws of the War on Terror—the USA PATRIOT Act (2001), National Security Strategy of the United States of America (2002), and National Strategy for Homeland Security (2002)—introduced a series of terms and categories into the political lexicon, many of which are cited by critics as evidence of the "state of exception" within which we now live: "enemy combatant," "battlefield detainee," "extraordinary rendition."[55] These categories name the novel forms of liminal, rightless subjectivity produced by the extra-juridical mechanisms of the U.S.-led War on Terror and experienced in Guantánamo Bay, Abu Ghraib, and untold secret prisons located throughout the world. The word *extraordinary* nicely captures the simultaneous newness and mundanity of the War on Terror's emergency formations—extraordinary as exceptional, and extraordinary as extra ordinary (*really* ordinary). In the latter meaning, the vocabulary of "enemy combatant" and "extraordinary rendition," the violence it names, represents an exceptionally acute manifestation of long-established norms, Manichean frames—civilization and barbarism, human and infrahuman—basic to colonial modernity.

It bears emphasizing here that my intention in this section is not to suggest any perfect congruence between this and that emergency formation; an emergency declared in response to a national disaster of course differs profoundly, in its political intention and effect, from an emergency declared in wartime or in the face of economic crisis. Rather, my purpose is to locate the contemporary proliferation of emergency—as a narrative and as a governmental form—within the longer history of emergency as a technique of state power. This argument about the politics of emergency mirrors the overall argument of this chapter, which sheds light upon the ways in which ostensibly discrete instances of security thinking and governance—Social Security and Homeland Security, for example—share a political genealogy and rationality, which can be traced to the advent of colonial modernity.

CONCLUSION

Summoning Walter Benjamin, and invoking as well the work of Giorgio Agamben, a common critical refrain insists that in the moment of the War on Terror the state of exception has become the rule.[56] The ongoing state of emergency declared by President Bush in the immediate aftermath of September 11 stands as compelling evidence in support of this thesis. As I have argued here, though, the contemporary iteration of emergency governance is not in fact exceptional but *proves* or *evinces* the rule. The exemplary sites or subjects of the "post-9/11" state of exception, such as Guantánamo Bay or "battlefield detainee," are contiguous with the longer history of modernity's exceptional violence—a violence perfected in the space of the colony. The racial logics of the contemporary moment—the synthesis of outright exclusion and "differential inclusion"—can likewise be traced to the early modern moment, and in particular to the settler-colonization of the New World. And contemporary modes of neoliberal depredation—the production and subsequent seizure of devalued or non-commoditized spaces and entities—are genealogically related to originary forms of primitive accumulation.

The security project arose concurrently with and in support of the settler-conquest of the New World, the establishment of the modern state form, and the emergence of the capitalist mode of production. Centuries later, new and old technologies of dispossession continue to propel capitalism into new worlds both fictitious and real; new and old racisms continue to shape human social life, delimiting and structuring the space of political belonging; and new and old narratives of crisis and emergency—of nature, of war, of economy, of culture—continue to inspire the innovation and intensification of state and market power. Intrinsic to each of these processes, security—as a political ideal and governmental technique—is also one binding thread between them. So too is terror. From its inception, the imperial security project has labored to elide the terror of its foundation and extant form. The history and contemporary expression of that terror is taken up in the chapter that follows.

TWO

"A General Principle of Democracy"

TERROR AND COLONIAL MODERNITY

In the New World, as in Africa and the Indian subcontinent, the advent of colonial power was justified via appeal to the inherent terror of the "state of nature." In the colonial imagination, the "state of nature" was a space imbued with the sublime—an unfathomable space, inhabited by infrahuman beings, that inspired a disorienting, even paralyzing admixture of astonishment, terror, and pleasure, and that invited and demanded the pacifying influence of Enlightenment rationality and colonial power. Empire, that is, was conceived by its architects as a project of "counterterror." The object of this project was not simply the terror intrinsic to the colonized world but the terror of anti-colonial resistance. The imperial state interpreted the latter as evidence of the former—which is to say that violent opposition to colonialism was explained, by the colonial imagination, as the expression of an essential native barbarism rather than as a rational political response to, or reflection of, the terrors of empire. In the context of the War on Terror, this paradigm persists. The neoconservative doctrine of preemption assumes that the innate terror of the enemy other will soon erupt. The enactment of military violence is required to negate both the latent and manifest instances of anti-imperial terror.

The term "counterterror" betrays the ways in which the state's response to terror is itself a form of terror. The duality of terror as at once within and without, fundamental yet threatening to the imperial state, was revealed with a particular clarity, as myriad historians have argued, in the moment of the French Revolution, and the transition therein from Jacobin to Thermidorean violence—from Robespierre's insistence that terror was "an emanation of virtue... a general principle of democracy" to its later redefinition, in the moment of counterrevolution, as the archetypal enemy of the state. For thinkers such as Arendt, as for Hegel and Kant, the relationship between terror and the liberal state is uniquely a problem of foundation. The abiding historical and philosophic question is whether the glorious ends of revolution justify its violent means. As the ongoing history of Euro-American imperialism makes especially plain, though, terror is a central technology of the mature and not merely nascent form of the liberal state. Terror is also, crucially, one basic *condition* for the birth of political modernity. The emancipation of the bourgeoisie in Europe was enabled by the terrors of primitive accumulation—the extraction of resources and exploitation of slave labor in the New World. In his reflections on primitive accumulation, Marx highlights the ways in which capital "comes *dripping* from head to foot, from every pore, with *blood* and dirt."[1] But just as Arendt confines the terrors of the liberal state to the moment of its beginning, Marx imagines the terrors of primitive accumulation as primordial rather than perpetual. Countering these conjoined historiographic elisions, my argument in this chapter highlights the enduring mutuality of state terror and primitive accumulation.

The essential and enduring terrors of capital and the imperial state give rise to violent resistance. In the event of the Haitian Revolution, the masses of slaves in revolt demonstrated, to the world, that the radical realization of Enlightenment universalisms would be made possible by the violent destruction—and not merely philosophic rejection—of chattel rationality. In the mid-twentieth century, in dialogue with the anticolonial energies then reverberating throughout the world, C. L. R. James summoned the example of Haiti's slaves—and that of their leader Toussaint L'Ouverture—into contemporary service. James reflected on the content of the revolution's form—the theoretical implications of its violent methods, and the immutable contradictions of its violent aftermath. Writing in rhythm with James, in an allied conceptual idiom, Frantz Fanon meditated on the possibilities of an anticolonial violence that would bring newness into the world without itself calcifying, in the wake of independence, into the perpetual terrors of capital and state. The insights of James and Fanon continue to resonate in the current conjuncture. The possibility of a subjective terror that transcends the objective terrors of imperial power, without being assimilated by the latter, is a problem today posed from multiple political positions by a diversity of actors and theorists.

In this chapter, I demonstrate that the politics of terror are expressed in and by three primary modalities—terror as a pretext for imperial power, terror as a method of imperial power, and terror as a form of resistance to imperial power. Critical reckoning with the "terror" concept requires that we examine the interrelation of these modalities, within the recent histories of capital and the security state, and within the broad frame of colonial modernity.

TERROR AND THE COLONIAL SUBLIME

Kant, Burke, and the Colonial Sublime

The modern genealogy of the sublime is commonly traced to Kant and Edmund Burke. For both thinkers, the sublime—as a political and aesthetic analytic—was clarified by the colonial encounter. Writing in the latter half of the eighteenth century—a moment of deepening imperial processes in the Americas and in South Asia—Kant and Burke employed notions of the sublime to theorize the European male subject's confrontation with the radical difference embodied in and by the state of nature.

In Kant's definition, the sublime refers to the "boundlessness" of nature—that which is, in comparison to other phenomena, "absolutely great."[2] This greatness inspires in the subject a mixture of awe, pleasure, and terror. The receiving subject, Kant argued in his *Critique of Judgment* (1790), is broken down by the fearful immensity of nature. But in response, he submits to the primacy of reason, thereby restoring both the self and the social order at large. In Kant's theorization of the "dynamic" sublime, the recognition of nature's terrible power conditions the ultimate ascendancy of reason and rationality—and of the European male subject who is understood to be the privileged owner of such properties.

Like the imperial imagination at large, the Kantian sublime simultaneously posits the terrible vastness of the natural world and enacts its domestication. This double movement was performed in a quite literal way by artists of the romanticist movement, who at once paid homage to the immensity of nature and confined that immensity within the manageable parameters of a picture frame. In nineteenth-century North America, the artists of the Hudson River School exalted the immense scale, uncorrupted emptiness, and great, terrifying beauty of the New World. But in reducing that scale to the confines of the painting—and permitting the consuming public to view it at a position of safe remove, in a gallery or domestic setting—they affirmed human mastery over nature, and testified to the imminence and essential righteousness of the continent's conquest. The depiction of empty landscapes symbolically cleansed the continent of its native inhabitants, at once eliding and providing visual proof of the epidemiological slaughter then well underway. Those paintings that did include, if not foreground, the representation of indigenous subjects imagined them as indistinct from the deep gorges, impenetrable forests, and rushing rivers—as evocative of terror and the "negative pleasure" that accompanies it, as less than human, and as subject to the inexorable destiny of white civilization. This rendering of indigenous subjects as a part of nature echoed Kant's own philosophy of racial difference. As Gayatri Spivak and other postcolonial critics have argued, Kant imagines the "Fuegan" or the "New Hollander"—"man in the raw," as he elsewhere terms the savage, colonized subject—as a potential source of, but incapable of being redeemed by, the sublime. (Women too are denied entry into the community of rational subjects for whom the sublime is "universally communicable.")[3]

According to Burke's earlier elaboration, the sublime is "whatever is in any sort terrible, or is conversant about terrible objects, or operates in a manner analogous to terror."[4] Burke allows that the terror of the sublime might also elicit feelings of pleasure—indeed, his own reflections share with Kant a basic understanding of the sublime as a displeasure that provokes feelings of pleasure—but its ultimate effect is disarming; the colonial subject is undone, his grasp of and power over the world threatened by the impenetrable and unfathomable vastness of what he confronts—an ascendant nature that exceeds, and demands the surrender of, humanity itself. In Burke's rendering, there is no second moment wherein the individual, and the reason he wields, reclaims his power over the sublime object.

Though Burke's 1757 treatise *A Philosophical Enquiry into the Origin of Our Ideas of the Sublime and Beautiful* is not explicitly staged within or addressed to any particular geographic context, the work is haunted by what would become one of the thinker's abiding political concerns: the ethical and moral consequence—for Britain especially but also for its colonized subjects—of the British imperial project. Throughout his entwined intellectual and political lives, Burke maintained a deeply ambivalent relationship to Britain's imperial projections in his native Ireland, in India, and in America. His extensive writings on Ireland and India in particular can be read, in good faith, as either a serious critique of empire or a primer on how to most effectively govern in the colonies—to rule, that is, in a way that reconciles the brutality of empire with the Enlightenment vocabulary in which it is clothed. Luke Gibbons situates Burke's *Philosophical Enquiry* against the backdrop of British colonial rule in Ireland. Burke was appalled, Gibbons notes, by both the violent tactics of the Whiteboy movement—which sought to protect tenant land rights—in the 1760s and by the colonial government's brutal reply.[5] The government's execution of Whiteboy agitators and suspected enablers was designed as a display of sublime terror, which would awe the subject population into an unquestioning reverence for the justice (or justness) of colonial rule. Burke advocated for a more measured mode of colonial power, one that would mitigate and obscure the object of terror, and one that would seek to enlist the colonized subject—via the judicious manipulation of the sublime—into the administration of the colonial regime, rather than simply seek their passive submission to its abstract dictums. Burke lamented, though, that social conditions in Ireland did not encourage the articulation of this more subdued, but still sublime, form of colonial power. The British imperial presence had so succeeded in suppressing local customs that no sound social fundament existed within which a more benign, more cooperative, colonial order might take root. Burke identified in India more fertile ground for his ideal imperial government. India, Burke famously avowed, was possessed of rules and principles equal in their legitimacy to, and endowed with an even greater historical weight ("tradition") than, those of Britain. In his speeches in support of the former Governor-General of India Warren Hastings's impeachment, Burke railed against the excesses of British power in India, abuses he attributed to the amoral mercantilism of the East India Company, and to the despotic tendencies of the Empire's "adolescent" foot soldiers. At once an impassioned plea for "sympathy" with the humanity and rights of the Indian people and a plainly orientalist affirmation of Britain's paternalistic relationship to them—an argument for cultural relativism that appeals to a universal morality and historicity—Burke's speeches and writings on India are a feat of rhetorical contortionism. In each of the meandering discursive paths down which he travels, though, Burke is guided by an abiding political-aesthetic concern with the sublime. As Sara Suleri observes, Burke deploys the trope of the sublime to describe the unknowable vastness of India (even as he attempts to construct around that vastness a taming taxonomic apparatus).[6] This vastness is, for Burke, doubly threatening. First, the terror *evoked* by the immensity of India threatens to overwhelm the imagination—undo the cognitive security—of the youthful agent of empire. Second, the sublimity of India is threatening because of the terror it *provokes*—the arbitrary, excessive, and punitive reassertion of colonial power. Importantly, at stake for Burke in both cases is the integrity of British social and political order, the danger posed to British society by its exposure and subsequent reversion to the unmitigated power of the sublime. In place of a colonial government guided by the naked pursuit of profit and propped up by the arbitrary exercise of force, the mode of rule Burke imagined would recognize the essential humanity and cultural singularity of the Indian people, and would conceal (or attenuate) the violence of colonial social relations with the "wardrobe of a moral imagination."

Whatever its politics, Burke's account possesses a keen dialectic sensitivity to the irrationality of rationality—the irrationality, specifically, of the putatively rational colonial response to the sublimity of the colonized (or soon-to-be colonized) world. While Kant imagines a second moment in the European confrontation with the sublime, wherein the male subject reestablishes his power over the boundlessness of nature through the exercise of reason, Burke recognizes that "reason" functions in the colonial context as euphemistic cover for the articulation of political terror (the synthetic sublime). The sublime power of nature is countered not with the ascendancy of reason but with the sublime power of the colonial state. Here we can glimpse the genealogical origins of the terror/counterterror cycle that structures the political present. The "terror" invoked in the rhetorical figure of the "War on Terror" signifies an ontological essence as much as a political practice. The legitimate violence of the state, in other words, is responding not just to the ideology and method of "terror" but to its intrinsic residence in the world's uncivilized spaces and peoples.

The Colonial Sublime Today

Burke's meditations on the political sublime anticipated the term's contemporary articulation, which evokes less the grandest canyon or tallest mountain and more the great terror produced by human technologies of mass violence. Today, the archetypal image of sublime terror is not a stormy sea or vast desert but the mushroom cloud left by the atomic bomb.[7] Importantly, though, these two manifestations of the sublime are not contradictory but allied, and their mutual entanglement was as much a feature of the eighteenth century as it is of the twenty-first. In the colonial context, the terror inherent to "first nature" required the production of "second nature" sublimity. Technologies of transport and communication were used to both inspire fear and compel subservience to the ideology of "development."[8] To borrow an example from Brian Larkin's *Signal and Noise*, the introduction of the railroad in Nigeria did more than transform the economic and cultural geography of the colony, tying together north and south and deepening the connection of the country at large to global processes of accumulation; it also provoked among the rural population a profound feeling of "fear and terror" at the limitless capacities of a colonial power that could transform the landscape itself.[9] Technologies of extermination were more unitary in their terrorizing effect. The exceptional space of the colony served as a laboratory for new methods of extermination, the lethalness and awe-inducing capacities of which could be tested on infrahuman subjects. In the New World, the introduction of repeating firearms—first the Colt six-shot revolver, and later the Spencer Carbine rifle—transformed the settler-conquest of the American West. Prior to their innovation, the superior horsemanship of Plains tribes such as the Comanche could match the cumbersome technologies and tactics of federal regiments; their advent altered the balance of power in battle and provoked new levels of terror in indigenous communities, for whom such weapons posed a cosmological as well as physical threat. In North and Southern Africa, the Gatling gun enabled the British Empire to expand spatially, and to "pacify" colonized populations terrorized by the specter of mass extermination. The first aerial bombs, meanwhile, were manually dropped from an Italian plane onto Tagiura, an oasis outside of Tripoli, in 1911. The bomb redrew the lines of the battlefield, incorporating civilians and cities into the theatre of war in previously unimaginable ways. It was also a perfect technology of sublime violence. The people lying in wait below turned in terror toward the heavens, pacified—the colonial strategists hoped—by a combination of reverence and fear. A communiqué released by the Italian Air Force in the aftermath of that first fateful attack claimed that the bombing "had a wonderful effect on the morale of the Arabs."[10] During the interwar period, the bomb was embraced by European imperial powers—most especially Britain—as an essential instrument of colonial governance. "Air control," or terror from above, preserved the lives of imperial soldiers by targeting colonized noncombatants.

In the metropole, the bomb carried both utopian and dystopian connotations. In the popular imagination, the potential it contained for mass destruction promised at turns planetary peace and the end of human (or European, or British) civilization. One common trope of early twentieth-century British science fiction imagined a "superweapon" that would cleanse the world of Anglo civilization's last resistors. Another recurring sci-fi narrative gave expression to darker fantasies; in the latter genre, the inferior races appropriate the "superweapon" and bomb Britain into savagery and oblivion.[11] This nightmare inversion of the colonial order of things contradicted the Kantian assumption that "man in the raw" was incapable of actively mediating, and being redeemed by, the sublime.[12] It also prefigured contemporary terror politics and its attendant narrative frameworks. In contemporary popular culture and governmental discourse, the "terrorist" is simultaneously imagined as primitive, prior to the temporality of modernity, and as a potential exponent of the most sophisticated modern weaponry. Before September 11, many prominent members of the U.S. foreign policy apparatus, more convinced by the Kantian formulation, thought such an attack ontologically impossible. In the spring of 2001, Paul Wolfowitz dismissed Osama bin Laden as "this little terrorist in Afghanistan"—a "man in the raw," in other words, whose natural habitat was a cave in Tora Bora. But the events of September 11 represented the realization of the imperial nightmare conveyed by those century-old pulp fictions: the colonized subject, seizing control of the sublime power of modern technologies and visiting a vengeful terror upon his colonial overlords.[13]

The attacks of September 11, 2001, were experienced by the United States government, and the global capitalist order embodied by the World Trade Center, as an "image defeat." The loss that event represented for the imperial state was, at base, symbolic rather than economic or geopolitical.[14] The United States' militaristic response—a response guided in part by capitalist and territorial logics—has been most profoundly registered in material terms: hundreds of thousands dead, millions displaced. But as the Retort group has put it, the War on Terror is also, at heart, "a war for the control of appearances." When the U.S. military invaded Iraq in 2003, it heralded a "shock and awe" spectacle, the irresistible sublime force of which would compel the swift submission of the Iraqi army and ideological allegiance of the Iraqi people at large. The theatrics of the War on Terror's opening months, in Afghanistan as in Iraq, appear now as the ironic preface to the brutal and protracted counterinsurgency campaigns that have followed. The battle for "hearts and minds" at the heart of counterinsurgency warfare has necessitated, in rural Afghanistan in particular, a reversion to the developmentalist sublime—the building of roads and bridges, communications and energy infrastructure. But the sublime power of outright terror is still central to the tactics of imperial militarism. The people of Waziristan, Somalia, and Yemen live in a state of perpetual fear—terrorized in the knowledge that they could be killed at any moment by a bomb dropped from the unmanned drones stalking the skies above.

IMPERIAL ACCUMULATION, STATE TERROR

From Hegel and Kant onward, the philosophic elaboration of terror has centered on the problem of foundation—the inherency of terror to political revolution, and the moral implications of that essential and historically abiding relationship. Since 1789, the event of the French Revolution has acted as the historical touchstone for this conversation. Hegel hailed the "glorious dawn" of the Revolution and considered its attendant Terror a righteous "rage against evil."[15] Kant balanced the regrettable loss of innocent lives against the sound "moral disposition" of the Terror's popular supporters. Though less than eager to see the Revolution's methodology replicated, he ultimately deemed that its world-historical ends justified its violent means.[16] Not all of the Revolution's contemporaneous commentators came to an allied conclusion. Many intellectual observers, such as Schiller and Goethe, determined that if the justness of the foundational violence was incontrovertible, the subsequent "Terrors"—even if provoked by counterrevolutionary pressures from within and without—could not be so easily absolved.[17]

Notable among terror's twentieth-century theorists, Arendt—writing in the wake of the Second World War, with an intimate understanding of its horrors—drew a distinction between the terror of beginnings, such as Robespierre's "terror of virtue," which could be justified, and the "totalitarian" normalization of terror.[18] Arendt's contribution is useful in that it resists the identification of terror with rupture and highlights instead those political contexts within which terror is constant and pervasive. She does not, however, move beyond a focus on Bolshevism and Nazism to address the naturalization of terror within the liberal state itself (though her profound insights into the imperial origins of European fascism do encourage such an inquiry). For Arendt, in other words, as for Hegel and Kant, the problem of terror as it bears upon the French Revolution—and the genealogy of the modern state more broadly—is confined to the moment of revolution. Terror, though, holds an intrinsic place within the extant and not simply embryonic morphology of the modern state. And as I am eager to stress, terror in its imperial form—in particular the terror of primitive accumulation—is also one basic condition for the emancipation of the bourgeoisie and the birth of political modernity.[19]

Terror and Primitive Accumulation

In Hegel's philosophy of history, the event of the French Revolution gives concrete form to the Enlightenment ideals of freedom, equality, and self-possession. The Revolution, Hegel famously argued, "received its first impulse from philosophy."[20] The Terror, in this rendering, is the necessary midwife of a constitutional order "established in harmony with the concept of right."[21] Though Hegel was a keen critic of the insidious nature of unfettered capital, he did not explicitly acknowledge the economic and specifically colonial processes that created the basis of material wealth upon which the nascent French bourgeoisie voiced their claim to power. "The fortunes created at Bordeaux, at Nantes, by the slave-trade," Jean Jaurès later observed, "gave to the bourgeoisie that pride which needed liberty and contributed to human emancipation."[22] This "sad irony of human history" is not foregrounded in the historiography of political modernity. The dialectical insight it contains, however, clarifies the relationship between two terrors: the terror of primitive accumulation, and the terror of the French Revolution. If the event of the French Revolution is commonly granted a causal role in the history of political modernity, it is also (like all causes) an effect—an effect, specifically, of the terrors of slavery, forced labor, and resource extraction in the New World, and violent procedures of proletarianization in Europe. The perpetual terror of empire, that is, made possible the foundational terror of the French Revolution.

In the final part of *Capital*'s first volume, Marx developed his theory of the "so-called primitive accumulation." At base, Marx held, primitive accumulation "is nothing else than the historical process of divorcing the producer from the means of production." But the narrative that follows this opening definition ranges well beyond those forms of expropriation that gave birth to a wage laboring population within Europe itself. Marx stressed the centrality of colonial operations to the emergence of the capitalist mode of production. "The discovery of gold and silver in America," he wrote, "the extirpation, enslavement and entombment in mines of the indigenous population of that continent, the beginnings of the conquest and plunder of India, and the conversion of Africa into a preserve for the commercial hunting of black skins, are all things which characterize the dawn of the era of capitalist production.

These idyllic proceedings are the chief moments of primitive accumulation." And as he put it elsewhere, "The treasures captured outside Europe by undisguised looting, enslavement, and murder floated back to the mother-country and were there turned into capital."[23] (The word "undisguised" is somewhat out-of-place here, as the naked violence of primitive accumulation was always cloaked in layers of moral philosophy and judicial right.) Whether focusing on the enclosure of common lands in the English countryside or the institution of slavery in the American South, Marx foregrounded the essential role of state violence—and, in his phrasing, the "terroristic laws" it enforces—in enabling the primitive accumulation of capital.

In attaching the modifier "so-called" to his invocation of primitive accumulation, Marx was critiquing the mythology of capitalism's genesis as narrated by classical political economy. According to Adam Smith and others, primitive accumulation was an essentially peaceful process; over time, certain forward-thinking individuals, possessed of a will to accumulate and propensity to save, expanded their stock, thereby differentiating themselves from the less calculating and less industrious majority, who, absent a proliferating enterprise of their own, were forced to sell their labor for a wage. Hence the capitalist division of labor is born. "In times long gone-by," Marx caricatured this origin story, "there were two sorts of people; one, the diligent, intelligent, and, above all, frugal elite; the other, lazy rascals, spending their substance, and more, in riotous living." Marx called this truism of political economy a "nursery rhyme" and likened it to the role played by the idea of "original sin" in Christian theology. Wary of this morality tale, and its imagining of a pacific transition to capitalism, Marx reminds us, again, that capital enters the world covered in blood and filth.[24] Though accenting the terror of capital's birth, Marx shared with classical political economy an understanding of primitive accumulation as a *specific* moment in the emergence and evolution of the capitalist mode of production. He did not, in other words, devote a great deal of attention to the not simply originary but perpetual importance of "so-called primitive accumulation" to the expansion and deepening of capitalist social relations. In *Capital*, the foundational terror of primitive accumulation gives way to the "silent compulsion" of the market. Once the division of labor and its attendant ideological armature are solidly established, the role of state violence recedes. This is all another way of saying that Marx's treatment of the violence of primitive accumulation, and its place within the history of capitalist modernity, mimics the historiographic logic that imagines terror as constitutive of colonial modernity only in the first instance. When Marx avows that "force is the midwife of every old society pregnant with a new one"—as he does in his reflections on the centrality of state terror to the unfolding of primitive accumulation—we can hear echoes of Kant and Hegel on the foundational terrors of the French Revolution. These two historiographic elisions are conjoined. Or put slightly differently, when we inquire into the endurance of primitive accumulation within extant capitalist processes we are immediately confronted with the continuity of terror as a technology of state.

Later thinkers, both avowedly Marxist and otherwise, have developed empirical and theoretical treatments of the ways in which primitive accumulation remains central to the maintenance, and perpetual reinvention, of capitalism. "The original sin of simple robbery," as Arendt observed, "must be repeated lest the motor of accumulation suddenly die down."[25] Arendt was reflecting back on the recurring economic depressions within the advanced capitalist world in the closing decades of the nineteenth century. In that moment, acute crises of overproduction compelled the bourgeoisie to search for new sources of raw materials and degraded labor, and new markets for the consumption or reinvestment of idle capital. Arendt's inquiry borrowed from the Marxist thinker Rosa Luxemburg, who argued for the essential importance of "noncapitalist social strata" to the expanded reproduction of capital; in order to survive, capital must constantly find and expropriate spaces outside of itself. "Imperialism," Luxemburg wrote, "is the political expression of the accumulation of capital in its competitive struggle for what remains still open of the non-capitalist environment."[26] Capital's imperial imperative moved the bourgeoisie to solicit the assistance of state power—to protect the exportation of capital, and to enable, via the enactment or threat of violence, the extraction of new raw materials and exploitation of new sources of labor. "Exported capital," Rudolf Hilferding put it, "feels safest when the state power of its own country rules the new domain completely."[27] When the necessity of imperial expansion to the engine of accumulation is made plain, Hilferding argued, a shift occurs in the attitude of the bourgeoisie. Historically, "economic life was to be completely free of state intervention; the state was to confine itself politically to the safeguarding of security and the establishment of civil equality.... [But] the desire for an expansionist policy," he continued, "causes a revolutionary change in the mentality of the bourgeoisie. It ceases to be pacifist and humanist."[28]

But as Hilferding's awkward "was to be" phrasing implies, the existence of a capitalist market free of state intervention, the ideology of laissez-faire, was always an illusion (as was the apparently "pacifist and humanist" countenance of the bourgeoisie). As Polanyi and others have reminded us, laissez-faire was crafted by the state.[29] The state is required both to establish the conditions for market mechanisms and to manage the social and economic effects of liberalization. The "disembedding" of the market from society—like the prior separation of the producer from the means of production—is a violent movement that results in generalized insecurity. In the moment of economic liberalization, the state is diminished in its role as a provider of social protections. It continues, though, to manipulate financial controls and evangelize on behalf of market ideology. And, most profoundly, it extends its powers of repression: the withering of the welfare state and expansion of the police state are reciprocal processes.[30]

Though (unevenly) manifest in both the domestic and colonial spheres, the inherency of state violence to the invention and reproduction of capitalist social relations—and perpetuation of "so-called primitive accumulation"—is, as Hilferding suggests, brought into stark relief when the more transparent terror of imperialism enters the political foreground. It is in the colony, Frantz Fanon observed in *The Wretched of the Earth*, that the essence and universality of capitalist violence is revealed.[31]

Terror and the American Century

The imperial logics governing European political order around the turn of the century culminated in the terrors of the Second World War. The return of colonial technologies of racial thinking and industrialized extermination to Europe was not an aberration from the progressive trajectory of enlightened modernity but rather one logical outcome of it—one possible manifestation of the terror intrinsic to it. In the postwar moment, the putative defeat of fascism and dissolution of Europe's imperial possessions did not in fact signal the transcendence of colonial rationality itself. Presiding over the rubble of Europe's crumbling empires, the United States announced its claim to global supremacy. It did so through the sublime spectacle of the atomic bomb, and through more mundane performances of its nascent economic and geopolitical ascendancy. The founding rhetoric of the "American Century" gestured toward the planetary tide of anticolonial sentiment and movement, and affirmed the right of all peoples to self-determination. The Keynesian economic consensus—underwritten and supervised by American or supranational financial institutions—seemed to signal the advent of a more humane era in the history of capitalism. Welfare states miraculously bloomed out of the ruins of Western Europe, and lending bodies such as the International Monetary Fund (IMF) guided the implementation of developmentalist strategies in the global South. But as thinkers such as Césaire and Fanon saw at the time, the ascent of the United States represented another stage in the extant history of colonial modernity, not a departure from or repudiation of it. "The hour of the barbarian is at hand," Césaire warned in *Discourse on Colonialism*. "The modern barbarian. The American hour. Violence, excess, waste, mercantilism, bluff, gregariousness, stupidity, vulgarity, disorder."[32] Beneath the veneer of democratic optimism and technological progress, old wounds festered. Black bodies swinging from trees, and the generalized racial terror of the Jim Crow South, betrayed an unsettling affinity between Nazism and the darker side of the American experiment. The existential imperatives of anticommunism, meanwhile, provided political and moral cover for the resumption and transmutation of imperial processes in Southeast Asia, Africa, and elsewhere. From Indochina to Central America, the United States labored to make the world safe for capitalism. When the ideology of "free enterprise" was met with resistance rather than passive submission, more coercive means were deployed to ensure the extension and deepening of capitalist social relations. In the proxy wars and counterinsurgency campaigns of the Cold War decades to come, the spread of "democracy" and the "free market" was enabled by the terror tactics of military and paramilitary "security forces." From our contemporary vantage, the atomic bursts over Hiroshima and Nagasaki appear not as the final, cleansing terror of the Second World War, but as the inaugural terror of the postwar capitalist order.

That the "Cold War" was a cruelly ironic signifier for the emergent nation-states of the Third World was evidenced not simply by the conflicts in Korea and Vietnam. Beyond those declared and direct interventions, the focal point of U.S. militarism in the 1950s and 1960s was Latin America, where the doctrine of "low-intensity" engagement was born—in Guatemala, in El Salvador, in Colombia, and indeed across the hemisphere. Fearing regional emulations of the Cuban Revolution, the United States worked in the early 1960s to arm and embolden security forces throughout the Americas.[33] Outside the public eye and ostensibly independent from U.S. military and intelligence forces, clandestine paramilitary units could do the dirty work counterinsurgency required with impunity. As with Churchill and Mussolini in Africa, in private communications or classified memoranda U.S. leaders were candid about the utility of terror tactics. In 1962, General William Yarborough counseled the Colombian government on the need for a paramilitary unit that would "execute ... sabotage and/or terrorist activities against known communist proponents."[34] In less discrete military enunciations, such tactics fell under the heading of "counterterror"—a term that seems almost deliberate in the profound ambiguity it betrays. Is "counterterror" a clumsy way of saying "antiterror"? Or does it, rather, signify terror's response to terror (as a counterpoint replies to a point)? Until the Cold War, the term "counterterror" carried, in both scholarly and journalistic contexts, the latter resonance. It was used, for example, to describe the call and response of Red and White terrors in the wake of the Russian Revolution, or Nazism's violent reply to resistance in occupied France, Norway, and elsewhere. But facing the conjoined specters of creeping communism and radical decolonization, the United States and its allies assimilated "counterterror" to a different narrative logic. Today, in official government discourse and popular consciousness across the world, "counterterror" simply refers to the efforts on the part of the state to prevent terrorist attacks. But however unitary its current definition, the "counterterror" trope still contains a subliminal acknowledgment of the ways in which terror is not merely the enemy of the modern state but a basic element of its historical and contemporary constitution. And beyond its discursive articulation, the empirical archive—from El Mozote to Waziristan to Gaza—is clear: the practice of "counterterror" continues to mimic, and produce, the very thing it purports to resist.

"Low-intensity" warfare, a key tactic of U.S. militarism in the early decades of the Cold War, became paradigmatic in the wake of Vietnam. The fallout from America's capitulation in Southeast Asia, after a protracted military engagement costly in both human and financial terms, precipitated a strategic shift toward conflicts waged out of the public glare, often without explicit legislative authorization, and through the funding of proxy forces.[35] This evolution in military doctrine coincided with the birth and incipient imposition of neoliberal rationality. In September 1973 in Chile—a few weeks after the last American combat troops had left Vietnam—the military and national police staged a coup that overthrew the elected leftist president Salvador Allende. In October of that same year, members of the Organization of the Petroleum Exporting Countries (OPEC) declared an oil embargo against the United States (and later Western Europe and Japan) in response to U.S. support for Israel in the context of the Yom Kippur War. The conjuncture of these three events would have extraordinary and enduring geopolitical and economic consequences. The coup in Chile—which the United States supported, via its covert destabilization of the Allende government—prefaced the first thorough application of neoliberal economic reforms on a national scale. And the torture and disappearances that accompanied the "Miracle of Chile" provided early evidence of the intimacy of state terror and neoliberalism. The energy crisis caused by the OPEC embargo, finally, had many immediate and long-term economic effects. Compounding the immense financial toll of the Vietnam War, it provoked stagflation in the United States. It also led to the dissolution of capital controls in the oil-importing countries and a correspondent growth in various forms of financial speculation. In 1973, all that is to say, both neoliberalism and the technologies of state terror that continue to condition its planetary entrenchment took shape on the horizon (even if the origins of both the former and the latter can be found in the more distant past).

1973 is one crucial year in the history of the political present; 1979, the year of the Iranian Revolution and Soviet invasion of Afghanistan, is another. Prior to the revolution in Iran, the United States embraced political Islam (Islamism) as a counterforce to secular nationalisms in the region, which it viewed as a proxy for Soviet power. In Egypt, for example, the Muslim Brotherhood accepted the support of the United States, and Nasser's secular-nationalist state hewed more to the socialist course. But for either political formation—the Islamist and the nationalist—such affiliations were an imperative of survival, as much as or more than they indicated a genuine fidelity to the orthodoxies of the West or the East. Both political Islam and secular nationalism spoke to the urgency of non-alignment—the need for developing nations to evade subservience, ideologically or economically, to the superpower at either end of the bipolar world. The clarity of this ostensible dichotomy was further obscured by the Iranian Revolution. The new regime in Iran was both Islamist and resolutely nationalist—and deeply opposed to American influence. From this point forward, the United States followed a less coherent formula in its search for allies in the region—lending its support, for example, to secular-nationalist dictators such as Saddam Hussein, and creating the conditions for the emergence of Islamist terror in Central Asia.[36] In Afghanistan, the United States encouraged and manipulated militant expressions of radical Islamism. Wary of direct involvement but hoping to entrap the Soviet Union in a draining—Vietnam-like—quagmire, the CIA cultivated the Afghan jihad, ideologically as well as materially, through various governmental and private intermediaries. "From this dynamic," as

Mahmood Mamdani observes, "emerged the forces that carried out the operation we know as 9/11."[37]

In the aftermath of September 11, countless commentators reminded us that al-Qaeda grew out of the CIA-created *mujahideen* in Afghanistan. This fact is invoked—by pundits, politicians, and scholars alike—in the context of arguments that deploy a sort of Frankenstein logic: we should be careful what kind of monsters we bring into the world, as one day they might turn on us, their maker. Or it is cited as yet further evidence of the truism that the United States will lend its military power and ideological blessing to even the most sinister forces if it suits the nation's geopolitical interests. There is undoubtedly some truth to these related lines of interpretation. But they obscure as much as they reveal—about the historical and contemporary entanglement of the United States and Islamist terror and, more generally, about terror and its relationship to the state. If extremist Islamism was a convenient ally of the United States in the 1980s, in the aftermath of the Cold War—when the foreign policy apparatus was in need of a new narrative to frame American global power—it would become a convenient enemy. The specter of terrorism occupied an increasingly prominent place in U.S. foreign policy discourse throughout the 1990s; and September 11 provided the conditions for the declaration of a "War on Terror"—a narrative that establishes the state project of "counterterror" as spaceless and interminable. This is all to summon again a basic argument of this chapter: "Terror" has utility for the state both as a method of violence and as a pretext for violence. For many of its architects and acolytes, the fact that the War on Terror has produced far more terrorists than it has eradicated—the Islamic State of Iraq and the Levant (ISIL), for example, was a fetal entity in 2001 but grew dramatically over the subsequent 15 years—is only partially an inconvenient truth.[38] Terror does threaten the imperial security state, by exposing its vulnerability and by holding up a mirror to its essential violence. But the production of terror is also essential to the war's imperial raison d'être, as it naturalizes the necessity of perpetual militarism.

Neoliberal Terror

Rosa Luxemburg argued that because the accumulation of capital requires the existence of non-capitalist strata, the notion of a truly universal capitalism is an oxymoron. She derived from this conclusion a theoretical certainty in the eventuality of capitalism's collapse. The perpetual expansion into and expropriation of the non-capitalist world is a logical impossibility. When there no longer exists an outside to subsume, accumulation will cease. She did not anticipate, though, neoliberalism's ingenious—if destructive and finite—solution to this apparently immutable contradiction: in the absence of an extant outside, one must simply be created. The purposeful devaluation of assets and labor, and the privatization of public services and industries, are two basic methods through which capital today forges—so as to re-assimilate and exploit—a synthetic outside.[39] Like the imperialist processes of which Luxemburg wrote, neoliberal methods of accumulation require the enactment of state terror. This terror is most explicitly evidenced by military interventions, from Haiti to Iraq, that clear any obstructions to the implementation of neoliberal policies. But it manifests itself in other ways as well. The generalized insecurity produced by the "disembedding" of the market from society, to once again summon Polanyi's formulation, requires the intensification of police repression. Neoliberal policing is designed to both discourage resistance through the display of potential force, and to contain—violently, if necessary—any actual challenges to the established capital-state nexus. The militarization of state and municipal police forces over the past several decades coincided with—is correlated to—the stagnation of real wages, increase of economic inequality, and retrenchment of social protections (among other symptoms of neoliberalism). Finally, the insecurity that neoliberalism generates does not simply provoke the threat or actuality of state terror; it is itself experienced as a sort of terror, the terror of living in perpetual fear of losing hold—suddenly or gradually—of one's means of survival.

In the neoliberal moment, Fanon's insight—that the ubiquity of capitalist violence is revealed in the space of the colony—acquires a different resonance. Writing at the highpoint of postwar social democracy, Fanon argued that in the metropole the educational system, the esteem attached to and derived from work, and the general "structure of moral reflexes" disguised the violence inherent to capitalist social relations. Today, though, as the promise of economic security recedes for the working and middle classes, the efficacy of these ideological apparatuses is diminished. When the "silent compulsion" of the market is rendered rather less compelling by deepening inequality and recurring economic crises, the state is obliged to intervene with more forceful methods of coercion. Thinking with but redirecting Fanon's observation, we might say that today the ubiquity of capitalist violence—the objective terror of capital in its global form—is clarified by the choc en retour of colonial rationality to the global North. Increasingly, it is not just in the colony but in the metropole too that "the agents of government speak the language of pure force."[40]

Writing in the postwar decades, Henri Lefebvre and Guy Debord described "the colonization of everyday life," the boomerang return of colonial instrumentalities to the space of the European metropolis. "Incapable of maintaining the old imperialism," Lefebvre wrote, "searching for new tools of domination ... capitalist leaders treat daily life as they once treated the colonized territories: massive trading posts; absolute predominance of exchange over use; dual exploitation of the dominated in their capacity as producers and consumers."[41] When there are no longer non-capitalist strata to exploit, to summon Luxemburg's phrasing, imperial capital turns inward. Lefebvre and Debord signaled the advent of neoliberal rationality, the globalization of colonial methods of accumulation (a trajectory of globalization that moves from the periphery toward the center, from South to North). The past tense with which Lefebvre alluded to territorial colonization, however, was premature. The "old imperialism" has given way to a new one. The contours of the "colonial present," as Derek Gregory has termed it, are particularly evident in the moment of the War on Terror—the forms of emergency governance, accumulation by dispossession, and racial thinking and practice enacted therein. Conceived as both boundless and endless, the War on Terror normalizes the mobile and constant military enactments that neoliberal capital demands—from preemptive war to protracted counterinsurgency to the less visible but still pervasive operations of private security forces. The bureaucratic permanence and narrative assumptions of "Homeland Security," meanwhile, enable the militarization of public and private police and generalization of the surveillance apparatus. In plainer terms, the conjoined logics of the War on Terror and Homeland Security reveal both the inherency of terror to the modern state and the processes of accumulation this terror continues to make possible.

TERROR AND RESISTANCE: ABSTRACTION AND LIBERATION

Hegel's affirmation of terror was not merely a symptom of his faith in the world-historical significance of the French Revolution. In *The Phenomenology of Spirit* (1807), Hegel elaborated an understanding of terror as central to the project of human freedom—because of its cleansing assault on the forces of the *ancien regime*, yes, but also, crucially, because of its powers of defamiliarization.[42] The *experience* of terror and not merely its enactment in the political theatre, Hegel argued, radically alters how the individual perceives the world and conceives of her subjectivity within it. Hegel developed this latter understanding of terror's ethical and political consequence in his meditations on the master and slave relationship (or lordship and bondage, as it is often translated). Because the slave is conscious of the master's inherent power over her life, she exists in a state of absolute terror. But the experience of this pure and perpetual terror is, in the Hegelian formulation, "the beginning of true human freedom"—a necessary step toward the liberation of the slave's consciousness and, by extension, toward the realization of universal self-consciousness.[43] The condition of terror causes the slave to see that what formerly presented itself as natural and given, most especially her own position of subjection, is in fact a product of contingent historical forces, and is thus potentially fluid. The slave, that is, comes to possess, via the intimate encounter with terror, powers of de-reification. Her affective assimilation of the objective terror of slavery affords the slave a unique insight into the totality of human social relations, and a unique sensitivity to the possibility of their transformation. But if the experience of plantation terror initiates the process of self-becoming, it is in the crucible of violent struggle—wherein the slave risks her life to destroy the old ontological order—that the self-consciousness of the slave and universal potentiality it contains is ultimately realized. The act of terror is a moment of absolute negation through which the will of the slave inserts itself into and founds anew the narrative of universal history. The logic here is, somewhat confusingly, both deductive and inductive: deductive in that the abstraction of absolute negativity makes the project of human freedom concrete; inductive in that the universality of human freedom is realized through the particular subjectivity of the slave. The movement of the master-slave dialectic—and the larger axiom to which it alludes: that the universal is found in the excluded particular—was a significant, if always challenging, source of inspiration for anticolonial thinkers of the twentieth century, who, in the spirit of immanent critique, transmuted Hegel's philosophy of terror and freedom for the intellectual and political project of decolonization.

Terror, Theory, and the Revolt against Slavery

C. L. R. James's seminal *The Black Jacobins* (1938; 1963)—written in rhythm with the anticolonial energies then reverberating across the world—chronicled the world-historical import of the Haitian Revolution and its leader Toussaint L'Ouverture. James's account performed a materialist revision of the Hegelian dialectic, one fitted to the urgent praxis—as well as romantic humanism—of anticolonial struggle. In the book's opening chapter, "The Property," James describes in devastating terms the terror of plantation slavery. "The difficulty," he writes, "was that though one could trap them like animals, transport them in pens, work them alongside an ass or a horse and beat both with the same stick, stable them and starve them, they remained, despite their black skins and curly hair, quite invincibly human beings; with the intelligence and resentments of human beings."[44] James's depiction of the brutality of the plantation speaks for itself. Key here, though, is the emphasis placed on the slave's "invincible humanity." James, of course, is highlighting the resilient human being of the slave, which endured in the most degraded circumstances. But his interest is not limited to how efforts to *negate* the humanity of the slave were resisted or even transcended. As David Scott has observed, *The Black Jacobins* pays concurrent, if less focused, attention to the ways in which slavery is a positive power; the terror of the plantation, in other words, *produced* particular—and particularly human—subjects.[45] In the appendix added to the book's 1963 reissue, James conceptualizes the plantation as a quintessential modern space, and the slaves that lived and labored therein as quintessential modern subjects. The life of the New World slave, James wrote, was "in its essence a modern life."[46] Reading the plantation as paradigmatically modern—rather than as an aberration from the modern, or as a retrograde vestige of the old order that would soon be overcome by it—James implied that the New World slave possessed a privileged insight into, and was an archetypal exponent of, the contradictions of capitalist civilization on a planetary scale. Rhyming in ways with Hegel's formulation—as indeed with Lukácsian theorizations of the proletariat's apprehension of totality—the 1963 appendix imagines the slave as an agent of anti-reification. Because she is immersed within, and because her subjectivity is produced by, the absolute terror of chattel slavery, she is uniquely sensitive to the constitutive place of that terror within enlightened modernity at large. She is, in other words, especially attuned to the dialectical truth that, as Benjamin so neatly phrased it, "every document of civilization is a document of barbarism."

As Nick Nesbitt has observed, though, for much of *The Black Jacobins* James depicts the masses of Saint-Domingue slaves as basically unreflective; their revolt, and the terror at its core, is the expression of a visceral rather than intellectual awareness of the brutal injustices of slavery.[47] The violence they visit upon their overlords is presented as a reflection of the objective terror of slavery rather than as a subjective response to it. "From their masters," James wrote, "they had known rape, torture, degradation and, at the slightest provocation, death. They returned in kind."[48] In such moments, the contradictions between the 1963 appendix—which imagines the slave as a modern subject, with modern sensibilities and desires—and the body of the original text—which contrasts the rather unthinking masses with the mature Enlightenment consciousness of their leader, Toussaint L'Ouverture—is most pronounced. But in another reading, the notion that the Revolution had "two thousand leaders" rather than one—as James retrospectively insisted in an auto-critical acknowledgment of the book's occasionally elitist tenor—is already latent in the original text. Consider the following passage, a letter from Toussaint to his then lieutenant Dessalines, written in a moment of deepening precariousness for the Revolution and its leader:

> We have no other resource than destruction and fire. Bear in mind that the soil bathed with our sweat must not furnish our enemies with the smallest sustenance. Tear up the roads with shot; throw corpses and horses into all the fountains, burn and annihilate everything in order that those who have come to reduce us to slavery may have before their eyes the image of that hell which they deserve.[49]

Toussaint's conversion to the exigency of terror, James concludes, came too late: "[Toussaint's] desire to avoid destruction was the very thing that caused it. It is the recurring error of moderates when face to face with revolutionary struggle."[50] Here James upholds terror, not as the reflexive vengeance of the masses, but as the only rational response to the intransigent terror of the plantation. Toussaint, then, has arrived at the very place the masses began. Crucially, the recognition of unrestrained terror as revolutionary necessity is inseparable, as Nesbitt contends, from an understanding of *slavery* as such—an understanding not simply of slavery's immediate terrors but of its world-systemic significance and, by extension, of its total antithesis: absolute freedom, universal emancipation.[51] As narrated by James, Toussaint's journey to this place of final and total enlightenment modifies the Hegelian formulation. In the master-slave dialectic, the slave apprehends and projects her own universality through the experience and subsequent enactment of terror. The moment of terror and the moment of abstraction, that is, are synchronous. Terror *is* theory. In the case of James's Toussaint, by contrast, the practice of revolutionary terror is the consequence of the moment of abstraction—a *theory* of slavery and freedom prescribes the *praxis* of violence.

As both Hegel and James convey, the problem of terror and the problem of theory are inextricable. Perhaps the *ultimate* terror of the Haitian Revolution was the existential fear it provoked in the guardians of the colonial order and nascent capitalist world-system, who were terrorized by the specter of a black planet. For those quivering elites, as Nesbitt argues, Haiti's postindependence constitution of 1805—a critical-theoretical document that defined blackness as the particular through which universal human freedom would be realized—was itself an instantiation of terror.[52] In the context of the Revolution and its immediate aftermath, in other words, theory (or abstraction) *is* terror, not something that precedes or follows from it—the obverse, then, of Hegel's terror as abstraction, but in the complementary rather than contradictory sense. The terror of Haiti's slaves in revolt opened up the space for new theoretical possibilities; and the Revolution's moment of arch theorization—the propagation of the independent republic's first constitution—was yet another stage in the revolutionary terror, not a post-hoc reflection of or testament to it.

Terror, Theory, and Anticolonialism

In the final pages of *The Wretched of the Earth* (1961), Fanon offers some concluding thoughts on the urgency, in the moment of revolution, of formulating new concepts, new liberatory ideologies, toward the ultimate end of creating a new humanism—a humanism, as Césaire phrased it, "made to the measure of the world." These new concepts are produced in and through the act of struggle. Why this struggle is inevitably and necessarily violent is the enduring, troubling question posed by *The Wretched of the Earth*. In the opening chapter, "On Violence," Fanon outlines his oft-rehearsed critique of the dialogue between colonial violence and anticolonial counterviolence. "The violence which governed the ordering of the colonial world," he writes, "which tirelessly punctuated the destruction of the indigenous social fabric, and demolished unchecked the systems of reference of the country's economy, lifestyles, and modes of dress, this same violence will be vindicated and appropriated." The colonial order is "violence in its natural state," and it "will only yield"—the colonized learn "as soon as they are born"—"when confronted with greater violence."[53] If the colonized possess an innate knowledge of the essential violence of the colonial condition, though, they are not able to simply evade implication in—or locate within the frame of totality—its alienating rationalities and ideologies. Colonialism disfigures every consciousness it touches, colonizer and colonized alike—reifying the settler as subject and the native as object, and causing the latter to internalize the inferior ontology assigned them. Any theory of liberation enunciated in such a context, however objectively true, will carry something of the "lie of the colonial situation."[54] What is required is an absolute epistemological break with the colonial ordering of the world. Particularly in settler-colonies such as Algeria, violence is, for Fanon, the force that will introduce such a rupture—an opening within which conceptual and practical pathways to a true human consciousness might be illuminated. Through the act of violence, the colonized reveal—to the world and most profoundly to themselves—the mutability of colonial power and its reified relations of domination. Through the act of violence, the colonized begin to cleanse themselves of the objectification they have internalized, and to recognize themselves as subjects capable of bringing newness into the world.

The Wretched of the Earth is two books in one. Its opening chapters meditate on the moment of anticolonial becoming—the tactical problems confronted, and the liberatory concepts emergent, therein. The book's penultimate two essays, meanwhile, develop a prescient critique of the contradictions of the postcolonial state—the rearticulation of colonial culture and process under the supervision of the national bourgeoisie. ("Colonial War and Mental Disorders," which concludes the volume, acts more as coda than narrative denouement.) This trajectory, from anticolonial emergence to postcolonial contradiction, evinces again the two forms of violence with which Fanon is concerned—the perpetual violence of imperial capital and the ephemeral violence of revolution. This opposition evokes the distinction drawn by Walter Benjamin, in his "Critique of Violence," between "mythic" and "divine" violence: "If mythic violence is lawmaking [or law-preserving], divine violence is law-destroying; if the former sets boundaries, the latter boundlessly destroys them."[55] The divine violence of revolution "appears as a clear, simple revolt, and no place is reserved either for the sociologists or for the elegant amateurs of social reforms or for the intellectuals who have made it their profession to think for the proletariat."[56] We can hear in Benjamin's words an anticipatory echo of Fanon's critique of intellectual elites in the context of anticolonial revolution—their complicity with the nascent national bourgeoisie, their pedantic and myopic approach to the exigencies of struggle, and their interest in reestablishing elements of the old political and economic order under the sign of independence. The notion of "clear, simple revolt," moreover, resonates with Fanon's meditations on the necessity of "spontaneity" to the early stages of the revolution. Fanon's vision, of course, extended beyond the moment of negation to the realization of a new humanity, the cultivation of a truly decolonized human community. When Fanon writes that the violence of colonial order will be "vindicated" by the violence of anticolonial struggle, he is imagining the absolute eradication of colonial rationality, the dissolution of all relations of domination, and the unification of self and other within a true—and truly universal—humanism. Fanon is concerned, in other words, not simply with the liberation of the colonized but with the liberation of the colonizer as well. The former is impossible without the latter. The divine violence of the anticolonial movement will "expiate" the agents of empire, precisely because it will destroy the legal order that enshrines the ontological division between settler and native. But Fanon is profoundly wary of the rearticulation of mythic violence in the form of the postindependence state, and within the broader framework of the new international division of labor. And indeed, the postcolonial contradictions that Fanon observed on the horizon in 1961—the mythic violence of an endlessly reinventive, and necessarily imperialist, capitalism—remain unsurpassed.

Terror and Resistance Today

In contemporary political discourse, the problem of terror and terrorism is habitually conflated with the phenomenon of Islamic fundamentalism. Where, then, do al-Qaeda or ISIL fit in the political and intellectual genealogies of anticolonial violence elaborated above? This question can be engaged through the lenses of both history and theory. Islamist terror was innovated with the help of the CIA in the latter stages of the Cold War. But Islamist terror is only one expression of radical political Islam, the deeper roots of which can be found in the moment, and political and theoretical milieus, of decolonization. The Egyptian Sayyid Qutb, perhaps the key intellectual figure in the contemporary flourishing of radical Islamism, regarded nationalism as a poisonous colonial inheritance that could not be redeemed by decolonial movement. In this, Qutb's thinking was discordant with Fanon's faith in the radical potentiality of national consciousness. Qutb did, though, share profound intellectual affinities with Fanon and other anticolonial thinkers, such as Césaire, who highlighted the moral and cultural bankruptcy of Europe. Ali Shariati, another Islamist thinker and one of the intellectual authors of the Iranian Revolution, was a student of Fanon's theorizations of anticolonial struggle and was inspired as well by Che Guevara and Latin American liberation theology.[57] As Susan Buck-Morss argues, Shariati's critical disposition was defined "by the object criticized—world imperialism, racism, and class exploitation—rather than any ideological form."[58] A distinction must be drawn, it should be needless to say, between the Islamism of Qutb and Shariati and Islamist terror. The critical Islamism elaborated by Qutb and Shariati imagines ijtihad—the interpretation of Islamic law within a democratic public sphere—as an open and continual process. By contrast, for the Islamists of al-Qaeda and ISIL, as Mahmood Mamdani has put it, "the gates of ijtihad are forever closed."[59] Even if appealing to the project of universal emancipation, the Islamism of al-Qaeda conceives of the moment or act of struggle—jihad—as the route toward the realization of an extant ideology rather than as a space within which new concepts will emerge. Islamist terror, that is, is an instance of mythic violence par excellence. It is also thoroughly incompatible with the Fanonian anticolonial formulation, which disavows all ideologies and insists that the theoretical precepts of a truly universal humanism will only be clarified in and through the time-space of revolution. Finally, one objective of contemporary Islamist terror, as it is enacted in Europe and America especially, is the provocation of a significant military reply—because the latter generates yet more anger at, and enlists yet more recruits to, the violent struggle against the presence of Euro-American power in the world. Whatever the long-term goals of ISIL, its immediate tactics—mirroring those of the imperial state for whom terror is a necessary enemy—seek the perpetual escalation of the terror/counterterror cycle rather than its transcendence.

Al-Qaeda and ISIL are of course not the only contemporary exponents of terror as resistance. This is particularly evident when we broaden our definition to encompass the notion of terror as an *effect* of violence. Benjamin, invoking Georges Sorel, cites the proletarian general strike as a quintessential example of divine violence. A violence of "pure means," the general strike makes no demands of or claims upon the state. It gestures beyond the existing legal framework without positing a new one.[60] The state may regard the strike itself as non-violent, but it also perceives within it, as Idelbar Avelar has put it, the specter of a "virtual, possible, future violence" and responds in turn, with an anticipatory counterviolence.[61] The general strike is "violent," in other words, because it terrorizes the psyche of established political-economic order, not because it poses any immediate corporeal or material danger to the structures or holders of power. Some of the most visible contemporary popular movements against neoliberal capital and its government enablers signal the potentiality of a cognate form of non-violent violence.

Provoked by the recurring crises and endemic social failures of neoliberalism, recent instances of "spontaneous" revolt—from Cairo to Athens to Madrid to New York—have given rise to a resurgent left-critical interest in the theoretical and strategic efficacy of terror, broadly conceived. The most amplified contributor to this conversation has been Slavoj Žižek. In his essay "Robespierre or the 'Divine Violence' of Terror," Žižek invokes the food riots in Brazil in the 1990s:

> When those outside the structured social field strike 'blindly', demanding AND enacting immediate justice/vengeance, this is 'divine violence'—recall, a decade or so ago, the panic in Rio de Janeiro when crowds descended from *favelas* into the rich part of the city and started looting and burning supermarkets—THIS was 'divine violence'. . . . Like the biblical locusts, the divine punishment for men's sinful ways, it strikes out of nowhere, a means without end.[62]

Elsewhere, though, Žižek has described the recent youth riots in London and the *banlieues* of Paris in rather less heroic terms, as random outbursts that possess "the spirit of revolt but not of revolution": "From a revolutionary point of view, the problem with the riots is not the violence as such," Žižek concludes, "but the fact that the violence is not truly self-assertive. It is impotent rage and despair masked as a display of force; it is envy masked as triumphant carnival."[63] What the riots reveal, Žižek argues, is that "the only available alternative to enforced democratic consensus is a blind acting out. Opposition to the system can no longer articulate itself in the form of a realistic alternative, or even as a utopian project, but can only take the shape of a meaningless outburst."[64] Fanon would have arrived at a different interpretation. That an alternative does not immediately present itself is evidence of the reified nature of the society within which we live. Whatever preconceived theories we bring to the barricades are contaminated by, "carry the lie of," the mystified contradictions within which they were formulated. But through the act of revolt, Fanon avowed, new—if "partial, finite, and shifting"—truths might emerge, from which new conceptual vocabularies and new utopian imaginaries might be elaborated. Žižek does hint, though, at the implicit (or potential) theoretical content of the riots: "To riot is to make a subjective statement, implicitly to declare how one relates to one's objective conditions."[65] Fanon's faith was that this latent consciousness would, in the course and aftermath of struggle, become manifest in both theoretical and structural terms. What he envisioned was a divine violence that would give way to a *law-making but non-mythic* violence—which would ultimately hasten the eradication of violence itself. In Benjamin's critique, the violence of the state is inherently "mythic" because the idea of the political—the idea of representational democracy, for example, or the notion of the sovereign itself—is a symbol that comes to supplant the thing it signifies.[66] People have such fidelity to the ideal that they are blind to the actual conditions and potentialities of political life. The bringing of new truths into the world, Benjamin warned, will only result in the displacement of one idolatrous symbolic regime by another.[67] Fanon, by contrast, imagined that the theories produced through—and by the agents of—revolutionary violence would not just be critical but *self*-critical, and thus anti-idolatrous.[68] Such theories would contain an inherent awareness of, and resistance to, the calcification of emergent concepts into another apparatus of reification.

In the colonial context that animated Fanon's account, violent resistance is manifold in its intention and effect—the attainment and enactment of the human subjectivity of the slave or the colonized; the revelation of the objective terrors of colonial power; and the elaboration of material or theoretical routes of transcendence. Put slightly differently, the terror of anticolonial resistance refuses the civilizationist narratives that imagine the colonized subject as a part of the "state of nature" (an embodiment of its intrinsic terror), and brings into view the essential and abiding centrality of terror to the imperial security state. In the spirit of anticolonial thought—and in contrast to the mythic violence of entities such as ISIL, who intensify rather than imagine a way beyond the terror/counterterror cycle—there do exist contemporary forms of resistance that strike terror in the guardians of imperial order precisely because they unmask the terrors of capital and the state, or because they signal or enact new human subjectivities and new truths that might constitute a new and other world. As thinkers such as Fanon and James perceived with a unique clarity, this latter terror might be achieved not merely via violence itself but through the theoretical or literary enunciation of critical witness or speculative imagination.

CONCLUSION

"Terror," like "security," is a keyword of political and economic modernity. It was a central philosophic problem, and a central political technology, in the moment of the emergence of the modern state and capitalist mode of production. And it remains essential to the conjoined, but never identical, rationalities of state and market—and the resistance to which they give rise. I have attempted in this chapter to illuminate the especial place of the terror concept within the history of a specifically colonial modernity. In the first instance, terror—the sublime terror of the state of nature—is a pretext for the imposition of imperial power. In the second instance, terror is a method employed by the imperial security state to establish and deepen its dominance, and to guarantee the conditions and outcome of capital accumulation. Finally, terror is a strategy of resistance to the colonial order of things—a tactic of violence that aspires, variously, to unmask, arrest, or provoke the perpetual terrors of imperial order.

We are living today in the time of the "War on Terror." The efficacy of the War on Terror as a narrative figure depends on the assumption that September 11, 2001, constituted a historical rupture—an abiding premise that obscures the connections between, for example, the long history of emergency governance and the current "state of exception," or early modern and contemporary processes of primitive accumulation. The amnesia encouraged by the trope of rupture is not unique to the event of 9/11 or the War on Terror to which it has led. The cultures of forgetting that today enable the reproduction of militarized accumulation compound modes of erasure and disavowal that are basic to modernity itself. What Lukács termed "reification"—the procedure, coincident with the universalization of the commodity form, that makes what is historically produced and contingent appear as natural and fixed—is one word for the essential and necessary relationship between the forgetting of modernity's foundational violence and the latter-day reinvention of that violence.[69] Historicist attempts to counter this erasure of the past often end up rehearsing its basic effect—highlighting the terror of primitive accumulation, but failing to recognize subsequent and contemporary forms of accumulation by dispossession; revealing the terror that inaugurated the modern state, but obscuring the ways in which that terror persists beyond the moment of foundation—and, relatedly, obscuring the terrors of slavery and colonial expropriation that conditioned the terrors of the French Revolution.

But there do exist alternative cultures of historical reckoning that locate the moment of the War on Terror within deeper intellectual and political genealogies. The first two chapters of this book have begun to essay such a reckoning. The three chapters that follow consider how works of contemporary theory and fiction locate the conceptual paradigms of security and terror, and the political and economic forms through which they are expressed, within the long history of colonial modernity. Several of the texts I examine enact, among other formal and epistemological innovations, alternative ways of imagining, inhabiting, and remembering the time-space of rupture. For writers such as Junot Díaz, Teju Cole, Mohsin Hamid, and Roberto Bolaño, the moment of putative rupture—whether September 11, 2001 or September 11, 1973—does not obscure the past but brings it into more expansive and focused view. In listening to the insights of Hegel, Fanon, and Benjamin, we have already encountered the basic lineaments of such an approach. For Hegel, the experience and subsequent enactment of terror introduces a psychological rupture that frees the slave's consciousness and denaturalizes the social relations within which her humanity has been negated.[70] For Fanon, in the moment of struggle the violence of colonial relations, and the historicity of that violence, is laid bare—and new routes of emancipation are illuminated. Fanon's reading of colonial order and anticolonial becoming can help us grapple with Benjamin's famous injunction in "Theses on the Philosophy of History": "The tradition of the oppressed," Benjamin wrote, "teaches us that the state of emergency within which we live is not the exception but the rule." When we "attain to a conception of history that accords with this insight" we will appreciate that "it is our task to bring about a real state of emergency"—a moment of rupture wherein the terror of capital and the imperial state will be revealed and demystified, and through which a revolutionary formation will "blast open the continuum of history" and "leap in the open air."[71] It is beyond the powers of this or any academic monograph, alas, to "blast open" the continuum, the relentless terror of history as progress. But the chapters that follow will continue, in dialogue with various works of theory and fiction, to "attain to a conception of history" that makes the continuum—and its contingency—visible.

THREE

"Choc en Retour"

SECURITY, TERROR, THEORY

Writing against the specter of Jacobinism, Edmund Burke warned that the uprising in France was "a Revolution of doctrine and theoretick dogma," a grave threat to the order of things because of its abstract dictums—the potential it contained for universal application.[1] Like "terror," "theory" was constitutive of the modern state; and like "terror," "theory" is today imagined by the guardians of political order as something foreign and dangerous.[2] Though one can trace its modern origins to the French Revolution and birth of the liberal state, theory in its contemporary incarnation is associated with another archetypal moment of French revolutionary ferment, 1968. The events of that May—which reverberated in concert with social upheavals across the world—signaled the possibility of a synthesized left politics that would integrate a fundamental resistance to capitalist alienation and exploitation with critiques of patriarchy, white supremacy, Eurocentricity, and allied relations or structures of domination. "Theory" was the umbrella term under which each of these critiques could intermingle. Upon its Atlantic crossing, theory was received by U.S. elites as an unwelcome foreign entity, one that called forth an entire history of revolutionary paroxysms—1789, 1804, 1848, 1871, 1917, even, perhaps, 1776—and betrayed the enduring bourgeois fear of Maximilien Robespierre, Toussaint L'Ouverture, and, most profoundly, Karl Marx.[3] Despite this outsider legacy, a common polemic of recent times, most famously voiced by Terry Eagleton, holds that the arrival of theory in the U.S. academy led to its declension. The critiques it historically denoted have devolved into an insidious and impotent form of postmodern identity politics, and have been fully assimilated into the logic of the marketplace. This declaration of theory's death was echoed from the right. Upon the fall of the Berlin Wall in 1989, Francis Fukuyama and others in the neoconservative intelligentsia announced "the end of history"—the end, it was implied, of the era of political conflict that had been inaugurated by the French Revolution two centuries earlier. The free market and electoral democracy had triumphed over all alternatives. Like ideology, theory was now redundant.

Contemporary theory is thus engaged on two fronts, struggling to counter the "death of theory" narrative—which is closely related to the "end of history" thesis—and to formulate a critical vocabulary apposite to a political moment defined by permanent war and generalized neoliberal degradation. If the "end of history" announces the global apotheosis of liberal democracy and the free market, which emanates outward from the West/North toward the East/South, theory is today tasked with revealing the dialectical underside of this triumphalist narrative—the globalization not of freedom and security but of terror and insecurity. Though the figures of "Homeland Security" and the "War on Terror" are central objects of contemporary critique, the discrete terms "security" and "terror" are under-theorized. The contemporary theorization of security and terror is less a direct and autonomous critical project than a synthesis of three categories of critique: the critique of spectacle; the critique of the politics of exception; and the critique of empire (qua global capital). How, this chapter asks, do these three critical strands help us to situate the paradigms of security and terror within the history of colonial modernity at large?

In chapters 1 and 2, I sought to locate the contemporary iterations of security and terror within the long history of European empire and its afterlives. I sought, more specifically, to resist the assumption that September 11, 2001, constituted a historical rupture, by demonstrating how the conjoined formations of "Homeland Security" and "War on Terror" represent the reproduction of extant colonial histories. My focus to this point has been on the temporal trajectories of colonial rationality. This concern will continue to guide the chapters that follow. But in this third chapter I want to foreground as well the spatial routes of the contemporary return of colonial culture and process. In one sense, the spatial logics of the new imperialism mirror that of the old—the brutal subjection of the nations of the global South by the political and economic powers of the global North. I am also keen to accent here, though, what Césaire termed the "choc en retour" of colonial rationality to the metropole—the boomerang return, to the postcolonial North, of imperial modes of governance and accumulation. The theory I critique below is conditioned by this choc en retour. The critique of spectacle is responding to what Debord termed the "colonization of everyday life"—the pervasion of the commodity form throughout the social worlds of the metropole. The critique of exception is an effect of the contemporary enactment by and within the liberal state of forms of emergency governance that were innovated and normalized in the space of the colony. And the critique of empire is symptomatic of the neoliberal application in the global North of methods of depredation that have long been the paradigmatic mode of accumulation in the colonized world. These particular instances of "return" betray a broader historical condition—the planetary generalization, in a moment of perpetual war and neoliberal crisis, of emergency governance and economic insecurity.

The conjoined critiques of spectacle, exception, and imperial capital, though, are unevenly revelatory of the colonial essence and history of contemporary culture and politics. This unevenness is an effect of theory's symptomatic nature—the ways in which theory often echoes the form of its critical object. The works I critically engage in this chapter are exemplary instances of this formal echo. In their critiques of spectacle, Jean Baudrillard and Slavoj Žižek reproduce the ahistoricity of the image, leaving untraced the genealogical routes that connect commodity ascendance in the postcolonial metropole to the pure articulation of commodity rationality in the colony. In their theorizations of bare life and the state of exception, meanwhile, Giorgio Agamben and Judith Butler affirm the exceptionalism of the War on Terror's political technologies. Finally, Michael Hardt and Antonio Negri's critique of an emergent imperial order adopts two abiding tropes of the "globalization" concept: the assumption of an imminent or achieved planetarity—the disappearance of the "outside" that is essential to colonial rationality—and the assumption that the defining political forms of this globalism originate in the advanced capitalist world.

SPECTACLE, CAPITAL, TERROR

As theorized by Theodor Adorno and others, the mass violence of the twentieth century redefined the aesthetic and political implications of the sublime. Kant and Burke recognized that performances of political violence could produce the sublime, but they reserved the term "nature" for the non-human world. Writing in the eighteenth century, they did not see, or anticipate, the profound reification of social life under capital—the ways in which historically contingent social relations, and the violence inherent therein, are rendered by the mythos of capital as *natural*. In the context of this "second nature," the sublime acquires a different resonance and effect. Spectacular instances of political violence, and indeed the relentless spectacle of commodity culture, do not permit the second moment in Kant's dynamic sublime, wherein human reason and rationality reasserts its dominance over the irrationality of nature—because the irrationality of "second nature" violence is inextricable from rationality itself, and because there is no longer a position of safe remove, an outside, from which one can regard and redeem the sublime.[4]

The naturalization of commodity rationality was a key concern of the thinkers of the Situationist International. Guy Debord published his seminal *Society of the Spectacle* in 1967. Debord named, in that book's title and in its interior contents, a new form of capitalism based on the subjection of ever more realms of human social life to the rationality of the market. In so doing he described one of the defining characteristics of neoliberalism before the neoliberal era had properly begun. (Most historians of neoliberalism locate its inception in the early 1970s.) The prescience of Debord's critique, and the endurance of the state of affairs he highlighted and foretold, has ensured that the *Society of the Spectacle* remains a relevant text, one with much to say about the culture and techniques of contemporary capital accumulation. The "colonization of everyday life" was enabled by the ascent of the image—as a commodity in itself and as a screen that conceals, like a fetish, the reality of capitalist social relations. Debord's use of the term "colonization"—and Henri Lefebvre's echo of it—might be read as proposing an obfuscatory analogy between the radically different modalities of commodity rationality in the colony and metropole. His choice of metaphor, though, evinces the historical articulation of, rather than collapses the distance between, colony and metropole. Invoking "colonization" rather than simply "commoditization" evokes the dialectical relation between the violence of extractive industry in the space of the colony and the saturation by the commodity form of all spheres of human social life in the consumerist societies of the overdeveloped world. It points, in other words, toward the history of colonial violence that conditions—is synchronically and diachronically connected to—cultures of alienation and exploitation in the postcolonial metropole.

Reflecting the televisual glare of the Twin Towers' collapse, several widely cited theoretical texts composed in the near aftermath of September 11 summon Debord's critique—notably Jean Baudrillard's *The Spirit of Terrorism* (2002), Slavoj Žižek's *Welcome to the Desert of the Real* (2002), and the Retort group's *Afflicted Powers* (2004). The contemporary critique of spectacle confronts the same theoretical aporia negotiated by Debord: How to highlight the primacy of the image without submitting to its power? How to reveal the ubiquity of commodity culture without reinforcing its omnipotence and reproducing its ahistoricity? The Retort group observes that "the colonization of everyday life" is simply "'globalization' turned inward."[5] The contemporary critique of spectacle, I want to argue, mimics rather than resists this inward turning.

The violence of spectacle expresses itself in both subjective and objective forms. Subjective violence, as Žižek has outlined this distinction, refers to "violence performed by a clearly identifiable agent"—the violence that shows up on the evening news, the violence that disrupts the peaceful workings of everyday social and political order.[6] Objective violence, by contrast, refers to the often-invisible violence of the system itself—the pervasive and perpetual violence of capital in its globalized form. Spectacular instances of subjective violence serve one of two contradictory purposes. The dramatic car accident viewed by millions on YouTube distracts from rather than directs our attention to the slow ecological violence of automobile culture. But the logic of the terrorist attack—and indeed, as Retort cites, that of "the ruined small farmer from South Korea, slashing his arteries in defiance on the barricades at Cancun"[7]—avows that another form of subjective violence is possible, one that will cut through the thick screens of fetishism and reification. The potentiality of the "image-event" in exposing and resisting the objective violence of commodity culture is one central concern of the contemporary critique of spectacle.

"The events in New York," Baudrillard writes in *The Spirit of Terrorism*, "have radicalized the relation of the image to reality. Whereas we were dealing before with an uninterrupted profusion of banal images and seamless flow of sham events, the terrorist act in New York has resuscitated both images and events."[8] The meeting of image and event, though, is not seamless. "At the same time that [images] exalt the event," Baudrillard contends, "they also take it hostage. They serve to multiply it to infinity and . . . are a diversion and neutralization. . . . The image consumes the event, in the sense that it absorbs it and offers it for consumption."[9] The force of the real event is correlated to the symbolic power of its proliferation as image. But the reduction of the event to its image denies the experience of the event as reality. Baudrillard elaborates this paradox by suggesting that the destruction of the Twin Towers elucidated the contest between, and entwined nature of, reality and fiction. For many observers, Baudrillard notes, September 11, 2001, represented the "resurgence of the real ... in an allegedly virtual universe" (a resurgence that corresponded with "the resurrection of history beyond its proclaimed end"). Baudrillard is wary of this reading, however, and insists instead that if reality appears, in the event of the Twin Towers' collapse, to overtake fiction, "this is because it has absorbed fiction's energy, and has itself become fiction."[10] The image precedes and surpasses the real event: "Rather than the violence of the real being there first, and the *frisson* of the image being added to it, the image is there first, and the *frisson* of the real is added."[11] The image delivers the real. In other words, the violence of September 11 does not represent the return of history or the return of the real. It represents, rather, the triumph of the symbolic.

In Baudrillard's reading, the image-event of September 11 was empty of political content. The political aims of its actors, the historical forces from which it emerged and to which it responds—all of this is eclipsed by the image. Every replay of the towers falling serves to further evacuate the event of its historical and political meaning. Yet in making this observation so central to his account, Baudrillard finds himself stuck in something of a critical cul-de-sac. His emphasis on September 11 as spectacle—and his corresponding neglect of the concrete social relations within which the spectacle operates—serves to reinforce rather than resist the fetishism of the image. The question his account ultimately prompts, then, is how to "[preserve] intact the unforgettable incandescence of the image"[12] without being blinded by it. This is not to condemn or dismiss Baudrillard's essay—a slim and narrow volume that does not aspire to any kind of comprehensive reading of global politics—but to shed light upon the ways in which the dominance of the image is reprised in the moment of critique.

Avowed materialists, members of the Retort group—a "gathering of antagonists to capital and empire," composed, in this instance, of Iain Boal, T. J. Clark, Michael Watts, and Joseph Matthews—distance themselves from the more symbolic register of Baudrillard's account. But if keen to "desacralize" spectacle, *Afflicted Powers*, a manifesto-like account of global political order after September 11, remains in thrall to its power.[13] September 11, Retort suggests, was designed and experienced as an "image event"; its psychological and political power was owed in great part to the spectacle it produced. Debord famously defined "spectacle" as "capital accumulated to the point where it becomes image."[14] Citing this aphorism, Retort asks, "What more adequate encapsulation of the process could there be than the World Trade Center (with its multiplication of the terminally gigantic by two)? And what other means of defeating it—its social instrumentality, that is, its power over the consuming imagination—than have it be literally obliterated on camera?"[15] This two-part question captures precisely, Retort argues, the logic of the terrorist event. Retort is careful to assert their own opposition to this tactical reasoning: *"We do not believe that one can destroy the society of the spectacle by producing the spectacle of its destruction."*[16] That said, they insist, the state does "[feel] the cold hand of the image-event at its throat"— the video repetition of the towers' collapse and dissemination of Abu Ghraib photographs are but two examples of "image defeat"—and responds accordingly, with its own "Shock and Awe" productions and with redoubled efforts at controlling the access to and framing of information.[17] On one level, as we have seen, the War on Terror is a war over material power. Its aims are the extension and deepening of U.S. geopolitical authority, an objective that is joined—if at times discordantly—to the project of facilitating and securing neoliberal accumulation on a global scale. On a different but related level, the Retort group observes, the War on Terror is a war "for the control of appearances."[18] *Afflicted Powers* sets out to articulate the ways in which these two spheres of struggle, the material and the symbolic, are interwoven with one another. "Military neoliberalism" is the term Retort uses to describe this convergence, the intersection of military violence, primitive accumulation, and information war.

Marx used the term "primitive accumulation" to indicate the operations of enclosure and dispossession—of land, resources, and people—that brought into being a mass proletariat and provided the materials necessary for the inauguration of capitalism as a mode of production. As I discussed in chapter 2, many contemporary critics—in accord with Hannah Arendt's observation that for capitalism to survive, "the original sin of simple robbery" must be perpetually repeated—have focused on the centrality of primitive accumulation not just to the origins of capitalism but to its continuing evolution in the present. (In Retort's treatment of this problem, they sometimes substitute for "primitive" the word "crude," in order to resist the association of the primitive with the past.) Retort's intention is to shed light upon the ways in which the imperial wars of the twenty-first century "set the stage for the trinity of crude accumulation: the enclosure and looting of resources; the creation of a cheap and deracinated labor force; and the establishment of captive markets."[19] The ceaseless process of crude accumulation requires permanent war. The War on Terror, a "forever war," represents one effort to normalize this permanence, "to maintain," as Retort puts it, "the image of war as an unexceptional part of the state's external life."[20]

In normalizing itself, Retort argues, permanent war also works to "relativize" peace. This has long been the case. Since the advent of the aerial bomb, "pacification"—the imposition of peace through the delivery of spectacular terror—has been a central tactic of imperial governance. The first aerial bombs were dropped by European planes onto European colonies, with the aim of terrifying empire's subject populations into "peaceful" submission. As Retort writes: "Peace and terror are, from the perspective of imperialists and civilizers, inextricable."[21] The spectacle of pacification via terror reached "apocalyptic extremes," Retort notes, in the mushroom clouds over Hiroshima and Nagasaki. Yet there were no cameras on hand to transmit the peace-bringing explosions that devastated Japan. The phenomenon of aerial bombardment as mass-media event is more recent. Its effects have been double. The popular entertainment of the Gulf War—the bombing of Baghdad live on network television—functioned within the realm of war's normalization. But in the course of the War on Terror, more undisciplined, unsanitized images of aerial devastation have circulated—through WikiLeaks and other alternative media—in ways that circumvent manipulation by the state. All this is to say that the proliferation and intensification of image culture is at once "the key form of social control in present circumstances, [and one] source of ongoing instability."[22]

Since the struggle over the "control of appearances" is of profound political consequence, it follows that spectacle is both an object and method of critique. Though clear in their opposition to the notion that the society of the spectacle can be destroyed through the spectacle of its own destruction, Retort does suggest that "military neoliberalism" is vulnerable to image critique. Abu Ghraib is one poignant and politically potent image of latter-day capitalist militarism. The devastation of post-Katrina New Orleans is another. Each of these images speaks for, and gestures beyond, itself; yet none of them alone can represent the totality of the conjuncture from which they emerged. The latter task cannot be achieved through the pyrotechnic event or even through the instantaneous (un)mediation of military and capitalist atrocity. It will involve taking time—claiming time itself as a terrain of struggle—to articulate together, historicize, and illuminate the materiality of the images that flash before us.

EXCEPTION AND THE POLITICS OF BARE LIFE

When Debord and Lefebvre invoked the "colonization of everyday life," they gestured toward a line of inquiry that would consider the boomerang return of colonial culture and process to the space of the metropole. They signaled, in other words, the efficacy of an analytic approach that would understand the neoliberal society of spectacle as but the latest iteration of an imperialist rationality that is essential to the commodity form. Such an approach would not deny the newness of the spectacle age but would rather use that newness as a lens onto continuity—the genealogical and dialectical connections, for example, between spectacular terror in the colonies and the mundane generality of capitalist rationality in the postcolonial metropolis. The possibilities of this deeper historical examination have been only partially realized by contemporary critiques of spectacle, which mirror and magnify the ahistoricity of the image itself.

Like the critique of spectacle, the critique of exception reproduces the formal logic of its object. In particular, the theorization of the "state of exception" in the moment of the War on Terror tends to affirm rather than resist the exceptionalism of the current conjuncture. As terms such as "enemy combatant" and "extraordinary rendition" entered political discourse, and as the juridical apparatus of the War on Terror was elucidated, the work of Giorgio Agamben emerged as a crucial source—perhaps the crucial source—for critics struggling to develop a conceptual vocabulary adequate to the moment. Most specifically, Agamben's reflections on the *homo sacer*—the figure, reduced to a condition of "bare life," who can be killed with impunity but not sacrificed—seemed to capture the precarious subjectivity of the orange-clad and shackled Guantánamo inmate, or the naked and leashed prisoners at Abu Ghraib. His related insights into the normalization of the state of emergency, and the history of the sovereign "decision," informed the critique of the War on Terror's juridical and governmental innovations. Though Agamben's work on the figure of the *homo sacer* and juridical forms of the "state of exception" is deeply genealogical, his engagement with the War on Terror encourages rather than contradicts the myriad critical appeals to the exceptionalism of the post–September 11 state of exception. In *Homo*

Sacer (1998), Agamben identifies the Nazi concentration camp as the space wherein the exception is realized as the paradigm of modern social order.[23] The camp, Agamben writes in the latter volume, is "the place in which the most absolute *conditio inhumana* that has ever existed on earth was realized."[24] In *State of Exception* (2004), Agamben suggests that there is an imperfect analogy to be drawn between the legal and ontological status of the Jew in the *Lager* and the detainee at Guantánamo. In either case, the prisoner has lost not simply their rights as a citizen but any legal identity whatsoever. But the absolute loss of personhood, Agamben contends, is even more purely realized in Guantánamo, as the Jews in the Nazi camp "at least retained their identity as Jews."[25] Echoing Judith Butler, Agamben observes that "in the detainee at Guantánamo, bare life reaches its maximum indeterminacy."[26] Agamben's subtle but significant affirmation of "post-9/11" exceptionalism magnifies the absence, in his genealogical framework, of a sustained or intensive engagement with the specifically colonial origins and essence—and specifically racial logics—of the politics of exception.

Central to Agamben's theoretical framework—as to the contemporary theorization of bare life and the state of exception more broadly—is a concern with "biopower," power that has taken hold over life itself. For Foucault, biopower—the subjection of biological being to both state and market power—is intrinsically bound up with the politics of security. The object of security, Foucault argued, is the biological life of an entire population. Working in concert with but expanding upon technologies of discipline, which act upon individual bodies, security conditions and controls—secures—the political community at large. The biopolitics of security permits and regulates particular ways of being and guarantees particular forms of life. Correlatively, the biopolitics of security decides which ways of being are not permitted and which lives are unworthy of life. And race, Foucault observed, is the mechanism that marks the boundaries between necessary and disposable life. In *"Society Must Be Defended,"* his 1975–76 lectures at the Collège de France, Foucault considers the reciprocal emergence of biopower and modern racial thinking. In the eighteenth century, the rise of natural scientific disciplines occasioned a turn toward the biologization of the political sphere. Ivan Hannaford has described this process as "the displacement of political differentiation in history by economic, social, physical, and psychological differentiation outside history."[27] This turn in social thought toward "natural" science and law coincided with and enabled the development of modern biological racism. In Foucault's formulation, concepts of race and techniques of racism are deployed in order to fragment and stratify the "biological continuum" that is biopower's proper domain:

> [Racism] is primarily a way of introducing a break into the domain of life that is under power's control: the break between what must live and what must die. The appearance within the biological continuum of the human races, the distinction among races, the hierarchy of races, the fact that certain races are described as good and that others, in contrast, are described as inferior: all this is a way of fragmenting the field of the biological that power controls.[28]

The break between what must live and what must die. Agamben's conceptualization of "bare life" marks, but elides the racial implications of, this fissure in ontological unity produced by the "biopolitical machine." Foucault, Agamben notes in *Homo Sacer*, discovered that "the entry of *zoe* into the sphere of the *polis*—the politicization of bare life as such—constitutes the decisive event of modernity."[29] Following from but amending this observation, Agamben asserts that the conflation of the biological and political realms is basic not just to political modernity in general but to the figure of *sovereignty* in particular. Objecting to Foucault's analytic decentering of sovereignty—and lamenting his failure to recognize the convergence of negative and positive, objective and subjective, power—Agamben argues that any theory of biopolitics must be at once a theory of sovereignty. "Sovereignty," Agamben summates, "presents itself as an incorporation of the state of nature in society, or ... as a state of indistinction between nature and culture, between violence and law."[30] This indistinction is related to another: the state of exception is essential rather than exceptional to juridical order. In Agamben's words, "The state of exception is ... included in the *nomos* as a moment that is in every sense fundamental."[31] Invoking Carl Schmitt, Agamben suggests that the "state of exception" denotes a "complex topological figure" in which "the state of nature and law, outside and inside, pass through one another."[32] The "sovereign decision" suspends the law, and "thus implicates bare life within it."[33] Agamben is alert, though, to the ways in which both bare life and the state of nature are produced by rather than prior to sovereignty. "The production of bare life is the original act of sovereignty," Agamben writes. And later, in *State of Exception* (2005): "There are not first life as a natural biological given and anomie as the state of nature, and then their implication in law through the state of exception. On the contrary, the very possibility of distinguishing life and law, anomie and *nomos*, coincides with their articulation in the biopolitical machine."[34] The production of both bare life and the state of nature enables the binary structuring of society. This important observation gestures toward, without explicitly acknowledging, the essentially racialized nature of bare life—the fact that the "break between what must live and what must die" is a racial break.

Agamben's neglect of race is correlated to his only ephemeral engagement with the history and political forms of European colonialism. In *Homo Sacer*, Agamben essays a genealogy of the camp—the paradigmatic space of modernity, "the hidden matrix and *nomos* of the political space within which we are still living."[35] Agamben notes that the concentration camp first appeared as a method of repression and control in the context of colonial wars, in Cuba at the close of the nineteenth century and in South Africa in the early years of the twentieth. "Historians debate," Agamben writes,

> whether the first appearance of camps ought to be identified with the concentration camps that were created in 1896 by the Spaniards in Cuba in order to repress the insurrection of that colony's population, or rather with the concentration camps into which the English herded the Boers at the beginning of the twentieth century. What matters here is that in both cases one is dealing with the extension to an entire civilian population of a state of exception linked to a colonial war.[36]

In the context of colonial war, that is, the camp enables and crystallizes the generalization of the state of exception. But Agamben does not bring this observation to bear on his primary historical-theoretical object, the Nazi concentration camp. Auschwitz was located in *occupied* Poland; and Nazism's war of conquest, as Enzo Traverso has argued, was a "colonial war whose ideology and principles were borrowed largely from those of classic nineteenth-century imperialism."[37] The problem of colonialism, though, does not figure in Agamben's reckoning with Nazism. The genealogical routes between the racialized state of exception in the space of the colony and genocidal violence internal to Europe—the precise choc en retour highlighted by Césaire—are, in Agamben's account, ultimately unpursued.[38] Agamben does not reflect upon the uniquely colonial nature of either the Reich's eastward march or the concentration camps that clarified Nazism's racial and genocidal logics. Reckoning with the coloniality of Nazi violence, though, can help us discern the synchronic and diachronic connections among European empire, the state of nature, bare life, the sovereign exception, and the camp as *nomos*. Indeed, all of Agamben's core concepts acquire a greater explanatory power—in the context of the War on Terror and in general—when the fact of their centrality to colonial articulations of law and violence is placed in the analytic foreground.

As I paraphrased above, one of Agamben's foremost concerns is the indistinction, or entanglement, of law and violence, inside and outside, sovereignty and bare life. And as Achille Mbembe notes, the colony is the space wherein this indistinction is most fundamentally realized: "Colonies are zones in which ... internal and external figures of the political stand side by side or alternate with each other." As such, Mbembe continues, "the colonies are the location par excellence where the controls and guarantees of judicial order can be suspended"—the zone, that is, where exceptional terror is normalized as an essential technology of the liberal state.[39] Agamben's historicization of the "state of exception," though, elides the colonial roots of emergency governance. Agamben traces the history of the sovereign exception to the birth of the French republic—the states of siege declared in the moment of revolution, and codified in law by parliaments and heads of state throughout the nineteenth century. From this origin point, Agamben's brief history ranges across the Euro-American world—from the U.S. government in the moment of Civil War to the participant states of the First and Second World Wars, and finally to the U.S. executive in the moment of the War on Terror. The Euro-American centricity of Agamben's genealogy does not merely obscure the colonial origins and essence of the politics of exception. It also distracts from the ways in which the colonial state of exception, and the figure in bare life that resided therein, were *constitutive* of the central forms and figures of political modernity. The emergence of the bourgeois state within Europe was made possible by the exceptional terror of colonial power in the New World. And the European development of the categories of "human" and "citizen" depended upon the racialized dehumanization—the reduction to the condition of bare life—of the colonized. This is all another way of saying that the political forms of the colony and those of the metropole are not just genealogically but dialectically entwined. Neglecting to read modernity as *colonial* modernity, Agamben overlooks the dialectical relationship between Europe and its constitutive outside. This historical and geographic myopia, as Michael Rothberg has observed, is related to the absence in Agamben's work of any theorization of political resistance.[40]

Aside from a brief but suggestive meditation on "the people" vs. "the People," the multitude of excluded others versus the unitary body politic, there is in Agamben's critique of biopolitics no dynamic interplay between power and its subject, no gesture toward a possible dialectical countermovement. Agamben's approach to the question of the alternative is guided by ethical imperatives. Returning to the space of Auschwitz, Agamben develops an ethics of witness. Agamben's *Remnants of Auschwitz* (1999) adopts Primo Levi's concept of the *Muselmann* (Muslim), the inhabitant of the Nazi concentration camp who has been so degraded they exist in a space beyond conscious suffering. They have lost the capacity and will to live and embody the threshold of, the indistinction between, the human and the inhuman. From the indeterminate being of the Muselmann, the aporia it denotes, Agamben suggests, an ethics of witness can emerge. For Levi, the Muselmann, the "drowned," was the representative figure of the camp—and the only true witness to its horrors. The Muselmann returns from the camp unable to speak, or does not return at all. But this muteness speaks, in that it testifies to the limits of witness, to what cannot be recovered or apprehended by language. "The value of testimony," Agamben writes, "lies essentially in what it lacks; at its centre it contains something that cannot be borne witness to."[41] At stake for Agamben is the question of how the human can be recognized at the threshold of its intelligibility, how bare life can express at once the condition of the inhuman and the presence of the human. But if the unique ontological status of the "drowned" can help illuminate the boundary of human and non—while exposing the political technologies that introduce the distinction—the humanity and agency of the Muselmann is conceded by Agamben as lost, ever submerged.

Judith Butler, one of Agamben's close interlocutors, has herself undertaken a sustained and generative engagement with the ethical and political consequence of the figure in bare life. In *Precarious Life* (2004) and *Frames of War* (2009), Butler reflects upon the imagination and delimitation of the human in the time-space of exception, and develops an ethical response that might enable a new, and politically effective, enunciation of human sameness—what Césaire termed a "humanism made to the measure of the world."

Like Agamben, Butler reads what she terms the "new war prison" as paradigmatic of a new configuration of state power—an articulation of governmentality and sovereignty that renders permanent and general the state of exception. The concept of "indefinite detention," Butler discerns, "does not signify an exceptional circumstance, but, rather, the means by which the exceptional becomes established as a naturalized norm."[42] She is attentive, that is, to the ways in which the emergency of the War on Terror is conceived by its architects as interminable. And she signals too the deeper origins of the state of exception—the "historical time in which sovereignty was indivisible,

... a time that we thought was past [but which] turns out to structure the contemporary field with a persistence that gives lie to history as chronology."[43] But the genealogical perspective signaled here is peripheral to Butler's account. In rhythm with so many other critics of the "post-9/11" security state, Butler affirms the exceptionalism of the contemporary state of exception. Tellingly, Butler imagines the sovereign exception as atavistic; its contemporary articulation marks the return of a *pre*modern form rather than the latest iteration of a governmental technology that is basic to political modernity. While she sees that because "the problem of terrorism is no longer historically or geographically limited ... the state of emergency is potentially limitless and without end," she does not conduct a corresponding investigation into how the exception has been normalized historically within the domestic institutions and imperial projections of the liberal state. The infinite horizon of the emergency is, in her reading, a feature of the future but not of the past. Butler does briefly note recent "international precedents" for the practice of indefinite detention—in particular the British detainment of Irish Catholic and Protestant militants who were judged a threat but neither charged nor convicted of a crime (an example cited as well by the Bush administration, which was keen to highlight the approval given such policies by European human-rights courts).[44] She does not, though, consider the specifically colonial genealogy of Britain's juridical negotiation of the troubles in and beyond Northern Ireland; nor does she tie it to the longer history of emergency governance within the British Empire. This is not to dismiss the force of Butler's insights into, or indeed to deny the newness of, the "new war prison." But as I am concerned to stress, the newness of the political forms of the War on Terror is obscured rather than clarified by the analytic assumption of their exceptionalism. The particular contours of the contemporary "state of exception" are brought into sharper relief when we address as well the historical continuities of emergency governance—within the recent history of the United States, wherein an unbroken series of emergencies has structured state power since 1933, and within the longer planetary history of colonial modernity.

In *Precarious Life*, Butler summons Agamben's suggestion that "bare life" is a state of existence to which every human is potentially relegated. This recognition contains, for Butler, a certain political potentiality: "If bare life, life conceived as biological minimum, becomes a condition to which we are all reducible, then we might find a certain universality in this condition."[45] The verb "becomes" in this sentence—where Butler might simply have written "is"—is crucial, as it gestures toward the ways in which certain previously secure bodies and populations are now vulnerable to the condition of bare life. There is an implicit recognition here of how the contemporary enactment of the "state of exception" represents the return to the global North of forms of insecurity and rightlessness that have long been the norm in the colonial world. But rather than tracing the historical and geographic trajectories of this choc en retour, Butler highlights instead the "out of the blue" (my phrase) events of September 11—a "sudden address" of terror from without, which permeated the Homeland's putatively secure borders, and magnified our essential bodily vulnerability. In the aftermath of that day, Butler observes, this heightened sense of vulnerability manifested itself in reactionary ways: "a radical desire for security, a shoring up of the borders against what is perceived as alien; a heightened surveillance of Arab peoples and anyone who looks vaguely Arab in the dominant racial imaginary."[46] How, Butler asks, might we respond to the experience of violence, and the feeling of insecurity that that violence engenders, not with racism and militaristic desire but with a renewed sensitivity to the distinctly human vulnerability of others? This is the second, more elusive, condition of the universality Butler imagines. Its attainment will demand, as Butler acknowledges, that we attend to the ways in which vulnerability to violence, and to the condition of bare life in particular, is unevenly distributed. In order "[to] critically evaluate and oppose the conditions under which certain human lives are more vulnerable than others,"[47] we must arrive at a deeper understanding of how "the human is understood differentially depending on its race, the legibility of that race, its morphology, the recognizability of that morphology, its sex, the perceptual verification of that sex, its ethnicity, the categorical understanding of that ethnicity."[48] And as Butler demonstrates, the problem is not simply how these signs of difference internally structure the category of the human but how they mark its boundaries. The latter question acquires an especial urgency in the context of the War on Terror, wherein the racial derealization of particular human lives enables their mass destruction.

How might "we" come to identify the lives being lived and lost in Afghanistan and Iraq, or detained in Guantánamo Bay, as fully human lives? Butler accesses this fundamental problem via Emmanuel Levinas, and through a consideration of how photographic images of violence stage an encounter with the other that, potentially, prefigures recognition of the other's humanity and expands the boundaries of the human. The face of the other, Levinas claimed, compels from us an ethical response.[49] It follows, Butler suggests, that "the norms that would allocate who is and is not human arrive in visual form."[50] "Accordingly," Butler continues, "our capacity to respond with outrage, opposition, and critique will depend in part on how the differential norm of the human is communicated through discursive and visual frames."[51] In the space of war—and, we might add, in the "society of spectacle" broadly conceived—the frames that contain and transmit representations of the other, of the being or suffering of others, often foreclose rather than provoke ethical responsiveness in the viewer. In moments, however, alternative frames are constructed that bring the precariousness of the human into view. "In the Vietnam War," Butler writes,

> it was the pictures of the children burning and dying from napalm that brought the US public to a sense of shock, outrage, remorse, and grief.... Despite their graphic effectivity, the images pointed somewhere else, beyond themselves, to a life and precariousness they could not show. It was from that apprehension of the precariousness of those lives we destroyed that many US citizens came to develop an important and vital consensus against the war.[52]

Whether or not Butler is correct in attributing such affective, oppositional power to images of suffering children in Vietnam, she introduces here one of her crucial insights: for representation to act in the service of the human, "[it] must not only fail, but it must *show* its failure."[53] This sentiment resonates quite clearly with Agamben's insistence that "the value of testimony lies essentially in what it lacks." Both thinkers, that is, highlight the efficacy of representations that evince the impossibility of representing or apprehending the human.

Returning her discussion to the War on Terror, Butler reflects on the iconic Abu Ghraib photographs—the condition of their creation and circulation, and the multiple political effects of this putative "image-event." The tortured prisoners depicted in the photographs, Butler observes, "are ... not conceptualizable in terms of the civilizational and racial norms by which the human is constituted."[54] The scene staged in and by the photograph renders and performs a three-fold process of dehumanization. The infrahumanity of the tortured makes possible the act of torture, which reaffirms, or "reinstitutes," the infrahumanity of the tortured.[55] Finally, capturing the scene in photograph fixes the infrahumanity being (re)constituted through the act of torture. Butler asks: can images created in the service of dehumanization act in the service of humanization, when they travel beyond the scene of their production into a more plural and contested discursive field? When *Salon* published the most extensive set of Abu Ghraib photographs in February and March 2006, the names of the victims were omitted and the faces of the victims were obscured, in order to protect their privacy. "What we are left with," Butler writes, "are photos of people who are for the most part faceless and nameless." Again channeling Levinas, though, Butler contends that "the obscured face and the absent name function as the visual trace—even if it is a lacuna within the visual field—of the very mark of humanity.... Their occlusion and erasure become the continuing sign of their suffering and of their humanity."[56] Butler is proposing that the possibility of the human is most pronounced at the exact point where its effacement is most radically visible, where the limits of representation are most starkly evident. But as Butler would no doubt acknowledge, we must not presume that in highlighting or inhabiting the space of negation we have succeeded in recovering or reconstituting what is missing.[57]

The elaboration in the present of a radical humanistic response to the War on Terror's technologies of derealization—the production of bare life enabled by the enactment of exception—will require reckoning not simply with the substantive *presence* of the absence of the human, but with the history of that negation and the possibility of its future transcendence. How has the human/infrahuman distinction been produced and reproduced within modernity? And how has that distinction been resisted by those who have been cast outside the boundaries of human belonging? Butler's persistent emphasis on how "we" might represent or perceive the humanity of the "derealized" other is unaccompanied, in *Precarious Life*, by a concomitant inquiry into how figures in bare life represent, to themselves and to the world, their innate human being. Butler does address this question, though, in *Frames of War*, through an evocative reflection on the poetry composed by detainees at Guantánamo Bay. A "network of transitive affects," these poems are "insurgent interpretations, incendiary acts" that through their very existence and survival convey the basic vulnerability and extant humanity of the prisoner.[58] Butler also engages the political possibilities of the figure in bare life elsewhere, in her reflections on the problem of precarity in the current conjuncture. In a brief meditation on the relationship between precarity and performance, Butler asks, "What does it mean to lay claim to rights when one has none?"[59] The question, in other words, is not how extant power is enacted, but how the moment of performance/enactment—such as the illicit composition of poems at Guantánamo—arrogates to the actor a power that did not exist before: "It is a question of acting, and in the acting, laying claim to the power one requires."[60]

Butler's gestures in this direction remind us that the move from the ethics of seeing the human to the politics of its self-reclamation is not foreclosed by the concept of "bare life." The modes of resistance born in what Mbembe terms "the zone between subjecthood and objecthood" have, for example, long been a central concern of anticolonial and postcolonial thought. Thinkers from Frantz Fanon to Paul Gilroy and Achille Mbembe have meditated upon the forms of struggle practiced by the infrahuman slave or colonized subject—the humanistic consciousness and politics that emerge from the absolute *conditio inhumana*. Locating his inquiry in the space of the (post)colony, Mbembe reflects upon how the state of occupation/exception premised on the production of real or social death engenders the practice of suicidal terror—voluntary death as an expression of freedom. But he signals as well the possibility of alternative narratives or practices of becoming and overcoming. In his discussion of the plantation, its economy of social death and modalities of potential resistance, Mbembe highlights the transformative power of an aesthetic practice that contradicts chattel rationality:

> Treated as if he or she no longer existed except as a mere tool and instrument of production, the slave nevertheless is able to draw almost any object, instrument, language, or gesture into a performance and then stylize it. Breaking with . . . the pure world of things of which he or she is but a fragment, the slave is able to demonstrate the protean capabilities of the human bond through music and the very body that was supposedly possessed by another.[61]

Through the act of performance, the slave evinces her own invincible human being, and thereby refuses the infrahuman status—the condition of bare life—to which she has been assigned.

In the context of the War on Terror, the U.S. government's punitive response to the victims of Hurricane Katrina serves as a revealing lens through which to consider the dialectic of domination and resistance within the state of emergency. In the aftermath of the hurricane, New Orleans's stranded residents, the great majority of them poor and African American, were effectively abandoned by the government. Abandonment, though, does not exactly capture the relationship between the state and the city's most marginal citizens. Those left to fend for their own survival in the storm's wake maintained a two-fold relationship to the law: they were at once banished from its institutional protections and vulnerable to its punitive violence. The military was called upon to police the city and soldiers were given the order that they should "shoot to kill," as vulnerability was equated with criminality. In this way, the subjectivity of those "abandoned" in New Orleans bore some analogic resemblance to that of the Guantánamo detainee: without recourse to the law but subject to it. This duality is central to the state of exception more broadly. The suspension of the law is coincident with and depends upon its invocation and enactment. The "disposable" inhabitants of New Orleans, however, fought against the entwined forces of repression and neglect—asserting their full citizenship and right to the city; struggling against forces of privatization and for the renewal of public institutions and services; and creating cultural works that document the experience of the storm and testify to the human and social being of its victims. In so doing, they signaled the ways in which a state of emergence—what Walter Benjamin termed "the real state of emergency"—might be founded in the space and time of exception.

GLOBAL CAPITAL, NEO EMPIRE

In the introduction to *Homo Sacer*, first published in 1995, Agamben writes that the book was conceived in "response to the bloody mystification of a new planetary order."[62] Agamben does not elaborate this periodization. But his implicit reference, we can presume, is to what Fukuyama termed, in a more celebratory tenor, "the end of history"—the global triumph, in the post–Cold War moment, of the capitalist mode of production and liberal democratic state. For Agamben, this new planetary order heralds the generalization of the state of exception, and the creeping indistinction of wartime and peacetime, foreign and domestic repression—a process of "globalization" redoubled, in his account, by the advent of the War on Terror and the normalization of emergency governance therein. Michael Hardt and Antonio Negri's *Empire* (2000)—composed, like *Homo Sacer*, in that ostensive caesura in historical time, the 1990s—makes an allied diagnosis. The age of modern imperialism and national sovereignty, Hardt and Negri argue in *Empire*, is over. In its place is a nascent *imperial* order, a "boundless, universal space" accompanied by a "notion of right that encompasses all time within its ethical foundation."[63] Though published in 2000, *Empire*'s emphasis on the radical newness of the current imperial order rhymed with the "post-9/11" trope of historical rupture. And indeed, the book's immense popularity in the century's first decade is owed in part to the affinity between its critical vocabulary and the imperial forms of the War on Terror.

Empire, that is, resonated with two putative ruptures: the "post-9/11" articulation of imperial militarism—led by the United States but expressive of a supranational capitalist order—and the post-1989 advent of the world market, under the sign of "globalization." "Globalization" is at once a set of concrete material processes and a narrative, a mode of representation. As a discursive trope, "globalization" contains several fundamental assumptions: different and distant parts of the world are increasingly connected and interdependent; this interdependence is leading, in a progressive fashion, toward the global generalization of particular political, cultural, and economic forms; the central source of these forms, the point from which they emanate, is the West and, most specifically, the United States. These assumptions are most pervasive in neoliberal or neoconservative enunciations of "globalization," which affirmatively trace or prophecy the universalization of "free" markets on the one hand and liberal democracy on the other. But they are present too in myriad left critiques of "globalization." Hardt and Negri's *Empire* trilogy—perhaps the most visible and influential critical theorization of contemporary global politics—affirms the basic assumption of a realized or imminent planetarity. Their diagnosis of imperial universality, however, does not lead to fatalistic dismissals of left possibility. On the contrary, and in an ecstatic tone, Hardt and Negri sketch in *Empire*—and subsequently in *Multitude* (2004) and *Commonwealth* (2009)—the becoming of a global revolutionary force and rudiments of a planetary democratic commons. Relatedly but more implicitly, Hardt and Negri reproduce the "diffusionist" premise that traces the global dissemination of Euro-American economic and political forms—cultures and technologies of "biopolitical" production and the imperial logics of U.S. constitutionalism.[64]

I echo Hardt and Negri's dialectical appeal to the utopian potential contained within global formations or imaginaries. But I want to resist their claim of an achieved planetarity, the idea that "there is no longer an outside."[65] The binaries that structured modern political order—between civilization and nature, self and other, the internal and external spaces of capital—are extant; they are not displaced by but operate in concert with "postmodern" narratives and practices that assume or perform the dissolution of the inside/outside distinction. And I want to challenge as well the "diffusionist" tendency that underlies Hardt and Negri's critical framework: the implicit or explicit suggestion that the paradigms of contemporary global order originate within the North Atlantic world, the United States in particular. "America," Hegel famously claimed, "is the country of the future, and its world historical importance has yet to be revealed in the ages that lie ahead."[66] Writing from one such age but looking toward the future still, Hardt and Negri affirm this insight. As I am concerned to stress, though, "globalization" is equally a process of the global North evolving toward the global South, as methods of accumulation and governance perfected in the (post)colonial world return to the metropole. The geographic trajectories of what David Harvey terms "accumulation by dispossession" offer one illustrative example. During the middle decades of the twentieth century, when old forms of extractive industry joined with new forms of financialized dispossession in the global South, the combination of industrial prosperity and labor-union power translated into a precarious defense of the social commons in the global North.[67] The bulwarks of this defense started to crumble, however, with the advent of neoliberalism in the 1970s. In the decades since, depredation has become—if in radically uneven ways—the paradigmatic mode of accumulation in the metropole as in the postcolony. "Empire" names—and its critique emerges from—not just the extension of transnational capital and its attendant post-national structures of sovereignty across the globe, from the nerve-centers of finance outward, but the revisiting of colonial methods of enclosure and exploitation upon the advanced capitalist world. Though conditioned by this choc en retour, Hardt and Negri's account—with its emulatory globalism and Euro-American centricity—obscures the contemporary instantiations of colonial rationality in North and South alike.

The realization of Empire, Hardt and Negri claim, marks the dissolution of the dialectic of inside and outside, which structured the reality and imaginary of modern sovereignty. The disappearance of the outside is evinced by multiple material and symbolic processes: the "civilization of nature"; the privatization of the public sphere; the assimilation of non-capitalist space; the incorporation of difference; the displacement of national sovereignty by the supranational sovereignty of Empire. "The binaries that defined modern conflict," Hardt and Negri write in one representative passage, "have become blurred":

> The Other that might delimit a modern sovereign subject has becomes fractured and indistinct, and there is no longer an outside that can bound the place of sovereignty. The outside is what gave the crisis its coherence. Today it is increasingly difficult for the ideologues of the United States to name a single, unified enemy; rather, there seem to be minor and elusive enemies everywhere.[68]

If the claim that "there is no longer an outside" seemed premature in 2000, the post–September 11 resurgence of Manichean thinking, and the declaration of a War on Terror, provided further occasion to trouble this axiom. But the U.S. invasion and subsequent occupation of Afghanistan and Iraq also affirmed many of *Empire*'s central arguments. With the decline of national-state sovereignty and emergence of planetary imperial order, Hardt and Negri write in *Multitude*, war "is becoming a general phenomenon, global and interminable."[69] The War on Terror was conceived by its authors in precisely this spirit, as spaceless and endless. Discussing late twentieth-century transformations in the sovereign "right of intervention," Hardt and Negri observe, "Now supranational subjects that are legitimated not by right but by consensus intervene in the name of any type of emergency and superior ethical principles. What stands behind this intervention," they conclude, "is ... a permanent state of emergency and exception justified by the *appeal to essential values of justice*."[70] Though the first author of the War on Terror is the United States rather than some broader supranational entity (the "coalition of the willing"), Hardt and Negri's invocation of "a permanent state of emergency" prosecuted under the pretext of universal values—freedom, democracy, justice—outlines quite presciently the discursive frame of contemporary imperial militarism. September 11 and its aftermath, they avow in *Multitude*, "did not create or fundamentally change this global situation, but ... did force us to recognize its generality."[71] What the maintenance of empire requires, and what the War on Terror brings to the surface, is "a war to create and maintain social order [that] can have no end."[72]

The spatially and temporally boundless nature of war within imperial order is clarified, Hardt and Negri argue in *Multitude*, by the security concept. *Multitude* traces a paradigm shift in the rhetoric and practice of U.S. foreign policy, from a "reactive and conservative" focus on "defense" to an "active and constructive" commitment to "security."[73] Security, in other words, signifies the neoconservative doctrine of preemptive—and permanent—war. In accord with Foucault, Hardt and Negri understand security as a form of biopower, "in the sense that [security] is charged with the task of producing social life at its most general and global level." The biopolitical project of security is, for Hardt and Negri, necessarily spaceless and interminable; it demands "a martial activity equally in the homeland and abroad."[74] This realization of total war is, Hardt and Negri argue, "specific to our era" (whether by "our era" they mean the moment of the War on Terror or the post-1989 epoch that frames *Empire* is here unclear).[75] The progressive militarization of U.S. domestic policing over the past three decades or so—a tendency accelerated and deepened under the sign of "Homeland Security"— is extraordinary; so too is the U.S. government's avowed commitment to an endless and boundary-less War on Terror. But the key question is whether what we have witnessed since 2001—or 1989—represents the advent of a new state form, a new imperial logic, or if, rather, contemporary imperial formations simply adapt and accentuate capitalist rationalities that are basic to colonial modernity. In the early modern period, the concept of "security" was crucial to philosophic explanations of the dual emergence of the bourgeois state and capitalist mode of production. The modern state arose to "secure" the conditions of capitalist accumulation in both the Old World and the New. Processes of enclosure within Europe, and the expropriation of human and natural resources on the periphery, were enabled and ensured by state violence. Like the capitalist procedures it facilitated, the project of security was in its inception—and by definition—preemptive, spaceless, and permanent. As Hobbes foresaw, the perpetual accumulation of capital requires the perpetual accumulation of political power. The "active and constructive" technologies of security governance, all this is to say, are not new to the current conjuncture. Hardt and Negri do bring this deeper genealogy of the security project into implicit view in *Empire*, in their historicization of the imperial essence of U.S. sovereignty. "The U.S. constitutional project," they write, "is constructed on the model of rearticulating an open space and reinventing incessantly diverse and singular relations across an unbounded terrain."[76] Hardt and Negri acknowledge a concurrent *imperialist* tendency in U.S. political order, which is evinced by the internal confinement and exploitation of black life and labor and external projections of punitive state violence in the Americas and beyond. The modern security project is defined in part by its integration of these two tendencies: the Lockean notion that "all the world was America," a state of nature ready to be subsumed by Enlightenment rationality and capitalist ingenuity; and the concomitant necessity of an outside that can never be incorporated, because it constitutes and delimits the space and subject of sovereign political order. But in the contemporary moment, Hardt and Negri argue, it is the former, *imperial*, essence of U.S. sovereignty that is paradigmatic on a planetary scale. "The contemporary idea of Empire," they write, "is born through the global expansion of the internal U.S. constitutional project."[77] This is one example of the *Empire* trilogy's diffusionist perspective.

The universality of the imperial security project is evidenced, in Hardt and Negri's account, by its biopolitical logics. In Foucault's genealogy, the biopolitical turn in modernity prefaces the innovation of modern racism, which introduces a rupture in the biological continuum—"the break between what must live and what must die." For Hardt and Negri, by contrast, the ascendance of the biopolitical enables the transcendence rather than clarification of the binaries that structure political order—not the annihilation of difference but its proliferation and incorporation. "Imperial racism," they write, "integrates others within its order and then orchestrates those differences within a system of control."[78] This "strategy of differential inclusion" imagines difference not as absolute and eternal but as "fluid and amorphous"— "never as a difference of nature but always as a difference of degree."[79] As I argued briefly in chapter 1, though, "a strategy of differential inclusion" and a strategy of binary exclusion coexist today, as they have throughout the history of colonial modernity. The contemporary security project toggles between these two forms of racial practice, casting redundant bodies or absolute enemies into the outside, while incorporating a "multitude" of others into the domains of personhood and wage labor.

Hardt and Negri's insistence that "there is no longer an outside" in the imperial imagination and management of race is mirrored by their contention that there is no longer an outside to capital. The universality of capital is again expressed, for Hardt and Negri, by the ascent of the biopolitical. When biopower becomes the paradigmatic mode of governance, the "mutual implication of all social forces that capitalism has pursued throughout its development has now been fully realized."[80] Hardt and Negri relate this idea to Marx's notion of the real subsumption of labor under capital—the total saturation of commodity rationality throughout the social relations of production. Hardt and Negri depart slightly from Marx, though, in reading the biopolitical modality of real subsumption as *disruptive* of "the linear and totalitarian figure of capitalist development."[81] As biopower "unifies and envelops within itself every element of social life," it moves the subject and event of resistance from the margins to the center of society.[82] Biopower "presents power with an alternative" because it is productive. Empire is founded upon, conditioned by, forces of biopolitical production that it cannot ultimately control—including especially those of labor. In contemporary imperial order, Hardt and Negri argue, biopolitical labor, "labor that creates not only material goods but also relationships and ultimately social life itself," is qualitatively hegemonic.[83] "The central role previously occupied by the labor power of mass factory workers in the production of surplus value," Hardt and Negri contend, "is today increasingly filled by intellectual, immaterial, and communicative labor power."[84] The implied geographic focus of this observation is the post-Fordist economies of the global North. But Hardt and Negri—once again conforming to the diffusionist premise—project the qualitative hegemony of "biopolitical production" onto the world at large. Though "immaterial labor constitutes a minority of global labor, and ... is concentrated in some of the dominant regions of the globe," they suggest, "[it] has imposed a tendency on other forms of labor and on society itself. . . . [Today] labor and society have to informationalize, become intelligent, become communicative, become affective."[85] Transcending ontological divisions (productive and reproductive labor), spatial divisions (the factory and its exterior), and temporal divisions (working time and leisure time), the concept of the "biopolitical" enables the elaboration of a truly universal laboring class, the "multitude."

The multitude is composed of a plurality of singularities. Its internal difference echoes and resists the "differential inclusion" of imperial racism. Comprising a multiplicity of differences that "cannot be reduced to sameness," the multitude "acts on the basis of what the singularities share in common."[86] Hardt and Negri, however, themselves reduce to sameness the differences of which the multitude is composed. Privileging the hegemony of the "biopolitical" obscures the immense differentiation in the organization and experience of labor that occurs under—or indeed cannot be assimilated by—that heading. If anticolonial and postcolonial theorists imagined the excluded particular as the source of the universal, Hardt and Negri's theory of the multitude imagines a universal that begins from the fact of inclusion, that subsumes rather than emerges from difference. This elision of difference is in keeping with the tenor of Hardt and Negri's broader theoretical intervention. Mirroring the form of empire itself, Hardt and Negri's critique operates almost exclusively, and unapologetically, at the level of the general and the global. Confronted with the totalitarian violence of empire, they insist, we must resurrect and redirect the radical aspirations contained within any planetary imaginary. Just as Marx identified in the advent of the world market the possibility of international proletarian revolution, Hardt and Negri derive from the global articulation of empire a fervent optimism: "[The] utopian element of globalization," they assert, "is what prevents us from simply falling back into particularism and isolationism in reaction to the totalizing forces of imperialism and racist domination, pushing us instead to forge a project of counter-globalization, counter-empire."[87] The struggle to avoid particularism, though, can sometimes manifest itself as neglect of the particular itself. Relatedly, the repeated invocation that there is no longer an outside relegates to the analytic margins those spaces and peoples that exist beyond the centripetal force of biopolitical production.

In *Empire*, Hardt and Negri summon Rosa Luxemburg in support of their contention that the imperialist era has given way to the order of empire. Luxemburg, Hardt and Negri write, recognized that "imperialism rests on . . . fixed boundaries and the distinction between inside and outside . . . [and thus] creates a straightjacket for capital."[88] If imperialism facilitates the expansion of capital into non-capitalist strata, Hardt and Negri deduce from this idea, it also prevents the realization of a world market. For capital to survive, Hardt and Negri assert, it must destroy the barriers between inside and outside; it must replace the imperialist order with the order of empire. Luxemburg's foremost emphasis, though, was not the limits of imperialism specifically, which might then be overcome (by empire), but the limits of capital accumulation more broadly. Because the accumulation of capital requires the existence of non-capitalist strata, Luxemburg argued, a truly universal capitalism—the very idea of Hardt and Negri's "Empire"—is impossible. "Accumulation of capital," she put it in plain terms, "is inconceivable in any respect without non-capitalist circles."[89] From this observation, Luxemburg concluded that the expansionary logics of capital would ultimately confront the finitude of the world itself, and accumulation would cease. As David Harvey has observed, though, capital "can either make use of some pre-existing outside (non-capitalist social formations or some sector within capitalism—such as education—that has not yet been proletarianized) *or* it can actively manufacture it" (emphasis added).[90] In the neoliberal moment, the enclosure of natural resources such as water and air—the commoditization of an extant outside—coincides with the privatization of public assets or services—the fabrication of an outside, which is then seized upon by idle capital. The predatory devaluation and subsequent reassimilation of capital assets and labor power is another example of the latter synthetic method.

In *Commonwealth*, Hardt and Negri connect Harvey's theory of "accumulation by dispossession" to Marx's distinction between the real and formal subsumption of labor. Formal subsumption describes the internalization by capital of non-capitalist relations or practices. Examples of formal subsumption include the residue of feudal forms of craft production in the early industrial moment in Europe, or the unfree labor of plantation agriculture and mineral extraction in the colonies. Real subsumption, by contrast, designates not simply the incorporation of capital's outside but its disappearance. Globalization is one term for the movement from formal to real subsumption, the progressive destruction of non-capitalist social forms. Hardt and Negri, though, observe in *Commonwealth* a "reciprocal movement" at work in the current globalizing moment, "from the real subsumption to the formal, creating not new 'outsides' but severe divisions and hierarchies within the capitalist globe."[91] This "return" movement corresponds to the reappearance in the present of various methods of accumulation by dispossession—the heightened importance of extractive industry in the global South and processes of privatization and devaluation in the global North. Hardt and Negri's discussion of the "reciprocal movement" from real to formal subsumption is brief but significant. In *Empire*, Hardt and Negri invoke the biopolitical realization of real subsumption. But in *Commonwealth* they subtly qualify the assumption of that achieved universality—bringing into view both the endurance and the synthetic creation of imperialist technologies, and the spatial structures to which they correspond, within the order of empire. Though Hardt and Negri maintain their insistence on the absence of an "outside" to capital, their insights into the reciprocal movement from real to formal subsumption evoke the ways in which "globalization" signifies not the transcendence of imperialism but the planetary realization, in the South and North alike, of colonial rationality.

*

The rupture that I am most concerned to critique, in this book, is that implied by the ubiquitous marker "post-9/11." But I am also eager to resist another ostensible historical break—that between the age of colonialism and its aftermath. The term "postcolonial," as I read and deploy it, signifies less an aftermath than an afterlife—the animate endurance, and not just the lingering residue, of colonial rationalities in the space and time of their supposed death. This understanding contrasts with Hardt and Negri's *Empire* trilogy, which conforms rather to the assumption of a radical rupture. What postcolonial thought misses, Hardt and Negri argue, "is a recognition of the novelty of the structures and logics of power that order the contemporary world. Empire is not a weak echo of modern imperialisms but a fundamentally new form of rule."[92] My own intention is not to dispute the newness of contemporary imperial forms, but rather to argue that that newness is an expression of—and thus acts as a lens onto—continuity. "It is the continuity of the deeper structure," to again summon Frederic Jameson's insight, "that imposes the experiential differences generated as that structure convulsively enlarges with each new phase." The novel political forms of the War on Terror both derive from and reveal the persistence of the long history of colonial modernity, and of the security project at its core.

CONCLUSION

In the first chapter of *Capital*, Marx observes that the principle of equality only emerges as a social or philosophical ideal at the moment in which the commodity form has been generalized. "The secret of the expression of value," he writes, "namely, that all kinds of labour are equal and equivalent ... cannot be deciphered until the notion of human equality has already acquired the fixity of a popular prejudice." This prejudice acquires the solidity of common sense, he continues, "only in a society in which the great mass of the produce of labour takes the form of commodities, in which, consequently, the dominant relation between man and man, is that of owners of commodities."[93] The principle of human equality and ideology of market equivalence are conditioned by the commoditization of labor power, the universalization of the commodity form. The materialism implied in this deduction, Stuart Hall has argued, "is surely correct ... to insist that no social practice or set of relations floats free of the determinate effects of the concrete relations in which they are located."[94] Hall insists, however, that the moment of economic determinism is not in the last instance but in the first. If the words "freedom" and "equality" derive their resonance in part from the common sense of market rationality, these concepts remain always contested, subject to redefinition and resignification outside of and in opposition to the rule of capital. The inverse is also true; capitalism has long proven itself adept at assimilating its own critique. Capital and its critique, like the state and theory—and indeed like the state and terror—are dialectically entwined.

As Retort observes in *Afflicted Powers*, the War on Terror is in one sense a war "for the control of appearances." Theory is an active participant in this contest. "Empire" serves as an illustrative example. Embraced by the left as an accurate descriptor for the post–Cold War synthesis of neoliberal globalism and American militarism, the term "empire" was affirmatively invoked in the aftermath of September 11 by prominent voices on the right—scholars, pundits, government officials—who argued for the necessity, and celebrated the possibility, of a new American imperium. As Hardt and Negri summarize this disagreement: "the *concept* of Empire is always dedicated to peace . . . [but] the *practice* of Empire is continually bathed in blood."[95] Theory, to borrow Marx's phrase, is engaged today as ever in a "battle between two rights." This is another term, perhaps, for what David Scott has described as the "tragedy of colonial enlightenment"—the echo of domination's lexicon in the vocabulary of resistance (and vice versa).

As I have argued in this chapter, this repetition is not merely rhetorical but formal—in the moment of diagnosis and in the moment of prescription. As authored by thinkers such as Baudrillard and Žižek, the contemporary critique of spectacle mirrors the ahistoricity of the image. Reflections on resistance to the society of the spectacle, meanwhile, focus on the critical potentiality of the "image-event." The critique of exception—composed and inspired by Agamben—also replicates the logic of its object, affirming, however subtly, the exceptionalism of the "post-9/11" moment. And I myself, invoking Benjamin, gestured toward the possibility of a "real state of emergency"—a state of emergence or revolution born in the time-space of exception. Finally, Hardt and Negri's theorizations of empire and the "multitude" emulate the globalism of capital, casting to the analytic margins the modes of social differentiation produced and elided by imperial power. Each of these formal echoes limits, without foreclosing completely, intensive pursuit of the routes of continuity between the colonial past and colonial present—the spatial and temporal choc en retour of colonial histories and culture.

One fundamental argument of this book is that the conjoined political formations of "Homeland Security" and the "War on Terror" are made of colonial substance, and can only be approached with clarity when situated within planetary histories of European empire and its afterlives. The genealogies developed in chapters 1 and 2 sought to locate the contemporary iterations of security and terror within the long history of colonial modernity. This third chapter turned to the question of how the extant history of colonial modernity—and the dialectic of security and terror that is so central to it—has been revealed and critiqued in contemporary theory. Through readings of several contemporary novels, the two chapters that follow will continue this engagement with the problem of representation. In accord with my approach to theory, I am concerned, in my reading of fiction, with the particular histories any given text brings into view and with the particular strategies of representation it employs. The novels with which I will enter into dialogue—Teju Cole's *Open City*, Mohsin Hamid's *Reluctant Fundamentalist*, Junot Díaz's *Brief Wondrous Life of Oscar Wao*, and a series of works by Roberto Bolaño—regard the political forms of the present through the lens of the long history of modernity at large. They do so by tracing both the history and contemporary projections of Euro-American power in the world and the choc en retour of colonial rationalities to the global North. Evincing the planetary reenactment of colonial histories, these texts demonstrate the critical efficacy of a narrative mode that works both genealogically and dialectically—that illuminates, for example, the colonial origins of the neoliberal present and the terror of security. But they also convey, through their formal substance and reflexive consciousness, the obstacles to and limits of historical recovery.

FOUR

"Vanishing Points"

POSTCOLONIAL AMERICA

"We're an empire now," an unnamed aide to President Bush—later presumed to be Karl Rove—told the journalist Ron Suskind in 2004. "And when we act, we create our own reality." Against the empirical and historical commitments of the "reality-based community," Rove identified the post–September 11 United States as not simply a world power but a world creator, a divine-like hegemon that shapes the planet in its own image. As Rove's carefully chosen words betray, the security project, its imperial form in particular, corresponds to an ontological and epistemological certitude—the ideological assumption that both our identity and the meaning of our actions in the world are secure, uncontestable. Though the U.S. foreign policy establishment has long distanced itself from the nomenclature of "empire," Rove's candid remarks are representative of the casual if calculated frequency with which that term was deployed by many rightist intellectuals (among them Max Boot, Niall Ferguson, and Philip Bobbit) in the lead-up to and early stages of the War on Terror. Importantly, the world-making empire Rove imagines blocks out the past. It is an empire without history. Proclaiming an imperial self-consciousness in the present yet diverting our gaze from imperial pasts, Rove's paean to American power evinces the historical myopia that characterized the dominant discursive tenor of the early War on Terror. As I discussed in the previous chapter, some of the most influential critical theorizations of the War on Terror's political forms reproduce this basic ahistoricism, echoing the temporal exceptionalism implied by the "post-9/11" trope. In this chapter, I engage works of fiction that counter both the ahistorical affirmation and ahistorical critique of U.S. empire with historicist renderings of the current conjuncture.

In particular, three postcolonial novels—three works that locate the present within the long history of colonial modernity—guide my discussion: Teju Cole's *Open City*, Mohsin Hamid's *The Reluctant Fundamentalist*, and Junot Díaz's *The Brief Wondrous Life of Oscar Wao*. In their meditations on history—history as what happened, and history as narrative—these novels are concerned at once with cultures of historical erasure, and with the possibilities and pitfalls of historical recovery.

A settler-colony that achieved independence in the late eighteenth century and an extant imperialist power, the United States falls outside the dominant postcolonial paradigm, which is concerned predominantly—though not exclusively—with the twentieth-century dissolution of European empire and consequent creation of independent nation-states in Africa, Asia, and the Caribbean. In a broader reading, though, the term "postcolonial" simply names the resumption or reinscription of colonial practice and ideology in the moment and place of its putative afterlife—a definition that encompasses the United States, a country in which settler-colonial imaginaries—of private property, of racial difference, of civilizational progress—continue to shape political life, and in which techniques of accumulation and governance innovated by European empire continue to evolve. "Postcolonialism," to again summon Simon Gikandi's definition, is "a code for the state of undecidability in which the culture of colonialism continues to resonate in what was supposed to be its negation."[1] Postcolonial theory, he continues, "is one way of recognizing how decolonized situations are marked by the trace of the imperial pasts they try to disavow."[2] In other words, the "postcolonial" does not signify a temporal or discursive rupture, but identifies the persistence of imperialist culture in the metropole and in the formerly colonized world.

The moment of independence—whether 1776 or 1960—is not a departure from colonial modernity but another iterative moment within it. The United States serves as an illustrative example. The first postcolonial nation, the United States is also the first neocolonial nation—which is another way of saying that independence is at once break and renewal, repudiation and reproduction.[3] The literature of the early United States is shaped by this particular paradox of settler-colonial history. Canonical nineteenth-century writers such as James Fenimore Cooper, Herman Melville, and Walt Whitman undertook the postcolonial task of defining in aesthetic form a nascent national culture, while simultaneously recognizing—in the vocabulary of affirmation or critique or ambivalence—the latent and manifest imperial content of that culture.[4] Writing in the early nineteenth century, the Native

American activist William Apess rebelled against the ongoing domination of native peoples—by both state and federal authorities—in a distinctive, pluralized political language. A member of the Pequot Nation and a Methodist preacher, Apess voiced his resistance in the spiritual vocabulary of Christian universalism and, at Methodist camp meetings, to ethnically diverse audiences of Native Americans, European Americans, and African Americans.[5] Firmly rooted in the "problem space" of the postcolonial, Apess highlighted the enduring presence of imperial rationality within, and embodied the complex contours of, an emergent national-cultural landscape.

If questions of postcoloniality were central to the period in which Apess lived and worked, so too did they permeate the other end of the nineteenth century—the period of reconstruction and its reactionary aftermath. In the latter moment, W. E. B. Du Bois meditated on the doubleness or "borderline" subjectivity of the African American—at once American and African, within and without, emancipated and subjected—and highlighted the persistence of racial violence, both discursive and structural, in the time of putative formal freedom. The conceptual vocabulary that emerged from Du Bois's elaboration of "double consciousness" anticipated, as Kenneth Mostern has argued, the key analytic concerns of late twentieth-century postcolonial theory and literature.[6] Du Bois published his seminal *The Souls of Black Folk* in 1903, five years after the Spanish–American War, which resulted in the U.S. acquisition of Cuba, Guam, Puerto Rico, and the Philippines. The year 1898 is commonly cited today—accurately or not—as the moment in which the settler-colonial ethos of perpetual expansion first found expression beyond the ostensible boundaries of the young republic. In that moment, the United States legitimated its colonial assertions in the Caribbean and South Pacific with anti-imperialist rhetoric. This basic contradiction conveys not just outright hypocrisy but a deeply held ambivalence—a uniquely postcolonial uncertainty about the identity of the new nation, in itself and in the world. Though the United States' recent imperial ventures did not receive explicit treatment in Du Bois's 1903 text, the cultural and political-economic consequence of American imperialism—and indeed imperialism in general—would become for him a guiding question.[7] In the early decades of the century, Du Bois deepened his intellectual and political engagement with emergent struggles for independence throughout the colonized world. He sought to articulate internationalist resistance to colonialism with the African American struggle for equal rights and full citizenship. Here the connection between internal and external processes of colonization—and internal and external forms of state terror—acted not just as a frame for critique but as a platform for transnational revolution. His 1928 novel *Dark Princess* dramatized the radical potentialities of a planetary anti-imperialist project, one that would clarify the global consequence of the color line and work toward its transcendence within a global field of political action. In the postwar period, Du Bois directly confronted the neocolonial foreign policy of the United States at the dawn of the Cold War. The essential contradiction of this settler-colonial predicament—the concurrence of the postcolonial and the imperial—was reenacted in the mid-twentieth century, as the United States asserted its dominion over the decolonizing world. Testifying in the aftermath of the Second World War to the universal right of "self-determination" and heralding the end of modern European colonialism, the United States founded an "anti-imperialist" imperium. Intervening in this moment, Du Bois and other thinkers highlighted the great gulf between the anticolonial rhetoric and imperialist practice of the United States at the dawn of the American Century. Du Bois, who in his criticism and fiction had long borne witness to this fundamental and enduring hypocrisy, accused the United Nations of sheltering an emergent, U.S.-led neocolonialism under the euphemistic cover of Enlightenment idealism. Du Bois pointed not just to embryonic structures of domination in the decolonizing world, but to the ongoing oppression of African Americans and other excluded peoples within the United States. In so doing, Du Bois called attention to one of the abiding concerns of postcolonial American literature—the relationship between internal and external processes of colonization. The multiple and intersecting histories addressed by postcolonial American literature bear out this bifocality: Native American histories of conquest and extermination, resistance, and renewal; African American histories of enslavement and exploitation, movement, and struggle; hemispheric or planetary histories of war and empire, migration and diaspora. Where on the spatial and temporal map of the colonial modern do these histories meet? And what is exchanged or revealed in the moment of their convergence? Engaging these and related questions, the contemporary postcolonial American novel brings into evidence the dynamic interrelation of different imperialist histories, some of which we mistakenly imagine as belonging only to the past, and others we fail to apprehend as they form within and constitute our evolving present.

The contemporary incarnation of postcolonial American literature is conditioned by a conjunction of political and intellectual transformations: the struggle for and realization of independence in the colonized world; the subsequent wave of migration from the global South to the metropoles of the global North; the resumption and revision of colonial culture and process—a renewal signaled by the rhetorical resurgence of both security and terror, as original colonial tropes of civilization and its outside were refitted for the imperialisms of the postcolonial moment; the movement for civil rights within the United States; the Vietnam War and the cultures of resistance it inspired; the rise of the New Left and attendant formation of new social movements; the emergence, in a scholarly context, of the "new social history"; the turn, again in a scholarly context, toward "transnational" modes of inquiry; the denouement of the Cold War and discursive ascendance of "globalization"; the advent and global entrenchment of neoliberalism, which is experienced in the global North as the choc en retour of colonial forms of dispossession; the enactment of neoconservative foreign policy doctrine, which again reproduces colonial tropes and methods. These intersecting forces have compelled a sustained literary reckoning with the imperial essence and global location of the United States. They have led, that is, to the crystallization of a new literary formation—one that historicizes U.S. power in the world from the perspective of its others, and provincializes the United States within colonial modernity at large.

Like the theory I examined in chapter 3, the novels I engage here were conditioned in part by the spatial and temporal return of intersecting colonial histories and logics. But if the theory I critiqued only begins to bring that choc en retour into view, Cole's *Open City*, Hamid's *Reluctant Fundamentalist*, and Díaz's *Oscar Wao* illuminate its effects with a unique clarity. Resisting the exceptionalism of the "post-9/11" frame, these novels reveal the colonial histories that haunt the present—in Brussels as in Lahore. But they also betray, in their form as well as their content, the persistent and pervasive force of the trope of rupture and related modes of erasure. Crucially, this reprisal is reflexive. Excavating hidden histories, Cole, Hamid, and Díaz simultaneously—and self-critically—dramatize the limits of witness, the *páginas en blanco*, as Díaz puts it, that remain so.

LAYERED CITIES

The term "open city" refers to a city in wartime, immanently under siege, that declares itself "open" in order to obviate the possibility of civilian deaths and physical destruction. An open city, in other words, is a city that has surrendered itself in order to secure itself. In Teju Cole's *Open City*—his debut novel, which was published to widespread critical acclaim in 2011—the narrator Julius visits Brussels, an open city during the Second World War, and thus a city whose contemporary built environment includes preserved medieval and baroque elements, as well as "the architectural monstrosities" thrown up by Leopold II in the nineteenth century. Julius's trip to Brussels is a departure from the novel's primary locale, and the true open city of its title, New York. As a signifier of New York, "open city" names a metropolis contiguous with the world (yet so often blind to it or in violation of it), inhabited by a multiplicity of peoples and layered with a multiplicity of histories—many of which are buried beneath an architectural landscape focused less on the preservation of the past than on its systematic erasure. Wandering around the city with a keenly observant eye, Julius, a young Nigerian American psychiatric resident, contemplates these concealed pasts, histories of slavery and genocide, war and empire—histories that echo through Brussels and Lagos, and histories that resonate with the more immediate memories of planes flying into towers and bombs over Baghdad.

New York

Julius's reflective walks around the city, which make up the bulk of the novel, take him—and the reader—from Wall Street to Washington Heights, from Brooklyn to the Bronx. Attuned at once to the mundane details of quotidian life in the present and the weightier remnants of the violent histories buried underfoot, Julius holds forth on the hidden origins of the modern metropolis, and on the recent events, such as September 11, that shape its current psyche. Julius's urban explorations are accompanied by erudite musings on music, literature, and visual art—cultural artifacts that, alternatively, distract him from his earthly surroundings, render these in sharper light, or provoke the retrieval of a dormant memory. Though Julius's intellect is exceptionally alive to the world, his narrative voice is *affectively* deadened—enacting the very repression that his insights both highlight and begin to counter. There is, in other words, a contradiction—generative rather than limiting—between the novel's content and form.

Walking through Lower Manhattan one day, Julius happens upon "a great empty space, the empty space that was the obvious . . . the ruins of the World Trade Center."[8] Pausing for a moment at this place "that had become a metonym of its disaster," Julius meditates on the longer history of the geography of ground zero. "This was not," he stresses, "the first erasure on the site."

> Before the towers had gone up, there had been a bustling network of little streets traversing this part of town. Robinson Street, Laurens Street, College Place: all of them had been obliterated in the 1960s to make way for the World Trade Center buildings, and all were forgotten now. Gone, too, was the old Washington Market, the active piers, the fishwives, the Christian Syrian enclave that was established here in the late 1800s.⁹

"The site," Julius observes, "was a palimpsest, as was all the city, written, erased, rewritten."

> There had been communities here before Columbus ever set sail, before Verrazano anchored his ships in the narrows, or the black Portuguese slave trader Esteban Gomez sailed up the Hudson . . . before the Dutch ever saw a business opportunity in the rich furs and timber of the island and its calm bay.¹⁰

The purpose and care with which the past has been covered up, each layer of the palimpsest neatly obscuring the one beneath it, is related, Julius suggests, to the "well-organized" nature of modern human violence, atrocities "carried out with pens, train carriages, ledgers, barbed wire, work camps, gas. And," Julius adds, "this late contribution, the absence of bodies." Aside from the falling ones, he notes, no dead bodies were visible on September 11. "Marketable stories of all kinds had thickened around the injured coast of our city," Julius recalls, "but the depiction of the dead bodies was forbidden."¹¹ As Žižek puts it in *Welcome to the Desert of the Real*, "while the number of victims is repeated all the time, it is surprising how little of the actual carnage we see—no dismembered bodies, no blood, no desperate faces of dying people."¹² Though acknowledging there are understandable reasons for this proscription, Julius intimates that the failure to reckon with or even see the past—a past that has been deliberately concealed—is connected to the failure to see and confront the terror unfolding in front of us, in New York as in Kabul.

On occasion, however, the sedimentary remains of the past do surface, even if unbidden. In 1991, construction of an office building at the intersection of Broadway and Duane Street revealed human remains. The building site, it was discovered, lay on top of a centuries-old African burial ground. Over four hundred bodies were unearthed from the six-acre plot of Lower

Manhattan, which once lay beyond the city's proper borders, "north of Wall Street and so outside of civilization as it was then defined," as Julius remarks.[13] A controversy ensued, as the imperatives of capital clashed with the proponents of civic memorialization. The resulting compromise did sanction the construction of a monument, designed by a Haitian artist, which, when Julius glimpses it, is cordoned off for renovations. Julius, though, is less concerned with the controversy surrounding the memorial or the merits of its design, and more with the "echo across centuries, of slavery in New York," with the histories evoked by the excavated bodies, many of which "bore traces of suffering: blunt trauma, grievous bodily harm," broken bones and disease. "How difficult it was," Julius reflects, "from the point of view of the twenty-first century, to fully believe that these people, with the difficult lives they were forced to live, were truly people, complex in all their dimensions as we are, fond of pleasures, shy of suffering, attached to their families."[14] The thought is both an indictment of our indifference to the past—to the lives of history's dispossessed and downtrodden—and a plaintive commentary on the intrinsic difficulties of any empathetic identification, across the centuries or across the street. If Julius's excavations bring buried histories into view, they also point to those lives and voices that we cannot so easily summon.

"Aboveground," Julius reflects, "I was with thousands of others in their solitude, [and] in the subway, standing close to strangers . . . all of us reenacting unacknowledged traumas, the solitude intensified."[15] Julius's solitude is interrupted, though, by the unavoidable, sometimes alienating, chance encounter, as well as by more patterned conversations with friends and patients—each of which is recalled with dispassionate precision. In the text's dialogic moments, Julius performs the part of the sensitive elicitor of the "unacknowledged traumas" of others. Just emerging from a relationship, Julius often summons stories from his time with Nadege, his ex-girlfriend. One recollection centers on a trip to an immigrant detention facility in Queens, taken with a group from Nadege's church. The "Welcomers," as the group is called, visit the facility—"a long, gray metal box," under the jurisdiction of the Department of Homeland Security but contracted out to a private firm—to hear the stories of its detainees, and lend them a sympathetic ear. Julius speaks with a young man from Liberia named Saidu, clad in an orange jumpsuit, who narrates his journey from war-torn Liberia to Guinea, to Morocco, to Spain, and finally to JFK Terminal Four and this detention facility. As in his work life, Julius listens with openness and patience to Saidu's story of hardship and hope. On the ride back to Manhattan, he recounts Saidu's narrative to Nadege. Now, revisiting the day in his mind, Julius speculates that "perhaps [Nadege] fell in love with the idea of myself that I presented in that story. I was the listener, the compassionate African who paid attention to the details of someone else's life and struggle. I had fallen in love with that idea myself."[16] It is a moment of stark honesty, but one that betrays an enduring gulf not just between self and other, but between self-image and self-knowledge. Sensuous and cerebral, Julius's wanderings around the city bring into evidence the invisible histories embedded in New York's topography, but his attempts at introspection—the excavation of the self—are fleeting and partial, and point to layers of concealment within the story of his own past.[17]

Brussels

Searching for some concrete connections to his family history, Julius spends a winter month in Brussels in the tentative hope that he might locate his maternal grandmother, with whom he was once close. Though Julius does not find his *oma*, his visit does compel further reflections on the layered histories contained in any urban geography, and on the place of the singular, living consciousness therein. Looking out his apartment window at a cityscape that appears preserved and transported from some earlier time—and recalling a conversation he had on the plane about Brussels and the Second World War—Julius imagines all four of his grandparents (Nigerian and German) in September of 1944, wherever they were, "with . . . eyes open as if shut, mercifully seeing nothing of the brutal half century ahead and, better yet, hardly anything at all of all that was happening in their world, the corpse-filled cities, camps, beaches and fields, the unspeakable worldwide disorder of that very moment."[18] Just as Brussels managed to avoid the brunt of "Europe's fatal tussles" despite its position at the heart of the continent, all of us—whether we live in 1944 or 2003—are capable of shielding ourselves from, disavowing, the slaughter and destruction unfolding just over there.

Once on the ground, Julius is occupied less by the insistent grandeur of the city's historical artifacts and more by the contradictions of its postcolonial multiculture. Or rather, he is interested—as in New York—with the animate histories of violence that condition but are elided by Brussels's built environment. The sense of anomie in the city is palpable, as is the undercurrent of nativist hatred flowing just beneath its pristine surface. Acutely aware of his own difference, and of the recent history of racially inspired violence in

Belgium, Julius is unusually ill at ease in his movements around the city, wary of the "inchoate rage of the defenders of Vlaanderen."[19] He is also, as in New York, closely attuned to the relationship between the composition of the contemporary city and its colonial past, a past at once repressed—it is the immigrants who are labeled the colonizers: "murdering, thieving, raping Vikings from North Africa," in one local blogger's words—and blithely enshrined. Walking through a deserted park on Christmas Eve, Julius pauses by a plaque depicting the first five Belgian kings, and bearing the inscription: "HOMMAGE A LA DYNASTIE LA BELGIQUE ET LE CONGO, RECONNAISSANTS, MDCCCXXXI."[20] There is a clear connection, Julius implies, between the brutality of Belgium's colonial history and the racial anxieties of its present, a melancholic failure to properly mourn the lost love object—empire, in this case—and reckon with one's attachment to it. Paul Gilroy has termed this condition "postcolonial melancholia," the symptoms of which include a reverence for the past, a longing for the restoration of national greatness and the security of ethnic purity.[21] The postcolonial melancholia observed by Julius in Brussels dovetails with another—the melancholic failure, most evident in the United States, to fully mourn and situate historically the events of September 11. In both cases, the lost object is "sectioned off, hidden in a crypt," as Julius puts it.[22] This sectioning off prevents a productive historical confrontation with the event and its aftermath. The convergence and imbrication of these two melancholic foreclosures obscures, and inhibits critical engagement with, both the imperialist militarism of the early twenty-first century and the longue-dureé colonial terror with which it is contiguous.

In Brussels, Julius's main interlocutor is a young Moroccan man named Farouq—a learned, politically impassioned former student of comparative literature currently working in an Internet and phone cafe. Their exchanges cover a wide range of topics—literature and theory, history and current events, the ethics of violent resistance, Edward Said and Walter Benjamin, the Israeli occupation of Palestine and the War on Terror, Hezbollah and Malcolm X. Julius, the less assertive party in these conversations, tacitly affirms Farouq's opposition to the war in Iraq, and does not contradict his new friend's thoughts on the urgency of difference—"difference . . . not as orientalist entertainment" but "difference with its own intrinsic value"—even if his own cosmopolitanism is anchored more by a belief in human sameness (or put slightly differently, by a dialectical understanding of difference as sameness).[23] Julius is unwilling, however, to accept Farouq's admission that while he abhors Al-Qaeda's method he cannot "cast judgment" on their absolute right of resistance. Julius's exposure in Brussels to "simmering, barely contained fear," to routine violence prosecuted "in the name of a monolithic identity," translates into a greater sympathy for—if not outright identification with—Farouq's more militant position. Julius hears, in other words, Farouq's Fanonian logic—his insistence that the objective terror of colonial rationality will only yield when confronted with a reciprocal violence. But Julius also detects an unsettling affinity between the ethnic absolutism of the anti-immigrant (anti-Muslim) crowds and Farouq's own ideological certitude, "attractive though his side of the political spectrum was." "He, too," Julius observes, "was in the grip of rage and rhetoric." Speaking in more general terms, Julius continues: "A cancerous violence had eaten into every political ideal, had taken over the ideas themselves, and for so many, all that mattered was the willingness to do something." An outright rejection of violence does not, however, resolve the ethical problem: "It seemed," Julius concludes, "that the only way this lure of violence could be avoided was by having no causes, by being magnificently isolated from all loyalties. But was that not an ethical lapse graver than rage itself?"[24] He lets the question hover. Ultimately, though, Julius—if an apparently empathetic consumer of Farouq's story—is dismissive of his new friend's intellectual and political subjectivity: "He was one of the thwarted ones. His script would stay in proportion."[25]

Reverse Hallucination

In Brussels—in large part because of Farouq, but also as a consequence of his alienation from the city's toxic racial atmosphere—Julius is drawn out to a greater extent than he is in New York, more willing to grapple intellectually, less passive in his political thinking. This subtle shift in his social demeanor, however, does not correspond to a parallel change in the depth of his introspection. Throughout the novel, Julius returns, in memory, to his childhood in postcolonial Nigeria: the death of his father when he was 14; his estrangement, not long after, from his mother; his high school years in a military academy. Following his time in Brussels, the frequency and duration of these mnemonic visits increase, but they remain vague and incomplete. In coming to the United States—for his undergraduate education, initially—Julius imagined himself reborn, wholly new, "fully on my own terms." Searching in memory for his previous self, Julius finds only fragments; and he is careful not to pick up or examine too closely the more painful shards, if they are visible to him at all.

Following his father's death (after a brief illness), Julius's mother "decided to take me with her into her memories." She speaks "[in] a faraway voice which, because it could not talk about the death that had just shattered us, had begun to describe long ago things."[26] Specifically, she tells Julius stories about her girlhood in Magdeburg, Germany. Born just days after the Russian takeover of the city in 1945, she could of course not remember "the begging and wandering with her mother through the rubble of Brandenburg and Saxony." She retained, though, "not the memory of the suffering itself but the memory of knowing that it was what she had been born into." This suffering she could not know but felt deeply would remain, throughout her childhood and indeed her life, only visceral: "The rule was to refrain from speaking: nothing of the bombing, nothing of the murders and countless betrayals, nothing of those who had enthusiastically participated in all of it." His mother, Julius reflects, had "been born into an unspeakably bitter world, a world without sanctity." Decades and a continent removed, "it was natural, losing a husband, for her to displace the grief of widowhood onto that primal grief, and make of the two pains a continuity." The one grief is compounded by, reincarnate in, the other, and the silence that engulfs that originary suffering is echoed by the silence that soon enfolds mother and son, a silence that "with the passing months turned into the rift that wouldn't heal." Now, years later, long out of touch with his mother, Julius strives to imagine the lost details of her childhood, "an entire vanished world of people, experiences, sensations, desires, a world that, in some odd way, I was the unaware continuation of."[27] Aware, in this instance, of his unawareness—the accumulated silences and repressed memories that are his inheritance—Julius is less attentive to the vanishings in his own story.

Browsing a supermarket in Union Square, Julius is approached by a woman who recognizes him but whom he cannot place. When she introduces herself as Moji Kasali, Julius remembers—she is the elder sister of a close childhood friend. Moji and Julius promise, after this brief encounter, to meet again soon—and the two do see one another socially several times in the following weeks. One night Julius attends a party at Moji's apartment, and on the balcony the next morning, watching the sunrise over the Hudson, he is joined by his host. She has something to say to him: "When she was fifteen, and I was a year younger, at a party her brother had hosted at their house in Ikoyi, I had forced myself on her." The trauma of that night, she says, has never left her; she has thought about Julius "either fleetingly or in extended agonies, for almost every day of her adult life." Expecting from

Julius only silence, but needing more, she implores: "Will you say something now? Will you say something?"[28] Julius continues gazing at the river, and as far as we know remains mute. At the center of the novel is a rape: a rape that Julius has repressed, to no apparent destructive effect; a rape that persists, as a chronic pain, in the body and mind of his victim. It is unclear whether this single recovered memory—a memory Julius continues to silence—will lead to further restorations, and to a deeper self-reckoning. In place of psychological confession, Julius cites, to himself and to us, an opaque Nietzschean parable. In accordance with the melancholic malaise that has taken over the city, Julius is unable or unwilling to bring the "sectioned off" corners of his past from shadow into light. Julius, though, does not make the connection between his own dormant memories and the historical erasures he observes all around him, entombed beneath the financial district and reified by Brussels's colonial grandeur. Julius's disavowal of his rape of Moji is in keeping with the general numbness of his narrative voice—an affective distancing that is complicit with the modes of concealment that his cogent observations work to redress. The form of the novel, all this is to say, dramatizes the very repression that the content of the novel is determined to undo.

Following the revelation of the rape, and the foreclosure of any reckoning with it, Julius returns to his natural way of being in the world—the careful but dispassionate observer, the intellectually keen but emotionally distant listener. The penultimate episode in the book is an extended exegesis of Mahler's Ninth Symphony, a moving performance of which Julius hears at Carnegie Hall. This final aesthetic reflection echoes the novel's opening pages, wherein Julius recalls an earlier encounter with Mahler in a busy record store. Despite the sensory excess of his surroundings, as Mahler's *Das Lied von der Erde* plays over the store's speakers Julius is able to "enter the strange hues of [the music's] world." Later, on the train, the symphony's final movement returns to him, "playing through with such intensity that it was as though I were in the store listening to it. I sensed," Julius continues, "the woodsiness of the clarinets, the resin of the violins and violas, the vibrations of the timpani, and the intelligence that held them all together and drew them endlessly along the musical line. My memory was overwhelmed. The song followed me home."[29] Julius's experience, in this moment, is a sort of aural hallucination. And that is one thing, *Open City* insists, that aesthetic objects can do—help us see or hear what is not immediately there, make visible or audible the ghosts, the "unacknowledged traumas," all around us. Listing to Mahler's Ninth Symphony months later at Carnegie Hall, Julius is again moved by the "deep sorrow of

Mahler's long but radiant elegy," the intensive recognition of which makes him feel as though he can "detect the intense concentration, the hundreds of private thoughts, of the people in the auditorium with me."[30] But following the revelation of the rape that he committed and repressed, Julius's invocation of his own extra-sensory powers of observation has here a new effect. The reader is moved not by Julius's insights into what lies beyond our immediate perception, but by his blindness to that which is obsessively there. Like all forms of imaginative representation, *Open City* demonstrates, fiction not only summons new worlds into being or into view; it is also capable of "reverse hallucination," the elision or denial of existent realities.

The novel's final pages, like the narrative at large, repeatedly impress the devastating consequence of this latter "reverse hallucination." Of the concert-going crowd, Julius acutely notes: "It never ceases to surprise me how easy it is to leave the hybridity of the city, and enter into all-white spaces, the homogeneity of which, as far as I can tell, causes no discomfort to the whites in them. The only thing odd, to some of them, is seeing me, young and black, in my seat or at the concession stand."[31] His fellow symphony patrons can see Julius but not themselves. And as ever, befitting his occupation, Julius is sensitive to the fact that "the lens through which the symptoms are viewed is often, itself, symptomatic"—so it is whether one is observing the rubble beneath Canal Street or the deepest interiorities of the self, composing a novel or reading one.[32] "What we knew," Julius reflects, "was so much less than what remained in darkness."[33] *Open City* unfolds as a series of historical excavations that lead not to recovery—or not just to recovery—but to yet further sites of erasure and imperception. The political consequence of these enduring layers of concealment, the novel insists, is profound. To again invoke the plaintive words of Julius's friend and mentor Professor Saito: "There are towns whose names evoke a real horror in you because you have learned to link those names with atrocities, but, for the generation that follows yours, those names will mean nothing. Forgetting doesn't take long. Fallujah will be as meaningless to them as Daejon is to you."[34]

THE RETROGRADE FUTURE

Julius's imaginative excavations locate an eighteenth-century African burial ground and post–September 11 immigrant-detention facility—the racial terrors of the historical and contemporary security state—on one shared cartography. *Open City* uses the novel technologies of historical effacement operative in the moment of the War on Terror as a lens onto the longer history of imperial erasure and reproduction. The novel, that is, discerns in the apparent newness of the current conjuncture the manifest presence of older imperial forms. As Julius observes, and as the Retort group has put it, the contemporary articulation of the imperial security project is characterized by a "lethal mixture of atavism and newfangledness."[35] Classically imperialist processes of conquest and dispossession—justified by retrograde appeals to absolutist narratives of culture and religion—are accompanied by the deployment of "hyper-modern" information technologies and by the innovation of ever more opaque modes of fictitious capital.[36] Bombs *and* images; resource extraction *and* credit default swaps; primitive accumulation *and* media spectacle.[37]

The contradiction contained in this doubleness—which is at once the newness of the old and the oldness of the new—is central to Mohsin Hamid's *The Reluctant Fundamentalist*. The recipient of significant scholarly attention across the anglophone world upon its 2007 publication, Hamid's novel chronicles the pre- to post–September 11 experience of Changez, a young Pakistani university lecturer, formerly a star associate at the prestigious Manhattan financial firm Underwood Samson. The novel's single setting is an outdoor café in Lahore. Here Changez (the novel's sole voice) conveys his story to an unidentified American (possibly a CIA agent, or some other covert operative, but possibly simply a businessman or even tourist) he has encountered in the bazaar, only apparently by chance. Though this mise en scène—to which we return at the beginning and conclusion of each chapter in Changez's narrative—is confined, the novel spans several continents and reaches several centuries into the past. Befitting Changez's current occupation, his monologue resembles a subtly didactic address. He is patient with his listener, even as the latter's unease deepens. But he is also clear in the historical and political substance he wants to convey. Narrating his own journey of political awakening, Changez aims to locate the imperialist projections of the contemporary United States within the longer history of European empire. He endeavors, in other words, to clarify America's relationship to Pakistan and the world at large—within the immediate context of the War on Terror and within the broader historical frame of colonial modernity.[38]

The Neoliberal Fundamentalist

Graduating *summa cum laude* from Princeton, a freshly minted denizen of the meritocracy's upper echelons, Changez is offered a coveted position at Underwood Samson. On his first day at work, Changez marvels out the window of his 41st-floor office, intensely aware that "supporting my feet were the achievements of the most technologically advanced civilization our species had ever known."[39] Moved by this recognition, Changez is moved as well by the knowledge that he himself now wielded the power of advanced and advancing capital. On one of his first assignments, Changez travels to Manila to valuate a record company. He and his colleagues develop a complex financial model, the output of which will determine the company's fate. "I felt," he recalls to his American dinner companion, "enormously powerful on those outings, knowing my team was shaping the future."[40] At stake, Changez infers, is not simply the future of this record company and the livelihood of its current employees, but the trajectory of history itself.

At times, Changez does reveal a latent sensitivity to the lives his work affects. Valuating a struggling cable company in New Jersey, evidently wary of the task—which is certain to result in layoffs—Changez is given a pep talk by his superior, Jim. "Time only moves in one direction," Jim reassures him. "Things always change. . . . The economy's an animal," he continues, "First it needed muscle. Now all the blood it could spare was rushing to its brain. That's where I wanted to be. In finance. In the coordination business. And that's where *you* are. You're blood brought from some part of the body that the species doesn't need any more. . . . Like me. We came," he concludes, "from places that were wasting away." Changez is impressed by Jim's sermon on the transition from material to immaterial production, if somewhat uncomfortable with its closing salvo—a reference to Jim's working-class background and Changez's Pakistani origins—and "the idea that the place I came from was condemned to atrophy."[41] With his faith and enthusiasm momentarily restored by Jim's words, Changez returns to the job at hand with a renewed ruthlessness.

In the aftermath of September 11, Changez is privately alienated by the backward-looking nationalism on vulgar display in New York, a city he always imagined as too immersed in the future and too cosmopolitan to be consumed by nostalgia. Work, in this context, offers a reprieve of sorts. The progressive (future-focused) mindset of Underwood Samson appears immune to, and acts as an antidote against, the "classical" tenor and vocabulary of the nascent War on Terror. "At work," Changez recalls, "we went about the task of shaping the future with little regard for the past." During that time, Changez notes, "I was never better at the pursuit of fundamentals.... Our creed was one which valued above all else maximum productivity, and such a creed was for me doubly reassuring because it was quantifiable—and hence knowable—in a period of great uncertainty, and because it remained utterly convinced of the possibility of progress."[42] Changez does not initially see how the backwardness he laments and the futurism he celebrates are analogous in their effects; each structure of feeling disables historical consciousness or understanding. Gradually, however, Changez does begin to recognize the ways in which the retrograde culture of the war and the speculative financialism of Underwood Samson are allied modes of U.S. imperialist power.

His gaze focused immutably on the granular details of his work, Changez is able to disengage from both the immediate human consequence of that work and its more global implications. He is able to repress, in other words, the knowledge that the structures of finance he is helping to design and implement are tightly entwined with the same imperialist power at that moment being manifested in Afghanistan, a country that neighbors his own. When the myopia of his corporate asceticism does begin to recede, Changez is shaken by the depth of his new vision. In Chile to valuate a publishing house, Changez strikes up a tentative but charged acquaintance with the company's director, Juan Bautista, who senses in Changez a troubled ethical and political consciousness. Over lunch one day, Juan Bautista offers Changez a history lesson on the subject of the janissaries: "'They were Christian boys,'" he explains to Changez, "'captured by the Ottomans and trained to be soldiers in a Muslim army.... They were ferocious and utterly loyal: they had fought to erase their own civilization, so they had nothing else to turn to.'"[43] Juan Bautista's words have their intended effect. "I spent that night," Changez recalls, "considering what I had become. There really could be no doubt: I was a modern-day janissary, a servant of the American empire at a time when it was invading a country with a kinship to my own."[44] Always peripherally aware, but now urgently so, of the relationship between financial and geopolitical power, of the fact that "finance was a primary means by which the American empire exercised its power," Changez resolves to leave his job and return to Pakistan, to resist rather than facilitate this "project of domination."[45] No longer in thrall to the inexorable logic of the financial fundamentals, to the world-making power of capital, Changez redirects his analytic energies toward—focuses his "ex-janissary's gaze" on—the deconstruction of American empire, its history, and its current manifestation under the sign of a War on Terror. The wars in Afghanistan, Iraq, and beyond, in Changez's encapsulation, were united by "the advancement of a small coterie's concept of American interests in the guise of a fight against terrorism, which was defined to refer only to the organized and politically motivated killing of civilians by *killers* not wearing the uniforms of soldiers."[46] As this pithy observation makes plain, Changez understands the rhetoric of "terrorism" as a means through which the imperial security state obscures the terror intrinsic to itself.

Atavistic Empire

Discussing the novel's form, Hamid has described *The Reluctant Fundamentalist* as a sort of one-man play.[47] The "dramatic monologue" delivered by Changez—to which the unnamed American listener, like the audience in a theatre, and indeed like the novel's reader, is captive—interweaves his personal story with reflections on local and global history, and with contemporary political criticism. Evocative descriptions of the Lahore marketplace that acts as the novel's set are accompanied by historical visits to the ancient Mediterranean, feudal Europe, and colonial North America. Delivered from an urban bazaar that symbolizes openness and fluidity, and that contains within it reminders of deep historical time, Changez's monologue highlights the inwardness and backwardness—the false spatial and historical consciousness—of the contemporary United States. Though his American listener is condemned to silence—a reversal of the War on Terror's dominant dialogic paradigm—Changez does respond to subtle shifts in his companion's facial expression and posture. "The frequency and purposefulness with which you glance about," Changez notes, "brings to mind the behavior of an animal that has ventured too far from its lair and is now, in unfamiliar surroundings, uncertain whether it is predator or prey!"[48] This observation prompts an extended commentary on the social geography of Lahore, one that stresses the ancient origins of the city's spatial order, and one that suggests some points of commonality with the urbanism of twenty-first-century Manhattan. Most immediately, Changez is hoping to allay his companion's evident anxiety, but more pointedly he is working to construct his narrative's historical frame. "[Acquiring] a certain familiarity with the recent history of our surroundings," he insists early on, "allows us to put the present into much better perspective."[49]

In the early years of the War on Terror, the orientalist desire to know the other expressed itself in multiple ways. The cultural anthropologist Raphael Patai's *The Arab Mind* (1973) was widely read and heeded by U.S. military officials keen on bending the apparatuses of occupation in Iraq and Afghanistan to fit the essential psychology of the occupied. For example, the idea that Arabs are especially vulnerable to sexual humiliation informed the atrocities committed by U.S. soldiers at Abu Ghraib.[50] In the American public sphere, meanwhile, novels such as Khaled Hosseini's *The Kite Runner* (2003) met a more liberal or cosmopolitan desire—generally still compatible with the call for intervention—for some empathetic identification with the people of Afghanistan. *The Reluctant Fundamentalist* responds to but subverts this contemporary orientalist impulse. Rather than pose the relationship between the United States and Pakistan as absolute difference or easy identification, Changez reveals the complex contemporary and historical interrelationship between the two places. His monologue, moreover, insists that his American listener—and we, the readers of the text—redirect the orientalist gaze inward. Understanding Changez and Pakistan, in other words, will require reckoning with how that part of the world was shaped historically by British empire, and is subject today to the direct and indirect effects of U.S. imperialist power. Though Changez presents his American listener with the opportunity to apprehend this history, his story also evinces how the narrative framework of the War on Terror—its historical and geographic myopia—disables the possibility of historical perception or comprehension.

Changez's critique of the War on Terror is, in one sense, an engagement with the conjoined—though never identical—problems of history and memory. He is concerned in particular with one pervasive symptom: the distortion of individual and collective memory, and thus history, by melancholic attachments. "It seemed," Changez recalls of the months following September 11, "that America was increasingly giving itself over to a dangerous nostalgia":

> There was something undeniably retro about the flags and the uniforms, about generals addressing cameras in war rooms and newspaper headlines featuring such words as *duty* and *honor*. I had always thought of America as a nation that looked forward; for the first time I was struck by its determination to look *back*.... What your fellow countrymen longed for was unclear to me—a time of unquestioned dominance? of safety? of moral certainty? I did not know—but that they were scrambling to don the costumes of another era was apparent.[51]

It is also apparent to Changez that the nationalistic nostalgia of "Homeland Security"—the longing for a lost innocence—is inflected with racist sentiments. Upon his return from Chile, Changez is once again alarmed by the retrograde cast of the imperial apparatus, and by his own denigrated place within it. "I was struck," he remarks, "by how traditional your empire appeared. Armed sentries manned the check post at which you sought entry; being of a suspect race I was quarantined and subjected to additional inspection; once admitted I hired a charioteer who belonged to a serf class lacking the requisite permissions to abide legally and forced therefore to accept work at lower pay; I myself," he adds, "was a form of indentured servant whose right to remain was dependent upon the continued benevolence of my employer."[52] Changez hears echoes of imperial antiquity in the United States of the War on Terror, but the nostalgia that pervades the public sphere works against any historicization of the present. This nostalgia discourages as well the emergence of a global humanistic consciousness, one empathetically invested in suffering taking place elsewhere in the world, beyond "the limited geography that would come to be called Ground Zero,"[53] beyond the walls of the Homeland. "As a society," Changez laments, "you were unwilling to reflect upon the shared pain that united you with those who attacked you."[54] The nostalgia ascendant in the post–September 11 moment, Changez implies, contributed to the enactment of spatial and not just historical occlusions.

This nostalgia is given allegorical expression by Changez's love interest in New York, Erica. In the aftermath of September 11, Erica descends into a deep melancholia that mirrors the melancholia of the city and the country. Still profoundly affected by the death, several years before, of her adolescent lover, Erica has difficulties with intimacy. She is beginning to open herself to Changez, but September 11 "churned up old thoughts that had settled in the manner of sediment to the bottom of a pond," and she retreats inward. "She was struggling," Changez recalls, "against a current that pulled her within herself, and her smile contained the fear that she might slip into her own depths, where she would be trapped, unable to breathe."[55] Erica's inwardness mirrors the inwardness of New York and the country—the failure of the city and nation, in its moment of grief, to look beyond itself and toward the world. Unable to fully mourn her lost lover, to comprehend her lingering attachment to him and reconstruct her fractured and diminished self, Erica falls into a darker and darker depression, ever less capable of human interaction: "She was disappearing into a powerful *nostalgia*, one from which only she could choose whether or not to return."[56] Erica does not return; she is admitted to a mental institution, from which she disappears, and is presumed dead after her clothes are found on a rocky outcrop over the Hudson. Now back in Pakistan, Changez retains hope that she is still living, and that she will one day shed her profound detachment and reenter the world. He harbors similar hopes for New York, the city he once adored, and for the United States.

Changez himself is not immune to the force of nostalgia. As a boy he possessed an intense longing "not for what my family had never had, but for what we had had and lost."[57] This familial nostalgia corresponds to a national nostalgia—a longing for the restoration of his culture's glorious history. "Four thousand years ago," Changez tells his American companion, "we, the people of the Indus River basin, had cities that were laid out on grids and boasted underground sewers, while the ancestors of those who would invade and colonize America were illiterate barbarians. Now," he continues plaintively, "our cities were largely unplanned, unsanitary affairs, and America had universities with individual endowments greater than our national budget for education. To be reminded of this disparity was, for me, to be ashamed."[58] He is speaking here from the perspective of his New York self, looking back toward his home, and feeling acutely the great gulf that separates the one world from the other. Returning to Pakistan, Changez feels not shame in his family's or country's decline, but pride in the richness of his people's heritage. He remains sensitive to the stark differences in wealth and power between Pakistan and the United States, but is newly focused on critiquing the imperial processes that condition such geographic inequalities. Though articulated in the vocabulary of national resistance, Changez's political activism highlights and affirms the ordinary reality of cultural fluidity and hybridity. Remarking once again on the jingoism of the early War on Terror, Changez addresses his companion and America at large: "You retreated into myths of your own difference, assumptions of your own superiority. And you acted out these beliefs on the stage of the world, so that the entire planet was rocked by the repercussions of your tantrums."[59] Though palpable, his anger is not invested in a reciprocal assertion of national absolutism. Speaking of his relationship with Erica and the ways in which he has been transformed by it, Changez remarks that "it is not ... possible to restore one's boundaries after they have been blurred and made permeable by a relationship: try as we might, we cannot reconstitute ourselves as the autonomous beings we previously imagined ourselves to be. Something of us is now outside, and something of the outside is now within us."[60] A meditation on interpersonal intimacy and its after-effects, Changez's words are also a metaphor for the futile, destructive fictions of monocultural exclusivity and Homeland Security.

Changez's coming to political self-consciousness is occasioned by his recognition of the reciprocal relation of market progressivism and retrograde imperialist militarism. *The Reluctant Fundamentalist*'s attention to the concurrence of the atavistic and the newfangled betrays its distinctly postcolonial consciousness. The postcolonial condition is defined by the oldness of the new—the reiteration of colonial ideology and colonial policy in the moment of colonialism's supposed negation. This paradox is evinced with a particular clarity by the history and present of the United States—a settler-colony and latter-day imperialist power that imagines itself the vanguard of history itself; a nation wherein the power of capital and the state carries the residue, and enables the rearticulation, of colonial social relations. Narrating his journey from Lahore to Manhattan and back again, from underprivileged student to agent of America's financial empire to opponent of America's presence in the world, Changez brings into relief the "deep and perplexing doubleness" identified by Retort, and in so doing illuminates the (post)coloniality of the United States and the War on Terror.

Calling attention to the convergence of retrograde and futuristic militarisms in the moment of the War on Terror, *The Reluctant Fundamentalist* simultaneously reveals the cultures of melancholia and nostalgia that disable historical critique of the present. The difficulties of historical redress are also evidenced by the novel's form. The silencing of Changez's companion accents, paradoxically, the latter's failures as a listener. As the tension in their encounter builds, it is the deafness rather than the muteness of Changez's American interlocutor that is most forcibly conveyed. Changez's personal and historical narrative is ultimately received, tellingly, not with a gesture of emergent understanding but with the suggestion of imminent violence. The novel ends as Changez's companion reaches into his jacket and flashes "a glint of metal"—perhaps something as innocuous as a money clip, but perhaps a knife or gun.

Open City operates in a concordant register—recovering histories of loss while formally dramatizing the difficulties of historical registration or transmission. Traveling between New York, Brussels, and Lagos, Julius sheds light upon the multiple pasts contained and concealed by any geography. But the archive of forgetting he so vividly renders is mirrored by the amnesiac recesses, the blank spots of memory, within his own history. His, in other words, is a voice of witness whose testimony brings into stark relief those voices that remain inaudible, those histories that remain buried. Each of these novels, that is, brings into view the intersection of different imperial histories and outlines—or formally figures—the cultures of erasure, and forces of myopia, that work to keep those histories out of view. The text I turn to below, Junot Díaz's *The Brief Wondrous Life of Oscar Wao*, is likewise possessed of this dual concern. A chronicle of one particular historical experience—the story of the New World, of originary colonial terror and its echo across the centuries and across the globe, as embodied in the narrative of one person and one family—*Oscar Wao* is also a self-conscious reflection on the possibilities and limitations of literary witness.

HISPANIOLA, 1492–PERTH AMBOY, 2005

The essential political and economic forms of colonial modernity, and of the security project at its core, were founded in terror. The auto-historiography of capital and the imperial state disavows this essential terror, or imagines it as belonging exclusively to the moment of foundation. Accenting and resisting this historical elision, the novels I consider in this chapter clarify the necessary connection between the silencing of modernity's inaugural violence and its perpetual reproduction. In *Open City*, the literal and figurative burial of imperial pasts enables their reenactment in the present. In *The Reluctant Fundamentalist*, the dual forces of nativist nostalgia and financial futurism obscure the original and extant terrors of imperial order. And in *Oscar Wao*, finally, technologies of archival erasure make possible the eternal return of colonial modernity's primordial violence. But *Oscar Wao* is, at the same time, a sustained meditation on the potentialities of archival recovery. Like Cole and Hamid, Díaz reveals the ways in which the question of archival erasure and recovery is at base a problem of form. *Oscar Wao* is interested, in other words, in the modes of narrative representation through which the past is concealed, and through which it might be brought into view.

In the End, in the Beginning

Stories of origin and apocalypse frame each of *Oscar Wao*'s overlapping narratives—of individual, of family, of nation, of hemisphere, of world—but one epochal moment, at once end and beginning, founds them all. As the opening lines of Díaz's celebrated 2007 novel read: "They say it came first from Africa, carried in the screams of the enslaved; that it was the death bane of the Tainos, uttered just as one world perished and another began; that it was a demon drawn into creation through the nightmare door that was cracked open in the Antilles."[61] *It* is the "fukú", the curse inaugurated by Columbus's arrival in 1492 on the island of Hispaniola, the island that "Oscar, at the end, would call the Ground Zero of the New World."[62] Fukú signifies the routes of continuity between the terror of colonial modernity's beginning and the terror of its twentieth-century iteration—in particular the state terror prosecuted by U.S.-backed security forces in the service of American geo-power and global capitalist regeneration. Díaz's novel strives to make visible the histories of violence that fukú names, in the faith that if the curse cannot be transcended, at least it can be borne witness to. Discussing *Oscar Wao* in an interview with Edwidge Danticat, Díaz remarked that "the real issue in the book is not whether or not one can vanquish the fukú—but whether or not one can even see it," whether one can recognize and acknowledge (here he cites Glissant), "'the past, to which we were subjected, which has not yet emerged as history for us (but that) is however, obsessively present.'"[63]

As imagined and undertaken by Díaz, the project of witness is plural in both medium and form. *Oscar Wao*'s formal flexibility acts as a counterpoint to the dominant narratives of state and nation, the methodological narrowness and univocality of which silence the stories of history's victims and elide the violence upon which the state is founded and through which it is reproduced. Making audible history's silenced voices, *Oscar Wao* implies, will necessarily involve not simply the multiplication of narrative perspectives but a concomitant proliferation of interpretive and representational modes.[64] *Oscar Wao* pays homage to and samples a multitude of forms, genres, and texts—fantasy, science fiction, comics, magical realism; *The Lord of the Rings, Beloved, X-Men, Watchmen, One Hundred Years of Solitude, Planet of the Apes*—a cultural bibliography that reflects Díaz's own history as a reader. One particular work to which Díaz's novel is indebted, and to which it bears an evident affinity—in its interweaving of familial, national, and Antillean histories; in its inventive usage of footnotes; and in its linguistic pluralism—is Patrick Chamoiseau's Martinican epic *Texaco*. In his "Letter to Chamoiseau," a lyrical tribute to *Texaco*'s achievement, Derek Walcott meditates on the particular understanding of history that lends the novel its power and its poignancy:

> Every island is circumscribed by that oceanic sadness called History, but the *histoires* recorded in *Texaco* are not related to the march, the rhythm, of some optimistic chronology which leads from slavery to emancipation to colonialism to independence, or the demand for it; rather these events are simultaneous,

they have only one meaning and one tense: perpetual suffering, habitual agony. The scansion of time is as simple as the monody of waves or the rhythm of two seasons. The squatters live only in one tense, the "is" of the novel's meter. It is this monody that increases the quality of myth in rejecting a linear law and calendar: it is *l'histoire*, not History but the story, the fable, the rumor, as opposed to times, dates, and places. Every event in *Texaco* is given a domestic but mythic resonance, not by the narrator-novelist, the bird-scribe, but by the agitations of rumor, by contradictory memory, and by the incantations of its characters.[65]

The sensibility Walcott describes here—one that assumes the presentness of the past, and one attuned to the dialogue of individual memory and collective history—is equally palpable in *The Brief Wondrous Life of Oscar Wao*. "It is believed," Yunior remarks on page one, "that the arrival of Europeans on Hispaniola unleashed the fukú on the world, and we've all been in the shit ever since."[66] *It is believed*: the passive construction is testament to an authorship that defies clear attribution, a way of transmitting history through, as Walcott puts it, "the story, the fable, the rumor."

In addition to Walcott's *histoire*—history as story, fable, rumor; the word-of-mouth (*radio bemba*, in the Cuban vernacular) compilation of memory and experience—two other modes of history are at work in *Oscar Wao*: history as embodied, as registered by scarred flesh (Beli), bodily transformation (Beli, Lola), and body mass (Oscar); and history as literature, as writing, as that which is preserved in the archive or available at the local comic-book store. *Oscar Wao*'s author (Díaz), narrator (Yunior), and lead protagonist (Oscar) are all writers. Each has taken up the burden of history as literature; and the task with which they are faced is to render in written form the fable and the rumor, the bodily inscriptions or atmospheric impressions of infinite history. In *Oscar Wao*, these three modes of history—fable, body, word—record and express the presence of the past, reckoning with the lingering resonance of colonial culture and history, recognizing the ways in which putatively decolonized bodies and places remain "marked," as Simon Gikandi has put it, "by the trace of the imperial pasts they try to disavow."[67]

Rumor's Incantations

In the "story, fable, rumor" mode of history, the question of collective memory, the question of, as Díaz phrases it, *who we are as a people and what has happened to us*, is taken up in the café and the schoolyard, at the barbershop and *sobremesa*, in stories whispered or shouted, breathed and absorbed.

Yunior's lessons in Dominican history—usually delivered in footnotes—illuminate not just crucial events, but real and mythological figures of the recent and distant past, from indigenous resistance leaders in the moment of the colonial encounter to Raphael Trujillo's cast of torturers: Hatuey, "the Taino Ho Chi Minh," leader of the indigenous resistance against "First Genocide"; Anacaona (also known as the Golden Flower), "One of the Founding Mothers of the New World and the Most Beautiful Indian in the World," another resistance leader, captured and hung by the Spanish; the Mongoose, antidote to fukú, bringer of zafa, "enemy of kingly chariots, chains, and hierarchies"; the "Faceless One" (or "The Man Without a Face"), harbinger of imminent doom; Joaquin Balaguer, one of Trujillo's "more efficient ringwraiths" and his eventual successor—"a Negrophobe, an apologist to genocide, an election thief, and a killer of people who wrote better than himself"; Felix Wenceslao Bernardino (Felix), "one of Trujillo's most sinister agents, his Witchking of Angmar"; and Johnny Abbes Garcia (Abbes), head of Trujillo's secret police, "considered the greatest torturer of the Dominican people ever to have lived"—later a henchman for Haiti's "Papa Doc" ("P-Diddy" to Yunior) Duvalier.[68] Each of these figures is brought to life through the stories and legends that circulate about them. Abbes, Yunior notes, "was rumored to have in his employ a dwarf who would crush prisoners' testicles between his teeth.... He is said to still be out there in the world, waiting for the next coming of El Jefe, when he too will rise from the shadow." Of Felix, he writes, "It was said that the power of Trujillo never left him; the fucker died of old age in Santo Domingo, Trujillista to the end, drowning his Haitian workers instead of paying them." On Hatuey's burning at the stake: "What Hatuey said on the pyre is legend in itself: Are there white people in Heaven? Then I'd rather go to hell." And on Anacaona's death: "A common story you hear about Anacaona in the DR is that on the eve of her execution she was offered a chance to save herself: all she had to do was marry a Spaniard who was obsessed with her.... Tragically old-school, Anacaona was reported to have said, Whiteman, kiss my hurricane ass!"[69] The grammar of Yunior's storytelling, in particular his consistent use of the passive voice ("was rumored to," "is said to," "it was said that," "was reported to"), and his allusion to sites of shared knowledge ("a common story you hear"), evokes Walcott's *histoire*, a history composed through *story, fable, rumor*, wherein every unique moment is charged "with a domestic but mythic resonance."[70]

"There are a zillion of these fukú stories," Yunior writes. But even if "everyone has one knocking around their family" there are gaps in the archive, gaps that inhibit efforts at complete narrative recreation.⁷¹ The story of the family Cabral has its own hazy chapters: "We are trawling in silences here," Yunior acknowledges: "Trujillo and company didn't leave a paper trail—they didn't share their German contemporaries' lust for documentation. And it's not like the fukú itself would leave a memoir or anything."⁷² On the matter of the torture and imprisonment of Oscar's grandfather Abelard—officially for saying something amiss about Trujillo in a nightclub, but more probably for protecting his daughter from El Jefe's sexual predations—"there is within the family a silence that stands monument to the generations, that sphinxes all attempts at narrative reconstruction."⁷³ When evidence and testimony are lacking, efforts at historical recreation must draw from the reservoir of popular mythology. "The rap about The Girl Trujillo Wanted," the story often invoked to explain the Fall of Abelard and the destruction of the family, "is a pretty common one on the island," Yunior writes, "so common that Mario Vargas Llosa didn't have to do much except open his mouth to sift it out of the air." It "might be trite as far as foundation myths go," Yunior concedes, "but at least it's something you can believe in, no? Something real."⁷⁴ The Girl Trujillo Wanted and other myths, stories that cast "a supernatural shadow," stories "with no solid evidence, the kind of shit only a nerd could love," do not condemn the large or small narrative to the status of the untrue or the unreal.⁷⁵ On the contrary, their fantastic or mythological quality is precisely what makes them so recognizably real. Critics have been divided as to whether *Oscar Wao* is an example of magical realism or a departure from it. Díaz has offered hints into his own reading of this debate, stating in an interview that "magical realism in a very simple definition is like using the fantastic to describe the real, and this book argues that the real is fantastic. Which is very different."⁷⁶ As Oscar asks, "What more sci-fi than Santo Domingo? What more fantasy than the Antilles?"⁷⁷

History and the Body

In *Oscar Wao*, story, fable, and rumor accent repetition, recitation, and return—this is how power is manifested, in history and in historical narrative. The constancy of the fukú is demonstrated by the recurrence of particular events (the canefield beatings of Beli and Oscar, the first and second U.S. occupations of the Dominican Republic—further echoed in the U.S. occupation of Iraq), particular figures (The Man Without a Face), and particular stories (The Girl Trujillo Wanted). The embodied form of history also reveals the force of repetition, but power is here most profoundly evidenced in and enacted by processes of transformation. In the story of the family Cabral/de Leon, the body both records and propels transformations within and outside the self.

A high school student in Bani, living with her aunt, La Inca, Beli is pretty but invisible, "a gangly Ibis of a girl"—until her sophomore summer, the "Summer of Her Secondary Sex Characteristics," when she hits "the biochemical jackpot" and is "transformed utterly" into a "terrible beauty... un mujerón total."[78] Initially overcome with shame, Beli soon comes to recognize "the undeniable concreteness of her desirability which was, in its own way, power."[79] The power Beli feels in herself because of the desire others have for her—a power, La Inca reminds her, that is also a great burden—is inseparable from her own desire to escape, to be someone else, somewhere else. What she wants to escape is clear: "having to wait until fifteen to straighten her hair, the impossible expectations of La Inca, the fact that her long-gone parents died when she was one, the whispers that Trujillo had done it, those first years of her life when she'd been an orphan, the horrible scars from that time, her own despised black skin," and so on.[80] Initially, the "escape" enabled by her newfound sexual power is merely a euphemism for romantic entanglement, first with her school crush Jack Pujols, and second with the Gangster—agent of the Trujillato, Beli's first true love (but not her first heartbreak), and the man either directly or indirectly responsible for her being beaten to near death in a canefield (saved only by a zafa from La Inca). Still alive but still in danger, Beli, on La Inca's insistence, leaves the island for Nueva York. She meets her husband, father of Oscar and Lola and her third and final heartbreak, on the plane to Diaspora.

Not Nueva York but Nueva Jersey, it turns out, is Beli's final destination. Physical exile does not help Beli shed the weight of the past—her own, her family's, her country's. In Paterson, Beli retains that familiar yet "particularly Jersey malaise—the indistinguishable longing for elsewhere"—a malaise, and a desire, shared by her daughter Lola.[81] Called into the bathroom by her mother—"*naked from the waist up, her bra slung about her like a torn sail, the scar on her back as vast and inconsolable as a sea*"—Lola, just twelve, touches the dual burden, the violence of the past and the present, written on Beli's body: the scars from her various beatings (the scars of Trujillo) and the newly discovered tumor in her breast, "*a knot just beneath her skin, tight and secretive as a plot.*"[82] Lola struggles to differentiate her mother from the history of violence resident in her body. Determined to flee the latter, she resolves to sever herself from the grip of the former. Lola's escape, like her mother's, is enabled by her supernatural (Na'vi-like) physicality—and like her mother, Lola runs to a boy, "beautiful and callow" ("like all boys"), but also violent. Desire, the transformation it engenders, is again bound up in pain.[83] Yet so too is it bound up in survival, and in the possibility of real liberation. The curse is passed from mother to daughter, but this reproduction also keeps alive the possibility of a final zafa, the redemption and rebirth of the Cabral clan. The scar on Beli's back evokes Toni Morrison's *Beloved* (1987), and the scar on Sethe's back, a scar that archives a history of violence, but a scar—in the shape of a chokecherry tree—that also signifies the hope of regeneration.

It Was Written

Oscar is another character who carries the weight of past and present suffering on his body, his obesity the register of so many afflictions, both personal and collective. Though Oscar embarks on the occasional weight-loss program, these efforts are not symbolic of a desire to shed the historical burden he bears, to be absolved of a history he did not commit.[84] On the contrary, Oscar's life, most profoundly his life as a reader and as a writer, is devoted to confronting and chronicling—bearing witness to—the fukú of his family and his world. A voracious reader of genre fictions and comic books, most of all, Oscar, from high school onward, is also an aspiring writer. Visiting Santo Domingo one adolescent summer, Oscar carries along "a stack of notebooks and a plan to fill them all up."[85] By senior year he is on to his fifth novel, and doesn't stop writing through college and beyond (undeterred by a lack of interest from the publishing world). Eight months after his death—this time the canefield is the end—two manuscripts arrive at the house in Paterson addressed to Lola: more chapters from his unfinished opus ("a four-book E.E. 'Doc' Smith-esque space opera called Starscourge") and a letter to his sister, the last thing he ever wrote. But in an enclosed note, there is also mention of a third manuscript on its way, which contains "everything I've written on this journey. Everything I think you will need. . . . (It's the cure to what ails us. The Cosmo DNA.)"[86] The third manuscript never arrives.

Oscar's is not the only missing manuscript. In the months before he was imprisoned, Abelard began work on a "book about the Dark Powers of [Trujillo]," a book in which he argues "that the tales the common people told about the president—that he was supernatural, that he was not human—may in some ways have been *true*."[87] A book, in other words, that may well have resembled, in spirit and in truth, Oscar's own lost text. Alas, all copies of the manuscript were destroyed, along with the rest of Abelard's papers and indeed his entire library ("You got to fear a motherfucker or what he's writing to do something like that").[88] Thus it falls upon Yunior, the writer who survives, to color the silences, to fill in the gaps left by the two missing manuscripts that bookend the Cabral fukú. In the absence of documentary evidence, the fictive imagination is required. Yunior is careful to highlight the moments of embellishment in the narrative. About the name of a city Beli was purported to have visited with the Gangster, Yunior writes:

> In my first draft, Samaná was actually Jarabacoa, but then my girl Leonie, resident expert in all things Domo, pointed out that there are no beaches in Jarabacoa. Beautiful rivers but no beaches. Leonie was also the one who informed me that the perrito (see first paragraphs of chapter one, "GhettoNerd at the End of the World") wasn't popularized until the late eighties, early nineties, but that was one detail I couldn't change, just liked the image too much. Forgive me, historians of popular dance, forgive me![89]

Yunior's is the novel's sole voice. But in questioning his own authority as witness and narrator, as Monica Hanna has observed, he calls attention to those voices that we hear only indirectly or not at all.[90] His account, in other words, foregrounds rather than elides the silent moments in the archive. Yunior's admission of fallibility and incompleteness is not an indictment of fiction but a testament to its urgency. All histories—both the ascendant History and subjugated *histoire*, in Walcott's formulation—are constructed. Yunior's faith, which he inherits from Oscar, is that the mystifying fictions of History can only be countered by the illuminating, if never definitive, fictions of *histoire*.

Sharing a dorm room at Rutgers, Yunior and Oscar engage in bouts of reciprocal pedagogy. Yunior imparts his machismo wisdom and Oscar, in exchange, his trove of fanboy knowledge. Both aspiring literary artists, they also read and comment upon one another's work. In *Oscar Wao*'s present tense, ten years after Oscar's death, Yunior is teaching creative writing at a community college in Perth Amboy and working on his own writing "from can't see in the morning to can't see at night," a diligence learned from Oscar.[91] He has also become the keeper of Oscar's archive: his manuscripts, but also his library, his games, his papers—all safely stored in four refrigerators in the basement. Yunior is waiting for the day when Isis, Lola's daughter, will come looking for answers, for the story of her family:

A light, a desk, a cot—I've prepared it all.
How many nights will she stay with us?
As many as it takes.
And maybe, just maybe, if she's smart and as brave as I'm expecting she'll be, she'll take all we've done and all we've learned and add her own insights and she'll put an end to it.[92]

Oscar Wao is a book about writing but it is also a book about reading, and about the power of the reader. Reading the words of her tío, perhaps Isis can begin the process of reckoning that might cleanse the family of its fukú—witness being a necessary prerequisite to transcendence, the possibility of "[putting] an end to it."[93] But as the book's penultimate ending intones, via a quote from *Watchmen*: "'In the end? Nothing ends, Adrian. Nothing ever ends.'"[94] This citation recalls as well the refrain that echoes throughout the final paragraphs of Morrison's *Beloved*: "This is not a story to pass on." *This is not a story to pass on* is another way of saying that this is not a story to die.[95] The story of Oscar—his family, his island, his hemisphere, his world—is not a story to let pass away, but a story to keep alive. *Nothing ever ends* is likewise a fitting mantra for the project of postcolonial witness, a project tasked with registering and transmitting, to again summon Díaz's citation of Glissant, a past that is obsessively present.[96]

Speculative Witness

Oscar Wao's three-fold modality of witness—fable, body, word—excavates and illuminates the past in the present. A meditation on the presence of history, *Oscar Wao* is also a history of the present. Yunior's treatment of Dominican and Antillean history is, in a broader sense, a commentary on the long history of colonial modernity, on the relationship between the origins of modern empire—the "discovery" and conquest of the New World—and more recent iterations of U.S. imperialist power within and beyond the hemisphere. The book's persistent references to the War on Terror (Santo Domingo is described in separate moments as "the Ground Zero of the New World" and "Iraq before Iraq was Iraq") are accompanied by offhand allusions to and more focused reflections on the manifestations of U.S. power in the world over the twentieth century. A U.S.-backed dictator, Trujillo "was Mobutu before Mobutu was Mobutu." And the Dominican Republic was Vietnam before Vietnam was Vietnam. The illegal invasion of Santo Domingo by U.S. forces in 1965 coincided with the escalation of hostilities in Indochina, and as Yunior recalls, "many of the same units and intelligence teams that took part in the 'democratization' of Santo Domingo were immediately shipped off to Saigon." "What do you think," Yunior asks, "these soldiers, technicians, and spooks carried with them, in their rucks, in their suitcases, in their shirt pockets, on the inside of their nostrils, caked up around their shoes? Just a little gift from my people to America, a small repayment for an unjust war. That's right folks. Fukú."[97] From Santo Domingo to the "paddies outside of Saigon" the fukú travels with the itinerant infantry of an empire on the precipice of decline. Some of that infantry was Dominican, and Yunior notes the cruel irony of immigrant soldiers losing limbs and lives—in Vietnam and the first Gulf War—in the service of the same imperial power that for so long held brutal sway over their native country. The relationship between the long history of colonial modernity and recent history of U.S. power in the world is brought into especially stark relief by the "two atomic eyes [that] opened over civilian centers in Japan," the "Ground Zeros" of the American century. However geographically distant from Hispaniola, the bombing of Hiroshima and Nagasaki prefigures the Cabral family's fall. "Even though no one knew it yet," when those bombs fell on Japan, Yunior writes, "the world was then remade." But this remaking is expressed not by the advent of a new curse but by the reappearance of the fukú of "the Admiral" (Columbus)—the fukú of colonial modernity itself. "Not two days after the atomic bombs scarred Japan forever," Yunior recounts, "Socorro [Abelard's wife] dreamed that the Faceless Man was standing over her husband's bed, and she could not scream, could not say anything, and the next night she dreamed that he was standing over her children too."[98] The bombs, as the apparition of the Faceless Man suggests, are a rupture that summons and reanimates a deeper history of violence. Conveying this history in writing, Yunior is working against a collective amnesia that elides the past and obscures the present. "You didn't know we were occupied twice in the twentieth century?" He asks. "Don't worry, when you have kids they won't know the U.S. occupied Iraq either."[99]

Just as the fukú of the family Cabral cannot be resisted until it is acknowledged, so too the fukú of the Admiral, the fukú of colonial modernity, must be borne witness to before it can be overcome. The three modes of history at work in *Oscar Wao*—fable, body, word—enable the reciprocal narration of family and world, past and present; the former terms are clarified through the lens of the latter, and vice versa. This act of witness is, crucially, an act of the imagination. Salman Rushdie, in his essay "Imaginary Homelands," writes that émigré writers, displaced in space and time, can only relate to or represent their place of origin through the practice of invention, through fiction, through imagination. The homeland, in other words, is for those who have left a purely imaginary place.[100] For Oscar, however, the homeland is not left behind but taken with. And the imaginary is not a portal to a lost world but a way of engaging with what is immediately present and real. For Oscar, that is, the imaginary functions not as the means through which one can inhabit what is distant in space, time, or consciousness, but as a language and a form with which one can make vivid and confront the otherworldly brutalities of everyday existence.

The epigraph to *Oscar Wao* is taken from Derek Walcott's epic poem "The Schooner 'Flight,'" which chronicles the broad sweep of Caribbean history through the polyglot voice of the sailor Shabine. The excerpt chosen by Díaz concludes with the line "either I'm nobody/or I'm a nation," a fitting encapsulation of Oscar's fraught subjectivity, at once anonymous and burdened with the history of an entire people. But perhaps another line from Walcott's poem might have been even more apt: "I've got no nation now but the imagination." This is Oscar—Oscar for whom there is no salvation in geography, Oscar the great exponent of the "speculative genres," the reader and the writer whose project of historical witness is imbued with the radical possibilities of what is to come.

When Oscar describes the island of Hispaniola, where Columbus made landfall in 1492, as "the Ground Zero of the New World," he is referring to the foundational terror of colonial modernity. And as Díaz's novel conveys, this is the colonial modernity within which we still live. The New World's originary terror is perpetually reproduced by the enduring synthesis of capital and the imperial state. The *eternal return* of colonial modernity (as terror) is figured in *Oscar Wao* by the histories of violence passed between, and experienced anew by, each generation of the Cabral line. But if the repetition of violence structures the narrative, so too does the repetition of survival. In *Oscar Wao*, that is, the trope of eternal return makes vivid not just the constancy of terror but the constancy of our struggle to bear witness to it, and ultimately to move beyond it. It is this latter inheritance, passed from Abelard to Oscar (via Beli), that awaits Isis in the Cabral archives in Perth Amboy.

CONCLUSION

In his book *The Blank Spots on the Map*, the artist and writer Trevor Paglen uncovers the hidden geography of the War on Terror, a network of secret prisons and research facilities that, officially, do not exist. Mapping the black sites of the U.S. security apparatus, Paglen discloses a landscape of violence existing beyond the reach of popular perception yet brutally real.[101] Another geographer, Derek Gregory, has used the term "vanishing points" to describe the unknown spaces of incarceration that, when brought into view, reveal the essential logic and method of the imperial war machine.[102] Gregory understands "vanishing points" not simply as disappearing spots on the literal or cognitive map, but as spaces of intersection, as sites wherein two separate modes of power—biopower and the law, for example—converge, evincing a new political form.[103] This latter understanding of a vanishing point as a site of convergence evokes as well the intersection of different histories of empire and its afterlives—the synthetic reverberations, in the moment and geography of the War on Terror, of New World settler-colonialism and European imperialism in Africa, South Asia, and beyond; the choc en retour of colonial histories to the space of the metropole. Both understandings of "vanishing point"—as a site of deepening invisibility, and as a site of political or historical convergence—are central to the novels I have discussed in this chapter, and are basic to the problem of postcoloniality as it bears upon the United States in particular.

Open City, *The Reluctant Fundamentalist*, and *Oscar Wao* illuminate darkened corners of space and time, the blank spots on the map and in the archive. They expose, simultaneously, the cultures and technologies of erasure through which those vanishing points are formed and reproduced. And they self-reflexively dramatize, in their form as well as their content, both the obstacles to and potentialities of historical reclamation. Cole's *Open City* demonstrates how the coloniality of the War on Terror is obscured by the disavowal or concealment of imperial histories—the actual burial of bodies and other historical artifacts, and the corresponding cleansing of individual and collective memory. The failure to comprehend the brutality of empire and its after-effects enables the ongoing reproduction of colonial rationalities, in Brussels as in Baghdad; the vanishing points of Hispaniola and Daejon condition the vanishing points of Abu Ghraib and Guantánamo Bay. The endurance of such vanishing points is conveyed as well by Julius's muted affect, which performs the repression that the novel sets out to resist. Hamid's *Reluctant Fundamentalist* elucidates the cooperation between ostensibly discrete modes of historical occlusion—from nationalistic nostalgia to the futurism of finance capital to the millenarian militarism of Karl Rove. But Changez's monologic attempt at historical redress is met not with affirmative recognition but with the implied threat of assassination. Resisting the physical absence of archival matter, Díaz's *Oscar Wao* insists that the extant presence of the fukú will remain invisible until its history—from 1492 to 2005, from Santo Domingo to Paterson—has been witnessed. Yunior, though, calls attention to the necessary artifice of his own attempt to fill the *páginas en blanco* that define our imperfect apprehension of the past.

These novels also suggest an understanding of "vanishing point" as a site of convergence or indistinction: the presence of the past; the atavism of the new; the concurrence of the postcolonial and the neocolonial; the imbrication of internal and external processes of colonization; the co-belonging of security and terror. All of these intersections are basic to the postcoloniality of U.S. culture and politics, a postcoloniality W. E. B. Du Bois first observed over a century ago and would continue to think about until the end of his life in 1963. In 1952, Du Bois published an essay entitled "The Negro and the Warsaw Ghetto."[104] In that short but evocative piece, a reflection on his 1949 trip to Warsaw's devastated Jewish ghetto, Du Bois presented a re-theorization of the global color line, articulating anti-Semitism and anti-black racism in an effort to revise and broaden our understanding of modernity's racial formations. A deep engagement with one singular place and time, Du Bois's essay resonates in a global register and addresses multiple temporalities—the postwar struggles for independence, human rights, and civil rights; the wartime experience of ethnic absolutism and genocide; the longer, entangled histories of racial thinking and Enlightenment philosophy. Díaz, Cole, and Hamid are doing something similar: speaking to a multiplicity of times—1492, 1626, 1885, 1916, 1945, 1965, 2001, 2005 (the conquest of the New World, the Dutch dispossession of Manhattan, the creation of the Congo Free State, the U.S. occupations of the Dominican Republic, the Second World War, Vietnam, September 11, and the War on Terror); speaking from a multiplicity of places—northern New Jersey, the Dominican Republic, New York City, Lagos, Manila, Valparaiso, Brussels, and Lahore; and addressing the intersection of different imperialist histories, all of which remain alive in the world, but not all of which we can see. As Julius demonstrates on his walks through Manhattan, as on his repressed journey into his own history of violence, there are vanishing points around every corner.

FIVE

"This Is Our Threnody"

WRITING HISTORY AS CATASTROPHE

The contemporary flourishing of colonial rationality and process is conditioned by the erasure or repression of imperial pasts. In the current conjuncture—a moment defined by a permanent War on Terror and generalized neoliberal depredation—the elision of imperial history and the obfuscation of extant imperial forms are encouraged by the prevailing narrative assumption that September 11, 2001, ruptured time. Though propagated initially by neoconservative pundits and politicians, this assumption rapidly acquired the fixity of common sense within American culture at large, and it continues to be reproduced by writers and critics from across the left-right spectrum. This book has sought to counter the assumption of rupture in two primary ways—first, by relocating the paradigms of security and terror, the central conceptual tropes of contemporary American and global culture, outside of the confining "post-9/11" frame and within the long history of colonial modernity; and second, by reflecting upon the strategies of representation through which this longer history is, or might be, brought into view.

Cole, Hamid, and Díaz trace the genealogies of empire and its afterlives that cohere in the moment of the War on Terror. This more expansive historical vision is accompanied by a heightened sensitivity to the dialectic of security and terror—the terror, and insecurity, that accompanies the imperial imposition of the modern security project. The writer to whom I turn in this chapter, Roberto Bolaño, is possessed of an allied historical and critical consciousness. Using moments of putative rupture as a lens onto the past and the world, Bolaño's fiction articulates together the two genealogies that guided my historical theorizations of security and terror in chapters 1 and 2—the hemispheric (and global) history of neoliberal counterrevolution and the planetary history of capitalist, colonial modernity. Like the novels I examine in the previous chapter, though, Bolaño's work is not only concerned with revealing the histories cast in shadow by the global reach of capital and empire. His writing simultaneously, and self-reflexively, meditates on literature's ambivalent relationship to cultures of historical erasure. Literature, Bolaño's fiction testifies and enacts, is both a mechanism through which the blank spots in our vision are formed and normalized, and an urgent site of resistance to the apparatuses of fetishism and reification.

THE OTHER SEPTEMBER 11

In the later 1960s and early 1970s, the forces of leftist possibility and rightist repression waged a constant battle in Latin America, as indeed they did across the world. Bolaño's fiction was shaped by this moment: by its romance, its tragedy, its brutality, and, perhaps most profoundly, by the residue of loss and dislocation that has accompanied its defeated comrades on their journey through the world in the decades since.

Two events in particular were critical to his political and aesthetic self-formation: the violent suppression of student-led uprisings in Mexico City in 1968—most profoundly, the government massacre of hundreds of students and civilians in La Plaza de las Tres Culturas on October 2 of that year; and the military coup in Chile on September 11, 1973, which ousted the socialist government of Salvador Allende and installed the murderous dictatorship of Augusto Pinochet. Taken together, these two moments, each of which Bolaño experienced directly (born in Santiago, he relocated to Mexico City with his family in 1968, before returning to Santiago in 1973, one month prior to the coup), symbolized, for the young writer, the triumph of rightist reaction and foreclosure of left political alternatives. Written primarily in the 1990s, Bolaño's fiction reflects upon the decades that led from that defeat, an era that witnessed the regional and global descent into a neoliberal state of siege.[1] In short, the nightmare vision that appeared on the horizon in 1968 and 1973 has attained a pervasive material form; the reciprocal powers of market fundamentalism and authoritarian governance—prosecuted in the name of security and against the specter of terror—have been generalized and normalized. Bolaño's novels at once lament this genealogical progression—a progression that connects Chile 1973 with millennial Juárez—and attempt to work through the problems posed by this particular history for the conjoined projects of literature and theory.

The years 1968 and 1973 provoked, for Bolaño and an entire generation of Latin American artists and activists, a radical reexamination of the place of oneself in, and impact of one's creations upon, the world. As Jean Franco has written, the military repression of left politics in Mexico, Chile, and elsewhere "ended the utopian dreams of writers and projects of literature and art as agents of 'salvation and redemption'.... Terms such as 'identity,' 'responsibility,' 'nation,' 'the future,' 'history'—even 'Latin American'—had to be rethought."[2] As part of this reexamination, new literary movements arose in opposition to the perceived acquiescence of the "Boom" writers to the entwined processes of neoliberal transformation and autocratic consolidation. The "infrarealist" movement to which Bolaño belonged in 1970s-era Mexico City sought to counter ossified "Boom" forms—which, according to Bolaño and his literary comrades, mirrored and magnified the rigidity of state power—and return literary praxis to the street, to vernacular life, to real and imagined spaces beyond and beneath the jurisdiction of the lettered city. Other writers pioneered a transition toward testimonial literatures, the more radical exponents of which, in Rory O'Bryen's words, "denounced literature *tout court* as an institution coextensive with authoritarian power and essential to the maintenance of social exclusion."[3] Bolaño's work contains a concordant, if not so final, critique.

In his representations of 1968 and 1973, two of which I consider in this chapter, Bolaño is concerned both with the immediate aftermath of these events, and with their legacy across space and time. *Amulet* (1999/2006), written in the voice of a woman who passes the Mexican Army's 1968 occupation of the National Autonomous University of Mexico (UNAM) in a bathroom stall, collapses multiple temporalities into one transcendent experience. *The Savage Detectives* (1998/2007) reflects upon the near afterlife of 1968 and 1973 from a position of further remove; Mexico City in the 1970s is the novel's point of departure, but the latter half of the book follows the exilic wanderings of scattered visceral realists through the Mexican state of Sonora, and onward to Europe, Africa, and Latin America. Looking back at the dawn of punitive neoliberalism from the apogee of its global realization, each work essays a history of the current crisis.

"This is going to be a horror story," the first line of *Amulet* reads. Auxilio Lacouture, Uruguayan "mother to all Mexican poets," is on the fourth floor of the Faculty of Literature and Philosophy in a bathroom stall when the army and police arrive. "Thanks to Pedro Garfias," she recalls, "and my inveterate habit of reading in the bathroom, I was the last to realize the riot police were on campus and the army had occupied the university, and so, while my eyes were scanning verses penned by that Spaniard who had died in exile, the soldiers and riot police were arresting and searching and beating up whoever they could lay their hands on."[4] Auxilio resolves to defend her territory, to stay in her stall, and continues to read, "slowly at first, word by word and verse by verse, but then my reading started to speed up and soon it sped out of control, the verses flying past so quickly I could hardly take anything in, the words were sticking to one another."[5] Just as the words on the page stick together, so too do the temporalities of past, present, and future. Reflecting on her life's journey from her bathroom fortress—"my watchtower, my bloody subway carriage ... my gigantic rainy day"—the grammar of what was, what is, and what would be "folded and unfolded itself like a dream": "The year 1968 became the year 1964 and the year 1960 became the year 1956. But it also became the years 1970 and 1973 and the years 1975 and 1976."[6] Remembering her future, Auxilio watches herself meeting Arturo Belano in 1970, "just a kid who couldn't hold his liquor ... proud that Salvador Allende had been elected president of his faraway Chile."[7] Auxilio sees as well the dream of September 1968, "an enormous, uninhabited valley," reappear in the dream of 1973; she sees Arturo Belano in Santiago, as Allende is overthrown, and fears for his life: "perhaps that lonely valley is an emblem of death, because death is the staff of Latin America and Latin America cannot walk without its staff." She remembers as well, prospectively, the return of Arturito, his silence upon his return, "as if what other people expected became incomprehensible to him or he simply didn't give a shit."[8]

Back in Mexico City, Arturo appeared outwardly the same person who had left only months before: "deep down," though, "something had changed or grown, or changed and grown at the same time."[9] (Arturo, of course, is an alter ego of the author—and as Francisco Goldman notes on the book's jacket, *Amulet* is Bolaño's most autobiographical novel). Mexico City in the 1970s was rich with literary culture; competing poetic camps navigated one common and charged milieu of readings, salons, parties. "One camp," the Mexican writer Carmen Bullosa recalls, "admired the demotic poet Efraín Huerta, famous for his 'minipoems' packed with humor and verve; the other looked to an exquisite magazine, *Plural*, published by the cosmopolitan intellectual and future Nobel laureate Octavio Paz"—the writers of the street, in other words, versus the aesthetes of the academy.[10] Bolaño, moved by the righteousness of youth yet jaded already by revolutionary foreclosure, ran with the Efrainite contingent—though always on its margins. The infrarealists—Bolaño's own band of iconoclastic poets, mythologized in *The Savage Detectives* as the "visceral realists"—staked out a position of radical autonomy, abjuring all stasis and embracing the ideals of chaos, speed, unmediated experience. In *Amulet*, Auxilio describes the literary crew with whom Arturo traveled upon his return from Chile: "sixteen-, seventeen-, eighteen-year-old kids, who seemed to have graduated from the great orphanage of Mexico City's subway rather than from the Faculty of Philosophy and Literature, ... a generation sprung from the open wound of Tlatelolco.... They were the children of the sewers."[11]

At multiple points, Auxilio refers to the story being told as a "horror story" or a "horror film"—the nightmare of past, present, and future collapsed into one narrative temporality. There exists the possibility, though, that the mediated quality of the nightmare might be transcended, the abyss between experience and its representation bridged or closed completely—not to mitigate the horror but to embody it and thus properly bear witness to it. This, anyway, was the insistent hope of the infrarealists, who set out to produce the identity of literature and lived experience. The first part of *The Savage Detectives* consists of a series of diary entries, spanning the period of November to December 1975, composed by a seventeen-year-old law student, Juan García Madero, who has been invited by Arturo Belano and Ulises Lima to join the visceral realists. A protagonist in his own right but more importantly a lens onto Arturo and Ulises, García Madero, as he's known to his friends, chronicles the visceral realists on the precipice of exile—children about to bid farewell to Mexico City and the version of themselves forged therein. In the "Infrarealist Manifesto," one of his first published pieces, Bolaño wrote: "Risk is always elsewhere. The true poet is always leaving himself behind. Never too long in the same place, like guerrilla fighters, flying saucers, and the white eyes of lifers. LEAVE IT ALL BEHIND, AGAIN. GO OUT ON THE ROADS."[12] Yet as García Madero notes in his diary, the visceral realists liked to walk backward, with eyes trained on an ever-receding point of origin: "'Backward,'" as Arturo puts it, "'gazing at a point in the distance, but moving away from it, walking straight toward the unknown.'"[13] There is an obvious allusion here to Walter Benjamin's Angel of History, eyes focused immutably on the wreckage of the past, hurtling blindly toward the future. The Angel of History is also with Auxilio in the bathroom stall at the university, yet this time her movement is arrested, the dialectic is frozen, and she sees past and future at once. There is radical potential in this cessation, what Benjamin called *Jetztzeit*, the "here-and-now." This is the goal too, perhaps, of the infrarealists—to interrupt homogeneous empty time, the unrelenting continuity of history as horror story, and locate the shards of utopia in the wreckage of the past. Or at the very least, to finally recognize the past for what it is, not a linear and logical unfolding—"progress"—but an ever-expanding pile of debris.

From the New World capital of Mexico City, Arturo and Ulises travel east, to the Old World, to Europe's refined melancholy, to North Africa's exigent antiquity. The second section of *The Savage Detectives*, the longest of the book's three parts, is made up of a multiplicity of voices (52, to be precise). In stark contrast to the singular narrative consciousness and matter-of-fact style of the book's opening, we are exposed to layer upon layer of cascading recollections, descending streams of testimony and autobiography that offer a murky window onto the mythic post-American wanderings of Arturo and Ulises. Arturo arrives to Barcelona in 1977; it is a confused city, euphoric at the passing of Franco yet still tinged with the pain of the revolutionary defeat that led to his reign, and feeling as well the competing reverberations of 1968—inspiration and repression—emanating from elsewhere on the continent, and indeed from the other side of the Atlantic. Ulises settles in Paris in the same year, in a dank and filthy bedsit. "I've never seen a worse *chambre de bonne*," an acquaintance recalls; yet he is content enough in his milieu, one poor poet in exile among a city full of them. Soon enough, though, both Arturo and Ulises are on the move again. After an interlude in Israel—which includes a prison stay in a town known for its nuclear-weapons facilities—Ulises returns to Central America. Accompanying a delegation of Mexican poets to early Sandinista Nicaragua, he gets lost in the revolution, misses the plane home, and only reappears in Mexico City months later, carrying a distant air and vague tales of a river-bound journey north marked by an archipelago of islands, each representing a different temporality—past or future. After years in Barcelona, working odd jobs and avoiding any literary entrapment, Arturo sets off again as well, this time heading south to Africa and the brutal tragedy of postcolonial war.

From Angola to Rwanda, Sierra Leone, and Liberia, Arturo travels through a political landscape fabricated and devastated by the cartographic power of European empire. Ostensibly writing freelance dispatches for a Barcelona newspaper, we learn little of Arturo's experiences in Africa or his reflections on them. We only glimpse his ephemeral and voiceless appearances in a closed world of European journalists, on hand to record and transmit the fractured remnants of the independence age wherein "revolution" has become a euphemism for permanent civil war. Arturo's journey recalls two other iconic African sojourns, both of which speak to Belano/Bolaño's literary and political formation—poète maudit Arthur Rimbaud's turn as an arms dealer in the Horn of Africa in the 1880s, and Che Guevara's failed revolutionary mission to the Congo in 1965. A witness to the Paris Commune, Rimbaud, like Belano, experienced revolutionary disappointment as a crisis of literary representation. His response was to leave the literary world behind, to engage on a more visceral level with the senselessness and violence of material reality and his complicity therein. In Africa, Philip Derbyshire observes, "Rimbaud becomes the colonial capitalist who best exemplifies the spirit of the post-Commune French empire." Belano's African narrative, Derbyshire notes, is more subtle—he is a passive observer of, rather than an active participant in, the theatre of imperial destruction.[14] But like Rimbaud, Belano has been rendered mute, in a literary sense, by the experience and spectacle of revolutionary catastrophe. Che Guevara, meanwhile, is evoked as both muse and counterpoint. Like Che, Belano is a child of the Southern Cone formed within the hemispheric crucible of leftist political struggle. Yet the two exiles inhabit opposite sides of the 1968/1973 divide. Che carries to Africa the memory of revolutionary triumph in Cuba and a romantic belief in the imminence of global liberation from capitalist imperialism. Belano carries the scars of rightist reaction and a more tragic theory of history. When we last see him he is disappearing into the bush with a band of young Liberian soldiers, not as their comrade or acolyte but as someone who can conceive of no other direction than deeper into the abyss.

The Savage Detectives' third and final part returns to García Madero's diary, at the exact point it left off, as he, Arturo, and Ulises take flight from Mexico City. In search of Cesarea Tinajero, the founder in the 1930s of the original visceral realists, the three poets head north to Sonora. On January 1, García Madero writes:

> Today I realized that what I wrote yesterday I really wrote today; everything from December 31 I wrote on January 1, i.e., today, and what I wrote on December 30 I wrote on the 31st, i.e., yesterday. What I write today I'm really writing tomorrow, which for me will be today and yesterday, and also, in some sense, tomorrow: an invisible day. But enough of that.[15]

Time has become jumbled; today is at once past, present, and future. "I don't know whether today is February 2nd or 3rd," García Madero records. "It might be the 4th or even the 5th or 6th. But it's all the same to me. This is our threnody."[16] The temporal mash-up experienced by both Auxilio and García Madero symbolizes the transformation of an entire generation's historical consciousness—the collective composition of a new philosophy of history based not on progress's inexorable march but on a more tragic, more radical, understanding of time's unfolding. In Bolaño's fiction, the events of 1968 and 1973 in Mexico City and Chile are registered as ruptures, but, crucially, as ruptures that reveal historical continuity, that direct the gaze toward the past—and toward the world—and challenge the observer to find the remnants of utopia buried in the detritus of homogeneous, teleological time. The visceral realists' journey to Sonora is guided by this Benjaminian imagination—an imagination that is present too in the novels of Teju Cole, Mohsin Hamid, and Junot Díaz that I considered in the previous chapter.

When the visceral realists do find Cesarea Tinajero, it is in Santa Teresa, a fictional Juárez, the city at the center of Bolaño's epic novel *2666*. In the latter work, Santa Teresa functions as the vanishing point at which two different historical movements, played out on two different spatial scales, converge and entwine. The city at the turn of the millennium, a pure space of capitalist violence, is an archetypal site of both global war and hemispheric repression.

UNIVERSE AT WAR

Bolaño's youthful literary and political exertions, distilled in the infrarealist movement, were responding to and directed toward regional problems of history and representation: the constant deferral in the post-independence Latin American state of true anti-imperial overcoming; the articulation of localized dictatorship and neocolonial expropriation; the promise and repression of leftist transformation; the struggle of literature to convey and confront the brutality—and beauty—of daily life in the lettered city. Both *Amulet* and *The Savage Detectives* depart from this regional, postcolonial position. Yet each novel ends up occupying, or gesturing toward, a distinctly global frame of historical and conceptual reference. For the novels' protagonists, as for their author, the events of 1968 and 1973 are locatable on local political trajectories but engender a deeper, planetary historical consciousness. In *2666* (2004/2008), Bolaño attempts to realize this global reconfiguration in literary form. The novel is also a self-reflexive meditation on the problem of representing totality. *2666* renders the universal condition of permanent war—the origins, antecedents, and apotheosis of a militarized neoliberal globalism—while calling attention to spaces and realities that remain concealed by the shadows of capital.

Composed of five discrete books and totaling some 900 pages, *2666* chronicles enlightened modernity's bloody twentieth-century crucible. Though spanning continents and decades, the novel centers on two moments in particular—Nazism in mid-century Europe and neoliberal terror in millennial Mexico. As mapped in *2666*, the relationship between Europe and Latin America does not abide the classical imperial binaries of identity and difference, core and periphery, self and other, colonizer and colonized.[17] Old World and New, rather, are imagined as inhabiting one common historical landscape—not to elide geographic difference or the inequities of colonial power, but to stress modernity's essential globality. Juárez in 2000 and Poland in 1944 are two unique expressions of one planetary history of terror. In *2666*, Mexico's northern frontier and Nazism's eastern front are connected by the figure of Benno von Archimboldi (né Hans Reiter; Archimboldi is a nom de plume), a German veteran of the Second World War and enigmatic novelist. For much of his career "an author whose books languished on the dustiest shelves in the stores or were remaindered or forgotten in publishers' warehouses before being pulped," Archimboldi has toward the end of his life achieved a measure of international renown and inspired a burgeoning critical industry. *2666*'s first book, "The Part About the Critics," follows four Archimboldian scholars—Pelletier, Espinoza, Morini, and Norton (the lone woman)—in their pursuit of one another and the writer to whom they have devoted their academic lives. Their quest for the Great Author mirrors the quest for the real, or for life itself: "They could read him, they could study him, they could pick him apart. But they couldn't laugh or be sad with him, partly because Archimboldi was always far away, partly because the deeper they went into his work, the more it devoured its explorers"—and it eventually leads three of the critics to Santa Teresa, where Archimboldi has recently been sighted.[18] In Mexico, though, it becomes clear that utter immersion in the work and biography of Archimboldi can obscure the history to and of which his life, and presumably his writing, speaks—Nazism and its planetary reverberations.[19]

The critics' host in Santa Teresa is Amalfitano, a Chilean professor of German literature forced into exile by the 1973 coup. The critics are initially skeptical of Amalfitano, whom they dismiss as "a castaway, a carelessly dressed man, a nonexistent professor at a nonexistent university, . . . a melancholy literature professor put out to pasture in his own field."[20] That Amalfitano taught for much of his career in cosmopolitan Barcelona only underlines, in the eyes of the critics, his current marginality. That he translated Archimboldi's *The Endless Rose* into Spanish raises his stature, but ultimately he is regarded by his European guests as inefficacious, "the unknown soldier in a doomed battle against barbarism."[21] Abiding the distinction between civilization and its outside, the critics are unable or unwilling to reflect upon the ways in which Santa Teresa—an exemplary space of late-capitalist violence—is not separate from Enlightenment culture but rather bound up with it, one instantiation of it. The routes of affiliation that Archimboldi's life brings into view—the intimacies of civilization and barbarism, the genealogical intersections and common imperial logic of Prussian militarism and neoliberal terror—remain for the critics opaque. Blind to the totality of colonial modernity, they divert their gaze as well from the geographic asymmetries, the stark divisions between North and South, that structure contemporary capitalist processes.

Beyond its basic otherness, the exotic shades of its adobe surfaces and desert sunsets, Santa Teresa holds for the critics no great interest. That Archimboldi may have traveled to Santa Teresa and its surroundings in pursuit of the same philosophic, aesthetic, or historical problems that animate his writing does not occur to them. They speculate instead that he came to Mexico as a tourist, or to visit an old friend, a war comrade perhaps. Bolaño's critique of literary criticism is concerned with much more than the academy, its ennui and near-sightedness. "The critics" also act as a synecdoche for a pervasive historical and geographic blindness, one endemic to the overdeveloped world—a blindness that obscures at once totality and singularity, the planetary condition of colonial modernity and its attendant forms of differentiation; a blindness that conceals the institutionalized terror of the metropolis behind the hysterical representation of chaos and disorder in the colonies, that disavows the destruction wrought by and in the name of Enlightenment rationality and that might also be diagnosed as an absence or deficiency of dialectical vision.[22]

2666's second book, "The Part About Amalfitano," examines the backstory and the current, precarious psychology of the exiled professor. The condition of exile, in Amalfitano's words, is "a natural movement, something that, in its way, helps to abolish fate."[23] Exile, in Bolaño's fiction, is associated not just with physical dislocation, but with a radical embrace of uncertainty, chaos, difference, insecurity, even insanity. Freedom, Amalfitano muses, is "no more than the perpetuation of flight."[24] This is the heroic conceptualization of exile that inspired the wanderings of the visceral realists in *The Savage Detectives*. When we meet him, though, Amalfitano is not setting out on the road, full of Ulises and Belano's youthful verve, but reflecting back, from a place of deep melancholy, on a life that is near its end. Exile may be a precondition of illumination, but what is revealed is often horrific. Amalfitano's travels through the twentieth century—from Pinochet's Chile to post-Franco Spain and neoliberal Mexico—have afforded him a unique insight into the brutality of modern and contemporary imperial order. He possesses the dialectical consciousness the critics so profoundly lack—an attention to the unity of civilization and barbarism—and embodies the intersecting histories they cannot see. This is not to say that disparate episodes of violence acquire, in Amalfitano, narrative coherence. As Brett Levinson has argued, *2666* unfolds through a series of interrelations that are at once dissociations. No single event can be reduced to any other.[25] Nor is there one moment of determinism that sets in motion a linear chain of cause and effect. The neoliberal violence of northern Mexico at the turn of the millennium is one logical outcome of the "disaster capitalism," to borrow Naomi Klein's term, inaugurated in Chile in 1973; and the presence of Amalfitano in both contexts does provide a sort of symmetry to that hemispheric story of neoliberal transformation. Yet the historical map painted by Bolaño in *2666* cannot be ordered through a tidy chronological connecting of the dots. As with Auxilio in the bathroom stall at UNAM or García Madero in Sonora, time in *2666* transcends tense. Amalfitano sees myriad moments simultaneously; "'history broken down,'" as a voice in his dream puts it, "'history taken apart and put back together again.'"[26] And it is because of this poly-focal sight, this attention to the "fragments, fragments," that he is overwhelmed by the fact of the universal. *2666* labors to achieve a dialectical vision equal to that possessed by Amalfitano, one that perceives at once the generalized violence of universal history and the particular moments or experiences that make it up.

Bolaño confronts the problem of how to keep in view both totality and singularity with an especial urgency in his representation of Juárez. *2666*'s third book, "The Part About Fate," chronicles the Santa Teresa interlude of Oscar Fate (né Qunicy Williams), an African American reporter for the Harlem newspaper *Black Dawn*. From Detroit, where he is researching a piece on an aging Black Panther, Fate is sent on assignment to Santa Teresa to cover a boxing match. Uninterested in the fight, he is drawn instead to the unsolved crime story of hundreds of young women, the majority of them maquiladora workers, murdered in Santa Teresa and neighboring cities over the past several years. Pitching a story about the "femicide" to his editor back in New York, Fate promises "'a sketch of the industrial landscape in the third world' . . . 'a piece of reportage about the current situation in Mexico, a panorama of the border, a serious crime story, for fuck's sake.'"[27] The narrative components Fate outlines in his pitch—the overlapping geographies of Third World, Mexico, Border, and the particular genre to which the story belongs—demonstrate the overdetermined nature of the murders, the ways in which they are made, in media or critical representations, to stand in for multiple social and historical forces. As a local reporter tells Fate, "No one pays attention to these killings but the secret of the world is hidden in them."[28] Bolaño's engagement with the murders, however, does not exactly abide and perhaps even resists this notion.

In the last interview he gave before his death, Bolaño described Juárez as "our curse and our mirror," a reflection of who and where we are as a people and as a world. But the mirror, as a technology of semblance, conceals as well as reveals. In *2666*, Bolaño is concerned simultaneously with the way Juárez reflects global reality *and* with the lives that exist behind, are hidden by, the mirror. He is, in other words, enacting a contradiction—one elucidated further by his implicit contention that the murders are symbolic of the violence of symbolic signification. The individual life lost acts as an avatar for all those throughout history who have been disappeared—in the bodily sense and by the apparatuses of representation.[29] And Bolaño is wary of this process of abstraction, which might reduce the femicide and its victims to mere metaphor, or even redeem the crimes by extracting the universal truth they ostensibly contain. *2666* accents instead the ways in which the moment of representation or theorization often obscures the very human beings alleged to possess the "secret of the world." The novel's fourth book, "The Part About the Crimes," documents each successive murder in an emotionless, clinical tone: the physical appearance and occupation of the victim; the names and occupations of surviving family; the forensic evidence; the method of disappearance. The repetitive prosody with which Bolaño depicts the discovery of each body and subsequent failed investigation, though devastating in its accumulative effect, does not bring into evidence the singularity of the individual lives lost. "The Part About the Crimes" highlights and performs a crisis of representation—the unrepresentability of the crimes themselves, and the illegible unique humanity of each woman murdered in Juárez. While not offering a way beyond this illegibility, Bolaño's detached rehearsal of each death directs our ear to the muteness of the individual victim, and begins to illuminate the gendered structures of reification that condition that silence.

At a diner in Santa Teresa, Fate overhears a conversation between two men on the subject of death across time. "In the seventeenth century," one man begins an extended monologue,

> at least twenty percent of the merchandise on every slave ship died. By that I mean the dark-skinned people who were being transported for sale, to Virginia, say. And that didn't get anyone upset or make headlines in the Virginia papers.... But if a plantation owner went crazy and killed his neighbor and then went galloping back home and killed his wife, two deaths in total, Virginia society spent the next six months in fear, and the legend of the murderer on horseback might linger for generations.... How come? ... The dark-skinned people who died on the ship weren't part of society.[30]

The victims of the murderer on horseback, he continues, "could be written," were legible human lives, while "everyone living in [Santa Teresa] is outside of society."[31] Though a theorization of modernity at large, *2666* sheds light upon the differential spaces of abjection and exclusion that exist within global imperial order, spaces cast in shadow by the universality of capital. The inhabitants of Santa Teresa are incorporated into global capitalist formations—the maquiladora is a paradigmatic site of neoliberal accumulation—but inhabit a liminal space of political subjectivity, at once subjected to and abandoned by the state, captured by its surveillance infrastructure yet invisible as rights-bearing citizens. In the aftermath of the Second World War, Hannah Arendt meditated upon the rightless subjectivity of Jews and other displaced people lacking any formal political belonging and thus lacking the rights of either human or citizen. In *2666*, Bolaño highlights what Arendt termed "the abstract nakedness of being human"—being in bare life—as an ontological moment that brings into particularly stark relief its own historical conditions of possibility.[32] Just as for C. L. R. James or Richard Wright the plantation slave possessed a privileged understanding of—and elucidated—the social relations and cultural logic of capitalist modernity, so too does the maquiladora worker in Juárez possess a privileged insight into the material and ideological apparatuses of capital accumulation in the neoliberal age. If imagining the female denizen of Juárez as an agent of demystification, though, *2666* ultimately refuses the idea that the murders act as a totalizing mirror of the world at large. The femicide and its conditions—material and symbolic processes that objectify women's labor and women's bodies as disposable—evince not planetary generality but unevenness and difference; the "abstract nakedness of being human," Bolaño's rendering of Juárez reminds us, is an inherently gendered category of existence.[33] And attending to this particularity, *2666* implies, is an imperative if we want to make vivid either the totality of global capitalist relations or the singular humanity of the femicide's individual victims.

2666 concludes with "The Part About Archimboldi," the heretofore invisible character at the heart of the narrative. Though an unusual child—obscenely tall, obsessed with seaweed, aware of his preternatural madness—Reiter (Archimboldi's surname at birth) is shaped most profoundly by his experience on the eastern front, the indeterminate borderlands of Germany's colonial lebensraum, during the Second World War. There he witnesses, and takes part in, the excess and banality of genocidal violence, and is forced to reckon with the reality of a world so thoroughly dehumanized that mass extermination is a logistical rather than a moral or ethical problem. Wounded in an advance on Sevastopol, Reiter finds himself, after a brief hospital stay, in Kostekino, a small Ukrainian village known for the purity and sweetness of its spring water. Here Reiter passes the winter of 1942, an anonymous man in an interstitial part of the world. Squatting in an abandoned building, he discovers, hidden behind the hearth, the diaries of Boris Ansky, a Ukrainian Jew and erstwhile Red Army soldier. Ansky's memoirs, which star a Soviet science-fiction writer named Ivanov, bring to the fore one of *2666*'s recurring themes, "semblance"—the revision or concealment of the real by mimicry, by ideology, by spectacle, by commodity fetishism. "It was all real," Ivanov puts it, "at least in appearance." "Semblance," Reiter tells himself,

> was an occupying force of reality, . . . even the most extreme, borderline reality. It lived in people's souls and their actions, in willpower and in pain, in the way memories and priorities were ordered. Semblance proliferated in the salons of the industrialists and in the underworld. It set the rules, it rebelled against its own rules (in uprisings that could be bloody, but didn't therefore cease to be semblance), it set new rules.[34]

Back in the war and armed with Ansky's papers—feeling weak and malnourished, yet also strangely liberated—Reiter vows "to prolong as far as possible this impulse toward freedom, toward sovereignty."[35] Or rather, like Amalfitano, he imagines the flight from sovereignty—from self-possession or national belonging, and the certitude of historical progress within which both are bound up—as an alternative, truer freedom. Nazism, a pure articulation of sovereign identification and aestheticized politics, "was the ultimate realm of semblance." "Only Ansky's wandering," he concludes, "isn't semblance." Thus, like Belano, Ulises, and Amalfitano, Reiter embraces the ideals of exile, perpetual movement, and *in*security—the only ideals, for Bolaño, that are capable of keeping pace with the real. After the war, Reiter vanishes into the world and into his new pseudonym, Archimboldi, penning obscure and probably minor novels from a succession of continental locales. When *2666* ends, Archimboldi is waiting to board a plane for Santa Teresa, for the border and for the desert— two spaces he has long inhabited in a metaphoric sense. In Bolaño's novels, as in his nonfiction prose, the geopolitical border is an emblem of great violence. But there also emerges in his work a more conceptual imagining of the border as a no-man's land where the fictions of nation and of self-possession lose their hold, a space of newness, of clarity—"that vast nonexistent territory where freedom and metamorphosis are common currency."[36] Archimboldi is on his way to a border more accurately described as a site of emergency than as a site of emergence; the metamorphoses unfolding in Santa Teresa—the monstrousness of capital's self-reinventions—are grotesque, an expression of domination, not freedom. But Archimboldi, a reconstructed subject of the Third Reich and a naturalized resident of "the no-man's land of the wide world," embodies the dialectic of the border—the border as an instance of violence and the border as a potential site of illumination, even liberation. He, like Belano, Ulises, and Amalfitano, has chosen a post-national, "extraterritorial," existence from which the "the hellish achievements of the twentieth century"—Nazism's genocidal-imperial logic and the brutality of neoliberal terror on the Mexico-U.S. frontier, in *2666*—can be borne witness to, if maddeningly and always imperfectly.[37]

In *The Lettered City*, the literary theorist Angel Rama writes, via José Martí, of two Latin American urbanisms, "one carried in the head while another moved beneath the feet": "the ideal city derived from well-known European prototypes, and the real city, expanding anarchically despite the efforts of those who wished to restrain and order its growth."[38] And as the Nicaraguan poet Rubén Darío wrote, "an ideal forest complicates the real one"; the utopian imaginary obscures the reality of social contradiction and disorder.[39] In Santa Teresa, the city that moves beneath the feet—the underside of the lettered metropolis—is fully above ground; the crisis of the nation-state and of the world to which it belongs is laid bare. Yet the ideal forest still complicates the real one. It does, certainly, for the trio of Archimboldian critics, who can only recognize Santa Teresa as a place of absence and lack, a place fundamentally apart from—not dialectically entwined with—Europe's cosmopolitan capitals. For Amalfitano, by contrast, the contradictions, in their nakedness, are all too glaring. Not blind to them, he is closer to being blinded by them. So too, perhaps, is Bolaño, who speaks often in his writing of a literature that "dares to venture into the darkness with open eyes" and does not flee or turn away from whatever then appears.[40] Such a literature, that is, will attempt to occupy the "vanishing points"—the spaces of erasure and obfuscation—that make possible the perpetual reproduction of colonial modernity's essential violence. And this literary immersion in darkness (as absence) might then illuminate the "vanishing points"—in that other sense of the phrase, as a site of formal synthesis or dialectical indistinction—of security and terror, civilization and barbarism: the barbarism of civilization, the terror of security. But if literature is capable of deepening our insight into these latter indistinctions, it is also, Bolaño suggests, complicit in them.

CIVILIZATION AND BARBARISM

Early in *2666*, Norton, Espinoza, and Pelletier—three of the Archimboldian critics—are sharing a cab ride in London. Upset at something the Pakistani driver has said—a vulgar insult directed at Norton—Espinoza demands that the car be stopped, drags the driver from the vehicle, and with Pelletier's help proceeds to beat him, proclaiming with each kick: "shove Islam up your ass . . . this one is for Salman Rushdie . . . this one is for the feminists of New York."[41] With the Pakistani man bloodied and unconscious on the sidewalk, the three critics reenter the cab and drive away, awash in a sort of post-coital euphoria. This shocking scene—which is less shocking when viewed from the latter pages of *2666*—speaks to one of Bolaño's abiding themes: the intimacies of literature and violence, the unity of civilization and barbarism. Literature possesses not merely the power of mystification but the power of destruction. While present throughout Bolaño's work, the mutuality of literature and violence is examined with a particular focus in two novels that center on Chile in the moment and aftermath of Pinochet, *Distant Star* (1996/2004) and *By Night in Chile* (2000/2003). The former's central player is a poet and a military pilot who writes fascistic Latin verse in the sky. The voice of the latter is a far-right priest notorious for the ideological purity of his literary criticism and for his role in educating the regime in Marxist philosophy.

When we meet him, Alberto Ruiz-Tagle (who will become, at a later stage of *Distant Star*, Carlos Wieder) is a young poet, a striking but reserved presence in literary workshops around Santiago. "He wasn't particularly talkative," the narrator recalls. "I was. Most of us there talked a lot, not just about poetry, but politics, travel, ... painting, architecture, photography, revolution and the armed struggle that would usher in a new life and a new era, ... the key that would open the door into a life of dreams."[42] This is the time of Allende, and literature is still inseparable from the romantic possibilities of individual and collective becoming. That Ruiz-Tagle is a peripheral figure in these conversations about the saving, reciprocal grace of revolution and literature prefigures his subsequent self-reinvention as the most public literary exponent of Pinochet absolutism—a synthesis of blood-soil nativism, reactionary Catholicism, martial repression, and vanguardist capitalism. Wieder's chosen medium is skywriting. He is an aviator-poet, combining the inscription of ephemeral verse—usually Latin, but sometimes Spanish; sometimes his own work, sometimes biblical passages—with feats of aerial trickery conducted in a German Luftwaffe plane from the Second World War. One early performance quotes from Genesis: "IN PRINCIPO ... CREAVIT DEUS ... CAELUM ET TERRAM ... DIXITQUE DEUS ... FIAT LUX ... ET DIVISIT ... LUCEM AC TENEBRAS."[43] *In the beginning ... God created ... heaven and earth ... God said ... let there be light ... and divided ... light from darkness.* Chile is a nation being reborn, and Wieder is acting as witness to that birth and as apostle to the earthly father of the new nation, Pinochet. Yet there is also room within his poetic sensibility for darkness. As he intones in what will be his final sky-poem, written against the opaque canvas of gathering storm clouds: "*Death is friendship ... Death is Chile ... Death is responsibility ... Death is love ... Death is growth ... Death is communion ... Death is my heart ... Take my heart*"—followed by his name, *Carlos Wieder* ("undaunted," our narrator adds, "by rain or lightning. Undaunted, above all, by incoherence").[44] The macabre tenor of this particular composition, confusing and obscured further by the darkened skies, does not result in any official reprimand. Wieder has been identified as the figure that will lend the retrograde futurism of the regime the cultural capital and aesthetic veneer of the avant-garde, and he is thus afforded a measure of artistic license. But his installation later that evening, part two of what was to be a grand and spectacular artistic statement in the capital city, elicits a more decisive, more punitive, response. A poet and an aviator in his public life, Wieder has been operating behind the scenes as an assassin, an agent of disappearance. The sequel to his afternoon performance, attended only by old school friends and a few military officers, is an exhibition of photographs—images of his mostly female victims, maimed and dismembered bodies, dead or on the precipice of death.

While his poems in the sky perform the labor of ideology, the aestheticization of the political, his actions on the ground enact not mystification but outright destruction. Yet the photographic exhibition points to a third potential function of art: the shock of revelation. That Wieder is a murderer, that he has been doing the regime's dirty work alongside its high-cultural work, is to his audience not the crucial provocation. What matters is the public display of the crime, the attempted translation of the crime into an object of aesthetic appreciation. While his productions in the sky are encouraged by the regime in part for their *anesthetic* or deluding effect, Wieder's exhibition demonstrates the extant demystifying potential of artistic presentation, the ways in which art—exhausted and degraded by its complicity with power—retains the ability to cut through the screen of semblance and expose the real. This is not to say that Wieder, after a change of heart, has decided to channel his artistic efforts against rather than in the service of the regime. On the contrary, his gambit is that the role of death in the reproduction of the political has been normalized to the extent that an exhibition of torture photographs will incite not alarm but affirmative recognition. Or at least he is curious as to what extent his performances in the sky have succeeded in altering the ethical or empathetic fabric of the general populace. For his troubles, Wieder is arrested and expelled from the Air Force. He becomes that most rare of things, an exile of Pinochet banished for the extreme cast of his rightist commitment.

"I am dying now," *By Night in Chile* begins, "but I still have many things to say." Father Sebastian Urrutia Lacroix is on his deathbed, propped up on one elbow, "rambling and dreaming and trying to make peace with myself."[45] A literary critic (under the pseudonym H. Ibacache), an occasional poet, and a prominent Opus Dei priest, Father Urrutia lends each of his multiple selves, if often ambivalently, to the Pinochet junta. As Ibacache he strives to "elucidate our literature . . . like a humble lighthouse on the fatal shore."[46] In less floral terms, he seeks to cultivate in the masses a rudimentary grasp of the nationalist literary-critical school (in *Distant Star* we learn that Ibacache provided, via an adulatory review, a significant boost to the literary career of

Carlos Wieder). As Father Urrutia, he is given the paradoxical task of educating the regime in Marxist philosophy; over a term of ten weeks, he lectures to a small group of ministers and generals—including Pinochet himself—on the critique of the commodity form, on dialectical reason, on *The Civil War in France*, and so on. Just as Wieder offered the regime the veneer of the avant-garde, Father Urrutia contributes a measure of intellectual legitimacy. Interested in knowing their enemy, the generals also possess a genuine (not immediately instrumental) desire to understand the key political and philosophic debates of the global twentieth century—an understanding they are certain Allende lacked. ("Magazines. All he read was magazines," Pinochet informs Father Urrutia).[47] At the conclusion of the course, Father Urrutia is overcome with doubt: "Did they learn anything? Did I teach them anything? Did I do what I had to do? Did I do what I ought to have done? Is Marxism a kind of humanism? Or a diabolical theory? If I told my literary friends what I had done, would they approve?"[48] His irresolute response to this episode and others, his repeated admission of a moral or ethical uncertainty, does not temper the primary resonance of his narrative: the profound complicity of his life, which symbolizes the complicity of literature and state terror.

One of Father Urrutia's final recollections captures this complicity—or "co-belonging," as Sergio Villalobos-Ruminott has put it—with great clarity. In the mid-1970s, Urrutia recalls, a woman named Maria Canales organized weekly literary salons at her home in Santiago, gatherings treasured by a community that had been dispersed or silenced by the junta. "How odd," he remembers thinking, "[that] the artists laughed, drank and danced, while outside, on the wide, empty avenues of Santiago, the curfew was in force."[49] In time, the conditions of this privilege are made plain. During one soirée, a guest wanders downstairs in search of the bathroom but happens instead, after trying several doors, on a naked man tied to a metal bed, in evident agony. Retracing his steps, turning off the lights behind him, the guest returns to the party, drinks two whiskies in quick succession, but doesn't say a word. Days or weeks or months later, the guest, a theorist of avant-garde theatre, tells a friend about the torture chamber in Maria Canales's house, and the story circulates. But the salon goes on as before. Urrutia is not shocked by the fact of the torture; Maria Canales's husband Jimmy is an American with rumored connections to the regime. He asks himself, though, why Maria Canales would permit the torture to take place during the hours of the salon, when anyone could get lost and encounter a scene that is meant to stay hidden. "The answer," Urrutia notes, "was simple: Because, with time, vigilance tends to relax. Because all horrors are dulled by routine."⁵⁰ In Maria Canales's house, literature and torture are cohabitants. This localized cohabitation is a metaphor for the "structural co-belonging" of literature and terror within the broader social order.⁵¹ The silence of the guests, the ease with which they see but choose not to see, is testament to the complicity of literature in the concealment of terror, or in the dulling of our ethical or moral response to it.⁵² Urrutia, too, sees but chooses not to see. His deathbed confessions are an exercise in selective sight, partial reckoning. The moment of disavowal is not just in the initial act of witness—the moment in which the door is closed on the tortured body in the basement—but in the repeated repression or denial of that original closure. "One has a moral obligation," Urrutia insists at the beginning of his narrative, "to take responsibility for one's actions, and that includes one's words and silences, yes, one's silences, because silences rise to heaven too."⁵³ Yet in the stream of memories that follows—his final gesture of self-revelation—the silences remain, echoing the larger national silencing of the past and its traces in the present.

Bolaño's engagement with the intimacies of literature and terror is addressed to multiple social or geographic scales. Most immediately, he is speaking to the national story of dictatorship and its aftermath in Chile—layers of erasure and forgetting that continue, in the moment of democracy and reconciliation, to keep uncomfortable histories buried underfoot. At the same time, and with an equal urgency, he is speaking to the broader Latin American history of authoritarian repression and neoliberal devastation, and the place of literature therein—the elevation and proliferation, by the literary establishment, of forms such as magical realism that, as Patrick Dove summarizes Bolaño's position, have "contributed more to the deadening of our sensibilities than to anything else ... [and] can only exoticize and banalize the experience of the real."⁵⁴ Finally, he is suggesting that the entanglement of literature and state power is one expression of global war; there is no longer an outside, a space of autonomy and difference, within and from which the literary can formulate critique and enact alternatives.

In the closing pages of *By Night in Chile*, Father Urrutia pays a visit to Maria Canales, after the time of dictatorship and decades after her salon. She asks her guest if he would like to see the basement. Urrutia is appalled by the thought, and declines. "They're going to knock the house down," Maria says. "They'll rip out the basement. It's where one of Jimmy's men killed the Spanish UNESCO official. It's where Jimmy killed that Cecilia Sánchez Poblete woman. Sometimes I'd be watching television with the children, and the lights would go out for a while. We never heard anyone yell," she recalls, "the electricity just cut out and came back."⁵⁵ Clearly shaken, Urrutia informs his host that he must leave. "That's how literature is made in Chile," Maria offers, by way of farewell. Urrutia nods in agreement, and later thinks to himself: "not just in Chile, in Argentina and Mexico too, in Guatemala and Uruguay, in Spain and France and Germany, in green England and carefree Italy."⁵⁶ That every document of civilization is a document of barbarism, as Benjamin put it, is a basic truth not only within this or that national context in this or that era, but within the long, global history of colonial modernity—from the invention and conquest of the Americas to the advent of a global War on Terror waged in the name of both theological right and Enlightenment universality.

CONCLUSION

The intersecting histories to and of which Bolaño's fiction speaks—the prehistory and afterlife of Nazism; revolution and reaction in Latin America; the global dissemination and intensification of neoliberal rationality—illuminate a series of dialectical interconnections: the mutuality, or "cobelonging," of literature and state violence, security and terror, civilization and barbarism. Reckoning with these overlapping intimacies, Bolaño's work insists, requires a formal escape—the explosion of, rather than confinement by, the trope of historical rupture. In Bolaño's fiction, the experience of 1968 and 1973 shatters the fiction of teleological time and with it the national or regional narrative of political overcoming. The events of those years in Mexico and Chile respectively are registered in Bolaño's novels as ruptures—but, crucially, as ruptures that provide a portal to, rather than block off, the past and the world. The exilic consciousness born in the moment of catastrophe perceives the genocidal and colonial logic at the core of enlightened modernity. Geographic and historical depth is symbiotically joined to the sharpening of dialectical consciousness and vision.

Within the auto-historiography of capital and the bourgeois state, the trope of rupture is closely entwined with that of *aberration*—the notion, for example, that the event of the Holocaust was an exception to the progressive teleology of enlightened modernity rather than one logical outcome, or one essential expression, of it. Conforming to the "post–World War I" periodization, inquiries into the emergence of Nazism commonly begin with an analysis of fascism's radical response to the specter of Bolshevism and reality of capitalist crisis. Dislocating the interwar years from deeper historical time, such accounts regard the rise of the Reich as the consequence of a conjuncture of recent events and forces. The crucial argument of the historian Enzo Traverso, though, is that, while not denying the hermeneutic import of conjunctural causes, we need to pay concurrent attention to Nazism's organic conditions of possibility, its genealogical origins.[57] We need to focus, specifically, on the ways in which intrinsic elements of colonial modernity—technologies of industrial extermination, imperialist ideologies of racial difference, and philosophies of "total war"—were "crystallized" within, and clarified by, the mid-twentieth-century phenomenon of Nazi violence. We need, in other words, to articulate the emergency of the discrete event with the emergency of modernity at large.[58]

Bringing a cognate genealogical method to bear on the "state of exception" we inhabit today, I have sought in this book to locate the defining forms and paradigms of the political present—the concepts of security and terror and the modes of emergency governance, capitalist accumulation, and racial thinking with which they cooperate—within the long history of a specifically colonial modernity. I have been interested, at the same time, in examining how this deeper history has been represented and critiqued in works of contemporary theory and fiction. One basic observation emerging from this latter inquiry, Bolaño's work affirms, is that narrative counterpoints to the trope of rupture possess a heightened sensitivity to the fallacy of aberration. The "state of exception" is not unique to the Homeland Security moment but rather is a basic mode of U.S. imperial governance, and indeed political modernity itself, over the longue durée. The emergency is the rule. Every document of civilization is a document of barbarism. Security is terror. When we escape the confining "post-9/11" frame and venture beyond the Homeland's fortified frontiers, these dialectical truths come into view.

EPILOGUE

RUPTURE AND COLONIAL MODERNITY

GROUND ZEROS

Richard Armitage's insistence that "history begins today" was later echoed by Defense Policy Board advisor Richard Perle, who declared to the journalist George Packer that "the world began on nine-eleven." Perle wanted to intimate, to Packer and his readers, that the long-nurtured philosophies and objectives of certain neoconservative thinkers in Bush's administration did not determine the narrative or policy program of the War on Terror. "There is no intellectual history," Perle avowed, to the substance of the Bush administration's military response.[1] If pressed, I trust, Perle would not deny the basic historicity, intellectual and otherwise, of the War on Terror. There is, though, a tactical advantage to be drawn from the calculated elision of the past. For the imperial state, the forgetting of the past is not an involuntary reflex that dooms one to repeat previous calamities (as George Santayana had it), but a willful mechanism that enables the reproduction in the present of various histories of violence.

Articulated in the first instance by politicians and pundits, the idea that September 11, 2001, constituted a historical break quickly attained, within and beyond the U.S. public sphere, the status of common sense. The assumption that "the world began on 9/11" was encouraged by the spatial and temporal metaphor of "Ground Zero," which came to signify not simply the locus of the September 11 attacks but the site of history's beginning. And it is signaled today by the ubiquitous phrase "post-9/11," which prompts and delimits myriad critiques of contemporary American and global culture and politics. I have endeavored, in these pages, to resist and counter this assumption of historical rupture—by illuminating the political and intellectual genealogies of the colonial present, and by examining the modes of representation through which those deeper histories are obscured or revealed.

Within political discourse that conforms to the "post-9/11" frame, the terms "security" and "terror" are utterly naturalized—constantly and ubiquitously invoked but seldom historicized. In the genealogies of security and terror I developed in chapters 1 and 2, I sought to bring into view both the early modern origins and more recent twentieth-century history of those key terms—accenting the terror that has always attended, discursively and structurally, the prosecution of security. The trope of rupture, I argued, reinforces an extant historiographic tendency that either denies or renders as merely ephemeral the foundational terrors of the modern security project—a project constituted, in its inception and today, by the liberal state (its imperial form in particular) and the capitalist mode of production. The terrors of the modern state's birth are not confined to the moment of revolution; they are basic to the prehistory and ongoing afterlife of the political emancipation of the bourgeoisie. The French Revolution was made possible by the terrors of primitive accumulation in the New World. And the state's apparatuses of violence—often enacted in the name of "security" under declared conditions of "emergency"—have enabled, in turn, the perpetuation of originary methods of accumulation. Just as the modern state labors to elide the terror that remains fundamental to it, the expansionary repetition of capital is enabled by intrinsic modes of erasure. As the concept of "reification" captures, the commodity form conceals the social history of its production—the exploitation and dispossession from which it emerged. Imperial capital, meanwhile, enacts on a global scale the erasure contained within the discrete commodity: the constant production of archival "vanishing points," which enable by obscuring the terrors of perpetual accumulation.

Perhaps the original erasure performed by the modern security project was the discursive and then actual depopulation of the New World. This "state of nature"—a space of essential terror in the colonial imagination—was doubly constitutive of modernity at large. It marked the racial boundaries of the secure political community and functioned as a key site of primitive accumulation. And if, in Locke's nostalgic words, "all the world was [once] America," an empty space awaiting and encouraging enlightened improvement, the security project requires that some of the world always remain America; the "outside" to capital and the liberal state must be continuously produced—even as it is subsumed by the colonization it demands and legitimates. In the contemporary moment, this necessary outside is reproduced by the War on Terror and by neoliberal capital. The War on Terror generates the very thing it purports to be fighting—creating the outside it promises to destroy—which ensures the enduring repetition of the terror/counterterror cycle and its attendant state of emergency. The perpetual emergency of the War on Terror, meanwhile, dovetails with the perpetual economic emergencies of the late-neoliberal moment. Capitalism's contemporary crises both derive from and unleash latter-day modes of accumulation by dispossession. When the bubbles created by liberated financial capital burst, the resultant "emergency" justifies the privatization of public assets and devaluation of labor—the fabrication, and subsequent seizure, of an outside to capital. The resultant expansion and deepening of precarity requires the intensification of the state's repressive apparatuses—the militarized policing of insecure spaces and populations. Just as the War on Terror produces more terror, which compels more war, the neoliberal response to economic crisis produces more crises, which compel more rounds of dispossession and heightened cultures of policing. In either case, the effect of this deliberate production of an "outside" is the further normalization of emergency, and the further enactment and revelation of the terror that is essential to the modern security project.

My emphasis throughout this book has been on the genealogical connections between the current conjuncture—a moment defined by permanent war and pervasive neoliberal depredation—and the long history of colonial modernity. The newness of contemporary political forms, I have argued, is an expression of rather than a departure from deeper continuities. The dialectic of inside and outside acts as one illustrative example. If the contemporary iteration of that dialectic is in one sense perfectly retrograde—the civilizationist rhetoric and imperialist militarism of the War on Terror, and the endurance of crude techniques of dispossession in the global South, reprise the spatial logics of modern empire over the longue durée—it does not precisely conform to the old geographic division between metropole and colony. The uniqueness of the current imperial moment is defined in part, I have been concerned to stress, by the deployment within the global North of various political and economic forms innovated or perfected on the colonial periphery: the pervasion of a pure and unregulated commodity rationality; the normalization of emergency governance; the production, and subsequent seizure, of non-capitalized spaces or entities. Importantly, though, this inward turning of imperial processes represents not a rupture with colonial rationality but its intensification and planetary generalization.

The critiques of spectacle, exception, and empire that I examined in chapter 3 are conditioned by, but unevenly revelatory of, the return of colonial logics to the space of the metropole. Each category of critique trenchantly diagnoses some of the key forms of the current political-economic moment. They are less attentive, however, to the colonial origins and essence of those forms. This historicist deficit, I contend, is owed to the tendency of these theoretical interventions to mimic the formal logics of their critical object. As authored by Baudrillard and Žižek, the critique of 9/11-as-spectacle, though illuminating how the "image event" obscures its own history, reproduces rather than counters the ahistoricity of the image. Agamben's theorization of the "state of exception," if located within a deeply genealogical framework, affirms the exceptionalism of the "post-9/11" moment—as does Butler's critique of "the new war prison." And Hardt and Negri's critique of empire, echoing the universalizing pretensions of global capital, announces the temporal closure of colonial modernity—the dissolution of its attendant binaries—and deduces in turn that "there is no longer an outside." The *Empire* trilogy mirrors the logics of its critical object in one other sense: if the neoliberal narrative of globalization celebrates the planetary radiance of Euro-American political and economic forms, the imperial order imagined by Hardt and Negri is itself defined by modes of governance and accumulation—specifically U.S. constitutionalism and biopolitical cultures of production—that emanate outward from the advanced capitalist world. I too am concerned with the global reach of Euro-American power. I have also worked, though, to clarify the inverse route—the choc en retour of colonial rationality to the global North. Attending to this choc en retour, we are reminded of the ways in which modernity has long been constituted from the periphery of the world-system. We are attuned, in other words, to Oscar de Leon's suggestion that the "Ground Zero" of colonial modernity—the modernity within which we still live—is found in the Antilles.

The fukú born in that moment is defined by the fact of its constancy, its eternal return, and by the cultures and technologies of erasure that enable its repetition. Abelard's book on the "dark arts" of Trujillo is presumed destroyed; Oscar's long-in-process epic of witness goes missing. "We are trawling in silences here," Yunior laments. And his unilateral attempt at documentary and imaginative recovery, however urgent, testifies as well to those voices that remain inaudible. *Open City*'s Julius likewise illuminates the gaps in our collective consciousness of the past: from the unmarked entombment of enslaved Africans in lower Manhattan; to the unspoken trauma of the Allied bombing of Germany during the Second World War; to the melancholic repression of the history and afterlives of empire; to the foreclosure of mourning, and elision of history, in the aftermath of September 11, 2001. But the work of historical illumination that Julius performs is contradicted by his own capacities for disavowal, as by a narrative voice that is intellectually alive but affectively remote. Both *Open City* and *Oscar Wao* are works of imaginative witness that self-reflexively narrativize the limits of witness, the impossibility of a complete redress of the "vanishing points" in the archive. So too is the third novel I considered in chapter 4, Hamid's *Reluctant Fundamentalist*. And as Hamid's novel insists, the burden of witness lies not only with the writer but with the reader, with the listener. Changez's didactic address to his silent American companion brings into view the routes of continuity between the moment of the War on Terror—the modes of racial thinking, emergency governance, and capital accumulation that are clarified therein—and the longer history of modern imperialism, in South Asia and beyond. But if Changez's narrative implores that—as another Pakistani, General Mahmud Ahmed, put it to Richard Armitage on September 11, 2001—"you have to understand the history," there is no indication that this call is registered by his American addressee. The possibility of a more receptive listener, though, is gestured toward by Díaz's Yunior, who has prepared the Cabral–de Leon archive, and an optimal reading nook, for Lola's daughter Isis. Just as the fukú of colonial modernity travels from one generation to the next, so too is the "weak messianic power"—to borrow Benjamin's phrase—of the witness passed on.

In an oft-cited footnote in *Oscar Wao*, Yunior meditates on the competition between writers and tyrants, a contest that is defined as much by intimacy, he suggests, as by antagonism: "*like, after all*," Yunior writes, "*recognizes like*." The writer, like his dictatorial adversary, aspires to or enacts absolute narrative power. More particularly, though, Yunior's reflection clarifies the dialogue between the fictions of "History" and the fictions of *l'histoire*. Cole, Hamid, and Díaz respond to the auto-historiographic fictions of capital and the imperial state with alternative fictions of witness and speculation. The question is whether this echo is divine rather than mythic, whether it opens up new liberatory routes or whether it instead replicates extant structures of power. This latter question is addressed with a particular urgency by Roberto Bolaño. Bolaño's work reveals how the conjoined modalities of historical erasure and historical blindness enable the perpetual reproduction of the modern security project's fundamental terrors. And as I discussed in chapter 5, Bolaño's fictions dramatize the complicity of literature in this work of concealment—in the burial and reburial of the evidence. If modernity's central political and economic forms are defined by their powers of mystification, so too is literature an essential technology of "semblance." But Bolaño's work also testifies to the possibilities of literature as a form of imaginative excavation and accounting, which might counter the "semblances" of colonial modernity.

The multiple historical trajectories that *2666* brings into view—the fascist and neoliberal counterrevolutions of the twentieth century; the long global history of permanent war—converge, in the novel, in 2001 in northern Mexico, less than a hundred miles from another "ground zero"—the site of the atom bomb's trial detonations in New Mexico's Jornada del Muerto desert in 1945. In Santa Teresa, Amalfitano finds among his unpacked possessions a book he has no recollection of acquiring, Rafael Dieste's *Testamento Geométrico*. Haunted by the volume's mysterious origins and interior contents—and inspired by Marcel Duchamp—Amalfitano hangs the book on a clothesline, so that Dieste's theories, through their unmediated exposure to the elements, might learn something of "real life." Each morning, Amalfitano observes the book as its sundried pages quiver in the breeze. And as the *Testamento* melds with the world to which it has been radically exposed, Amalfitano himself undergoes a process of decomposition that first presents as an ever more acute madness. But in "losing his mind," Amalfitano yields to a less alienated psychic state. Just as the wind speaks through Dieste's book, Amalfitano hears and submits to a voice—emanating from far away, from the bottom of a deep ravine, below a sky that "was purple like the skin of an Indian woman that has been beaten to death"—that narrates the deconstruction of history itself: "'history broken down . . . history taken apart and put back together again.'"[2] As Amalfitano trades his sanity for his sight in Santa Teresa, and as Archimboldi awaits his own flight to the border, the soldiers of civilization are marching into formation on the eastern front, preparing for the first battles of the War on Terror. The United States, under the sign of Homeland Security, is fortifying its southern frontier, guarding against the intrusion of "illegal aliens." The "pile of debris before [them]," to again summon Benjamin, "grows skyward." But their unblinking gaze might, perhaps, not simply register the immensity of the catastrophe but constellate the discrete fragments that make it up.

FROM ORIGINS TO AFTERLIVES

Barack Obama campaigned in 2008 on an ambivalent foreign policy platform, promising to close the detention facilities at Guantánamo Bay and pledging to end the "wrong" war in Iraq but properly finish the "right" one in Afghanistan. In March 2009, two months into President Obama's first term, the Department of Defense officially retired the phrase "War on Terror" as the overarching signifier of the United States' global military ambit, replacing it with the rather more muted heading "Overseas Contingency Operations." As president, though, Obama escalated the drone war in Yemen, Pakistan, Somalia, and beyond, failed to close the detention center at Guantánamo, and undertook an unprecedented prosecution of whistleblowers who had brought into public view some of the routine brutalities of the contemporary security state's conduct in the Homeland and in the world. But irrespective of Obama the candidate's evasive positioning, and Obama the executive's militaristic substance, his ascension did signal popular rejection of the Bush administration's bellicose military adventurism, which had burdened the country with two disastrous and protracted wars and contributed to the onset of the financial crisis in 2008. Obama's election, in other words, provided a certain "sense of an ending" to Bush's War on Terror.[3]

This symbolic denouement to the War on Terror was compounded by subsequent events. In December 2010, a Tunisian street vendor named Mohamed Bouazizi immolated himself in protest of his harassment by, and the corrupt meddling of, local municipal officials. In the days and weeks following, demonstrations against government repression and autocracy erupted across the country, eventually leading to the resignation in January of President Zine El Abidine Ben Ali, who had been in power for 23 years. The revolution in Tunisia inspired the emergence or escalation of popular movements across the region in the spring of 2011. The demonstrators who occupied Cairo's Tahrir Square in January demanding the ouster of President Hosni Mubarak sought redress for deepening social and economic insecurity and a rigidly anti-democratic political culture. One primary object of the protestors' critique was the perpetual "state of emergency" under which Egyptian society lives, a judicial enactment justified in the present context by the threat of "terrorism" and emboldened by the U.S.-led War on Terror—a military project to which the Mubarak government had lent its pliant cooperation. The Arab Spring, its early manifestations in particular, demonstrated that meaningful democratic transformations in the region would be realized through popular struggle, rather than imposed from above via U.S. warplanes. It suggested as well that the political and social movements driving such change would explicitly reject the ameliorative pretensions of U.S. imperialism, and the role of local regimes as a proxy for America's geopolitical designs.

Following the Arab Spring and the election of Obama, a third event added to the sense of the War on Terror's redundancy, nearly ten years after its advent. On May 2, 2011, U.S. Navy SEALs stormed a compound in Abbottabad, Pakistan, and assassinated Al-Qaeda leader Osama bin Laden. His death, which was met with ecstatic celebrations in the United States, encouraged revisionist readings of the War on Terror's first, disastrous decade. Whatever one might say about the immeasurable devastation and ongoing tragedies of the wars in Afghanistan and Iraq, a certain line of thinking went, Saddam and bin Laden are gone. The killing of bin Laden affected Obama's reelection odds more than it did the trajectory of the War on Terror's conduct. But the vengeful negation of the most notorious architect of the September 11 attacks added to the feeling that the moment of the War on Terror had reached, or was reaching, its end.

The assumption that September 11 constituted a historical rupture made possible the swift advent of the War on Terror as a narrative and as a military project. Obscuring imperial histories, the trope of rupture enabled the reproduction in the present of colonial rationality. The false rupture of the War on Terror's end is neither as pervasive nor as stark. But it has encouraged similar processes of historical amnesia or distortion. The labor of re-visioning the War on Terror as a discrete, past-tense moment has been performed with an especial enthusiasm by Hollywood. Films such as Peter Berg's *Lone Survivor* (2013) and Kathryn Bigelow's *Zero Dark Thirty* (2012) begin to construct a narrative framework that will displace the disastrous wars in Iraq and Afghanistan with the ultimate triumph of American honor and might. In such texts, in other words, we can perceive the strategies of historical obfuscation that will absolve—or simply erase—the ongoing brutality of the War on Terror, and thereby condition future reenactments of imperial militarism.

Lone Survivor, which is based on actual events, chronicles a doomed—but ultimately redemptive—Navy SEAL operation in Afghanistan. Setting out to locate and kill the Taliban leader Ahmad Shaw, a four-man reconnaissance team is ambushed by local Taliban forces. Only one American survives—and only because of the courage and kindness of a local villager, who discovers the wounded soldier, hides him in his home, and helps fight off the insurgents who storm the village in his pursuit. The SEALs were ambushed, the film implies, because they decided—after much debate—to release three goat herders with whom they crossed paths in the forested hills above the village. They owe their deaths to this act of mercy. But at the same time, the film infers, the morally pure decision to spare the herders' lives is what makes the larger American triumph possible, even guaranteed. That the Pashtun villager mirrors this act of kindness functions as a neat allegory for the reconciliation of occupier and occupied, the United States military and the people of Afghanistan, which is recast here as the mutual embrace of host and guest.

Bigelow's *Zero Dark Thirty*, a taut and stylish thriller that was met with both controversy and acclaim, portrays the years of intelligence work, driven by one pathologically obsessed CIA agent, that—in the official version of events—revealed the location of Osama bin Laden.[4] The film was praised in reviews for its narrative tension, realist aesthetic, and stark depictions of "enhanced interrogation." It was criticized, however, for implying a causal link between the use of "enhanced interrogation" and discovery of bin Laden's Abbottabad coordinates. In *Zero Dark Thirty*, which was made with the blessing of the CIA, the protracted torture of bin Laden's courier produces the crucial knowledge. Numerous members of the intelligence community have contradicted this version of events, highlighting the fact that the information generated by torture is generally unreliable, as it was in this particular case. (Though to argue the latter point, however true it may be, is to engage in a fundamentally *a*moral debate about the effectiveness of torture—rather than to insist on its inherent *im*morality). Bigelow, for her part, responded to this criticism by claiming that "depiction is not endorsement"—an argument that elides the importance of narrative. What matters is not simply the fact of torture's representation, but the narrative within which that representation is embedded.[5] In *Zero Dark Thirty*, torture is rendered as brutality, but it is also presented as necessary to the eventuality of bin Laden's assassination. In very basic terms, the triumphant end justifies the exceptionally violent means. This is another way of saying that in *Zero Dark Thirty*, as in *Lone Survivor*, we can discern the rudimentary outlines of a narrative framework that redeems the carnage of the wars in Afghanistan and Iraq and the broader exigencies of U.S. power in the world.

A third recent film, Clint Eastwood's *American Sniper* (2014), reproduces key elements of this narrative logic. Based, like *Lone Survivor*, on the nonfiction account of a former Navy SEAL, *American Sniper* is a meditation on the ethical and moral burden carried by the soldier who decides when to pull the trigger and when to let it rest, when to kill and when to let live. As in *Lone Survivor* and *Zero Dark Thirty*, the political complexities of the War on Terror are here reduced to a series of tactical and moral decisions made by unique individuals in discrete moments. Imagined as a series of ticking-time-bomb scenarios, the War on Terror is purged of any political content. Myriad reviews described *American Sniper* as a "human story"—a designation that signals the erasure of political or historical context.[6]

As the film opens, the American sniper, Chris Kyle, has his sights trained on a young boy who is carrying a grenade toward a group of U.S. soldiers. As the audience registers the ethical burden carried by this lone gunman, Kyle pulls the trigger, killing the boy. When a woman then picks up the grenade, Kyle kills her too. Just as *Zero Dark Thirty* implies a causal link between torture, the death of bin Laden, and the preservation of American lives—and just as Obama claims of the drone war, which has killed hundreds of civilians, that "simply put, these strikes have saved lives"—*American Sniper*'s opening scene presents the murder of the enemy, an agent of terror, as a necessary condition of "our" security.[7]

American Sniper, however, departs from the narrative logic of *Lone Survivor* and *Zero Dark Thirty* in one important way—by refusing any easy sense of closure. After his initial deployment, Kyle returns to Iraq three times. On his fourth and final tour, he kills, with an improbable shot, the skilled insurgent sniper who has haunted him throughout the film—a death, one of Kyle's officers suggests prior to its realization, that would "win the war" for the good guys. This putative final triumph, though, does not serve as the conclusion of Kyle's story. *American Sniper* follows its hero back home, where he struggles to adjust to the mundane demands of civilian life. Kyle's recurring trips to Iraq convey the ways in which the War on Terror is interminable. And the difficulties he faces in his domestic life elucidate, relatedly, the ways in which the war—for the people who wage it, and most especially for the people upon whom it is waged—will not be over when the last soldier returns home.[8] Both over there and back here Kyle's experience evinces the war's eternal return rather than the fantasy of a final cleansing and peace-bringing act of violence.

American Sniper gestures toward—without quite joining—an ever-burgeoning genre of veterans' narratives, a body of texts that interrupts the cycle of rupture and reproduction by making plain the ways in which the War on Terror is a present-tense phenomenon. In popular consciousness, the war after the war is understood through the vocabulary of post-traumatic stress disorder (PTSD). This association has an acute empirical basis. More than 2,300,000 members of the U.S. Armed Forces have served in the Afghanistan and Iraq wars. One-fifth of these War on Terror veterans have reported symptoms of PTSD or serious depression. The actual incidence of PTSD amongst Afghanistan and Iraq veterans is almost certainly far greater. Wary of being branded as mentally damaged—a stigma that can lead to discrimination in the workplace and elsewhere—many returning soldiers are reluctant to seek diagnosis for psychological conditions. Women veterans especially—one in four of whom suffer from military sexual trauma (MST), a form of PTSD—are often hesitant to pursue treatment for a condition that is socially ostracizing and not sufficiently understood. And the military and Department of Veterans Affairs (VA) are often reluctant, for primarily financial but also political reasons, to make the diagnosis. As one VA psychologist plainly put it in an internal communication in 2008, "Given that we are having more and more compensation seeking veterans, I'd like to suggest that you refrain from giving a diagnosis of PTSD straight out."[9]

Though the condition now described as PTSD is likely as old as humankind—in different historical moments "soldier's heart," "shell shock," "war neurosis," "combat fatigue," and "stress response syndrome" have been used to signify similar symptoms—the term itself was introduced in the mid-1970s, following the Vietnam War. In the latter half of the '70s, films such as *The Deer Hunter* and *Apocalypse Now* and memoirs such as Philip Caputo's *A Rumor of War* gave cultural expression to emerging public consciousness of post-traumatic stress. In the decades since, the corpus of cinematic and literary representations of PTSD has evolved alongside "trauma studies," an expansive academic field that integrates the disciplines of psychology, philosophy, literature, and history. By the time of the War on Terror's 2001 advent, "trauma" in general and "PTSD" in particular were well established as keywords of contemporary culture.

Growing public awareness of PTSD as a condition has corresponded to the standardization of PTSD as a narrative. The soldier—who is, in the archetypal narrative, almost always a man, despite the fact that both male and female veterans suffer from post-traumatic stress—returns home from war mentally damaged. A door slamming or engine backfiring summon, with a painful vividness, memories of violence, and indicate a heightened sensitivity to its ever-present threat. The soldier struggles to reconnect with his loved ones, who empathize with but cannot ultimately relate to his experience. The soldier is alienated not only from his family but from civilian culture broadly conceived, the routines and values of which strike him as meaningless. The war was horrible, but it was a horror in which he felt at home, a horror that made him feel alive. The source of his PTSD, then, is not simply the war itself, but the great phenomenological gulf between the front and the home front. If redemption is to be found, it comes in the form of a renewed intimacy with his spouse and children—a renewed commitment to their lives—and a rediscovered civic or occupational purpose beyond the domestic sphere. The homecoming story in *American Sniper* follows this narrative trajectory to the letter.

There do exist, though, many veteran narratives that resist these genre conventions. Ben Fountain's novel *Billy Lynn's Long Halftime Walk* (2012) reveals the ways in which the pathology/disorder inheres not in the individual but in society at large. When we meet nineteen-year-old Billy, he and the other hungover soldiers of Bravo Company are in a white Hummer limousine en route to Texas Stadium for a Thanksgiving Day contest between the hometown Cowboys—"America's Team"—and visiting Chicago Bears. Bravo, we learn, became national heroes after an intense firefight with Iraqi insurgents—subsequently dubbed the "The Battle of Al-Ankasar Canal"— was caught on video by an embedded Fox News reporter and beamed into living rooms back home. With higher-ups in the chain of command keen to capitalize on Bravo's popularity, Billy and his surviving comrades are dispatched on a two-week PR tour, of which this visit to Texas Stadium on the day the novel unfolds is the grand culmination. Bravo have been accompanied on their agitprop jaunt—"this huge floating hologram of context and cue"[10]—by a Hollywood player who has claimed the rights to their story and is struggling to sign up some A-list stars and secure studio financing before the company redeploys to Iraq. Alas, for Bravo, the war plays better in Dallas—where "the troops" are met with eager affection—than it does in Hollywood (Iraq War films, as of the novel's 2004 staging, have disappointed at the box office).

Billy Lynn is fundamentally concerned with how war is manufactured for consumption in the Homeland, how the War on Terror in particular is constructed and naturalized through pop-culture spectacle and the reduction of complex conceptual, historical, or geographic language—"terror," "democracy," "9/11," and "Iraq," for example—to empty or dissembling signifiers. At halftime, the soldiers from Bravo Company are thrown onstage with Destiny's Child and made to march around in some approximation of a military exercise as Beyoncé, leading with her hips, swerves and thrusts through the hit single "Soldier": "I know some soldiers in here... where they at, where they at." This decadent and depraved halftime performance—a dizzying admixture of vulgar nationalism, PG-13 pornography, and authentic American excess—crystallizes the technologies through which the war is transmuted into commodity form and rendered as enjoyment.

Throughout this most exhausting of days, Billy is confronted by earnest assertions of untroubled, and thus troubling, faith: his hometown pastor sends him Bible verses via text message; a Cowboys executive outlines for Billy the simple maxims that guide a life lived in pursuit of non-diminishing profit margins; and legions of Texas Stadium patrons, fans of the Cowboys and The Troops, greet Billy with declarations of their unwavering support for Operation Iraqi Freedom. Billy isn't sure. He's not sure about all this Christianity stuff. He's not sure about that other American religion, free enterprise. And he's not sure what Bravo is doing over there—he's not sure about the war. "Here at home," Billy perceives, "everyone is so sure about the war. They talk in certainties, imperatives, absolutes." The security of knowledge that attends the Homeland Security apparatus is one expression of an abiding social pathology—a collective conviction in vapid symbols such as "the troops" that precludes any meaningful reckoning with the actual substance of the military intervention in which "the troops" are involved. At base, *Billy Lynn's Long Halftime Walk* is a novel about the insanity of the culture to which the soldier returns, rather than the insanity of the returning soldier. "A kind of abyss," Billy reflects, "separates the war over here and the war over there."[11] But the yawning gap between the appearance of war and its reality also describes the *mutuality* of "the war over here and the war over there," the ways in which the cultures of militarism that prevail in either theatre are bound up in the other. The violence unfolding in Iraq, as *Billy Lynn* conveys, is conditioned by our blindness—or the dullness of our moral response—to it. The passivity with which the public back home consumes the war is itself an important form of participation in the military project.

The assumption of the domestic sphere and the battlefield as discrete spaces governed by radically different cultural logics—one trope of the standard PTSD narrative—is troubled as well by Atticus Lish's novel *Preparation for the Next Life* (2014). In key ways, *Preparation for the Next Life* echoes myriad other veteran narratives. Skinner returns home from the war nervous and depressed. He numbs the pain and anxiety with alcohol and pills, and keeps a loaded pistol under his mattress in the basement room he rents in

Queens. His emotional life is awakened by Zou Lei, a half-Uighur, half-Han immigrant from a remote region of northwest China with whom he falls in love. But this familiar story of acute psychological injury redeemed by domestic embrace is, in Lish's novel, ultimately unrealized. Skinner's story ends like that of so many non-fictive veterans, in suicide.[12] The radicalism of *Preparation for the Next Life*, though, lies less in its narrative shape and more in the expansiveness of its social imagination—the rich texture of its cartographic approach to the multifarious insecurities and terrors of twenty-first-century America and the world at large.

Like Skinner, Zou Lei is a veteran of the War on Terror; she spends three months in an immigrant detention facility, and once released lives in perpetual fear of Homeland Security. She longs for legal recognition and the more secure existence it promises. But she is also at home on the margins, "where everyone is illegal." Perhaps it is enough, she reflects, "to be free and on the street."[13] A native of rural Pennsylvania, Skinner too gravitates toward the periphery of the metropolis, where the vulnerability everywhere around him mirrors and melds with his own. The routes he and Zou Lei improvise on their epic walks through the outer boroughs chart a landscape of pervasive precariousness and alienation, of latent and manifest terror. But the density and scale of urban space contains within it, alongside infinite stories of loss, the sheer fact of mass survival, and the hope of perpetual escape:

> The city was uncontained. It covered a massive area and graded out into the world. There was no definite end at the horizon. There were more buildings, miles of them covering the earth on into the distance.... [Zou Lei] saw the complicated shape of the shoreline, the lack of contrast between the brown city and the water, as if it were all part of one thing, which it was, the geography of the earth, which you could move across as you lived.[14]

Against the violent borders of the Homeland, and the inequities of its internal contradictions, Zou Lei imagines a more fluid existence. Her momentum and desire has a westward trajectory, but this is not the standard American dream of upward mobility and proprietary selfhood. What she yearns for is a life "outside the reach of the authorities"—a life in which freedom refers to the absence of walls rather than to one's privileged place within them. The reality that Zou Lei and Skinner daily confront, however, is defined by exploitation and exhaustion—the proliferation of barriers literal and figurative rather than the possibility of their imminent transcendence.

The genre-conforming PTSD story focuses on the echoes and reverberations, in one mind, of a singular event or experience. *Preparation for the Next Life*, by contrast, illuminates the traumatic effects of everyday violence. Skinner's post-traumatic stress is a consequence of his multiple tours in Iraq—the deaths he witnessed, the death he narrowly evaded, and the death he produced. But the social world to which he returns is shot through with individual and collective psyches scarred not by war—or not only by war—but by the relentless terrors of life on and under capitalism's knife edge. The novel reveals, moreover, the connections between ostensibly disparate sites of American social order in its late-neoliberal moment—the prison, the military, the kitchen of a fast-food restaurant in Queens. These spaces are incorporated in common, global processes of political and economic securitization (qua terror). And the proper subject of each—the inmate, the infantryman, the undocumented wage-laborer—is marked by a profound corporeal and psychological insecurity.

Preparation for the Next Life is frequently described by its reviewers and critics as a "post-9/11" story. The novel does imagine New York as a deeply wounded city, and it does invoke the institutional and narrative particularities of the Homeland Security project. The new world it most vividly summons into being, though, is not the one left behind by the events of September 11, 2001, but rather the one inaugurated when Christopher Columbus blundered ashore on the islands of Hispaniola, the Bahamas, and Cuba—the planetary modernity of capital and empire within which we still live.

This book has argued that the trope of historical rupture enables the erasure and reproduction of imperial rationalities and forms. Yet in tracing the genealogies of security and terror to the settler-conquest of the New World—and even more precisely to the mythic and brutal year of 1492—it itself relies on one epochal "before and after" moment. There is one other rupture I am eager to affirm—the possibility of a final break with colonial rationality and culture. Decolonization, though, is a long revolution—a protracted war of position more than a concise war of maneuver. This book is my small contribution to that deep and urgent project.

NOTES

INTRODUCTION

1. PBS Frontline transcript, http://www.pbs.org/wgbh/pages/frontline/taliban/etc/script.html. Accessed October 12, 2013.
2. Jay McInerney, "Brightness Falls," the *Guardian*, September 15, 2001, http://www.guardian.co.uk/books/2001/sep/15/september11.usa1. Accessed September 17, 2010.
3. Teju Cole, *Open City* (New York: Random House, 2011), 71.
4. As used herein, the term "colonial modernity" signifies the inherence of colonial forms of culture, governance, and accumulation to the constitution—the origins and enduring essence—of modernity at large. An alternative scholarly use of the term "colonial modernity" describes the modern institutions and rationalities imposed upon or generated by colonized societies in one specific geographic context, for example colonial India or colonial East Asia.
5. Hannah Arendt, *Origins of Totalitarianism* (New York: Meridian Books, [1951] 1958), 148.
6. See David Harvey, *A Brief History of Neoliberalism* (Oxford: Oxford University Press, 2005), 156–58.
7. David Theo Goldberg, *The Racial State* (Malden, MA: Blackwell, 2002).
8. Though ubiquitous in political discourse, the term "terror" defies simple definition. In one sense, terror is another word for fear; relatedly, terror is a rhetorical figure, a trope that works discursively to structure or disrupt political order through the cultivation of fear; and finally, terror is a strategy of violence, which we can loosely define as the deliberate targeting of civilians, within and beyond the legally inscribed confines of the battlefield, for calculated political gain. These three—nonexhaustive—meanings of the term terror are intrinsically bound up in one another. The exercise of state terror, for example, is today enabled and obfuscated by the narrative of a "War on Terror" and the atmosphere of fear it produces and exploits.
9. Cited in Martin Gilbert, *Winston S. Churchill* (London: Heinemann, 1976), companion volume 4, part 1.

10. Telegram of June 8, 1936. Cited in Enzo Traverso, *The Origins of Nazi Violence* (New York: The New Press, 2003), 67.

11. Cited in Marc Redfield, *The Rhetoric of Terror: Reflections on 9/11 and the War on Terror* (New York: Fordham University Press, 2009), 74.

12. See, for example, Niall Ferguson's *Colossus: The Rise and Fall of the American Empire* (2005), Philip Bobbitt's *The Shield of Achilles: War, Peace, and the Course of History* (2002), in addition to John Gaddis's *Surprise, Security, and the American Experience* (2004).

13. As used herein, the term "global South" refers to those nations and regions of the world that have been subject to colonial or neo-colonial assertions of European or American power, and whose "developing" or "underdeveloped" status is a consequence of that historical and extant relationship of dominance and exploitation.

14. Jean Baudrillard, *The Spirit of Terrorism: Requiem for the Twin Towers*, trans. Chris Turner (London: Verso, 2003), 27.

15. Ibid.

16. Ibid., 4.

17. Giorgio Agamben, *Homo Sacer: Sovereign Power and Bare Life*, trans. Daniel Heller-Roazen (Stanford: Stanford University Press, 1998), 166–80.

18. As used herein, "Guantánamo Bay" refers specifically to the military prison established by the administration of George W. Bush in 2002, in the early stages of the War on Terror, and not to the longer history—dating to the Spanish–American War of 1898—of the United States' claim to the Cuban land upon which that prison is today located. Though as I am keen to argue, the politics of exception signaled by the contemporary invocation of "Guantánamo Bay" is contiguous with, and powerfully evokes, earlier articulations of U.S. imperial power in the Caribbean and beyond.

19. In Hardt and Negri's account, "imperialism" and "colonialism" are prosecuted by nation-states while "Empire" is a supranational project of planetary capital. For other theorists, such as Robert Young, the crucial distinction is not between imperialism/colonialism and empire but between colonialism and imperialism. "Colonialism," in Young's definition, signifies a project of either settler-conquest or commercial domination that is not entirely controlled from a metropolitan center. "Imperialism," by contrast, is bureaucratically managed from the center and is a project that interweaves political and economic objectives, and that contains a distinct ideological rationality. My own account does not set out to emulate or reject either of these distinctions, but rather to argue for the common inclusion of the "colonial" and the "imperial"—however one defines those terms—within the broad framework of colonial modernity. Colonial modernity encompasses manifold expressions of economic and political domination by territorial and extra-territorial entities—from the settler-colonization of the New World, to European imperialism in Africa, Asia, and the Caribbean, to neo-colonial or neo-imperial forms of capitalist or military power.

20. "Rebuilding America's Defenses: Strategy, Forces and Resources for a New Century," a report of The Project for a New American Century, Washington, D.C., September 2000, iv.

21. Ibid., 51.

22. The criticism of post–September 11 literature has likewise abided the trope of rupture. In an essay on the possibilities of American fiction after September 11, Richard Gray argues that if post–September 11 fiction has registered a profound transformation in our collective consciousness, it has not yet articulated, or found the language to articulate, the new worlds both imaginary and real that might acquire incipient form in the "yawning gap between before and after." Contemporary American literature, in other words, claims that everything has changed, that the walls between America and the world have crumbled, without venturing beyond the old boundaries or reflecting upon the altered social and cultural conditions of their interiority. Gray suggests, in his essay's prescriptive moment, that the ethical potential of contemporary American literature will only be fulfilled through an engagement with otherness, with difference. Michael Rothberg concurs, but furthers Gray's critique in arguing that what is needed is not simply a "deterritorialized" fiction, one that acknowledges the presence of difference within the domestic sphere, but a literature of "extraterritorial citizenship" that maps and engages the "the outward movement of American power, . . . the prosthetic reach of that empire into other worlds." Gray and Rothberg also agree in their diagnosis that contemporary American literature has registered an epochal change without itself changing. The problem for both critics is in the latter stasis. The persistent emphasis on a radical rupture, though, paradoxically works against the transformations in both literary form and content Gray and Rothberg seek. American literature, Gray and Rothberg contend, has made only cautious steps into the new world left behind by the catastrophe. But even more importantly, I argue, it has struggled to enter the world and the histories from which the event emerged. Territorial provincialism and historical myopia are allied symptoms. See Richard Gray, "Open Doors, Closed Minds: American Prose Writing at a Time of Crisis," *American Literary History* 21.1 (Spring 2009): 128–48; and Michael Rothberg, "A Failure of the Imagination: Diagnosing the Post–9/11 Novel: A Response to Richard Gray," *American Literary History* 21.1 (Spring 2009): 152–58.

23. Another reading suggests, more affirmatively, that the bodies captured by the camera are forever falling, forever in motion; at once frozen and alive, the falling figure in fact compels us to see this moment as part of an extant history and narrative. See Laura Frost, "Still Life," in *Literature after 9/11*, eds. Ann Keniston and Jeanne Follansbee Quinn (London: Routledge, 2008), 201.

24. The synthesis in contemporary imperial forms of the "atavistic and the newfangled" is noted by the Retort group, in their book *Afflicted Powers: Capital and Spectacle in a New Age of War* (London: Verso, 2005). Retort observes how, in the current moment, classically imperialist processes of conquest and dispossession are accompanied by hyper-modern information technologies and financial instruments.

25. Édouard Glissant, *Caribbean Discourse: Selected Essays*, trans. J. Michael Dash (Charlottesville: University of Virginia Press, 1989), 63.

26. Simon Gikandi, *Maps of Englishness: Writing Identity in the Culture of Colonialism* (New York: Columbia University Press, 1996), 14.

27. Jenny Sharpe, "Is the United States Postcolonial? Transnationalism, Immigration, and Race," in *Postcolonial America*, ed. C. Richard King (Urbana: University of Illinois Press, 2000), 181.

28. With the exception of the epic novel *2666*, which was first published in Spanish in 2004, all of Bolaño's fiction was written prior to September 11, 2001. His fiction was first translated into English in 2003, the year in which he passed away at the age of 50, when his short novel *By Night in Chile* was published by New Directions.

29. Roberto Bolaño, *Amulet*, trans. Chris Andrews (New York: New Directions, 2008), 32.

CHAPTER ONE. "ALL THE WORLD WAS AMERICA"

1. Fredric Jameson, *Valences of the Dialectic* (London: Verso, 2009), 380.
2. Mark Neocleous, *Critique of Security* (Montreal: McGill–Queen's University Press, 2008), 30.
3. John Locke, *Two Treatises of Government* (New York: Hafner, [1689] 1947), 134.
4. Ibid., 139.
5. Ibid., 135.
6. Thomas Hobbes, *Leviathan* (Peterborough, ON: Broadview Press, [1651] 2010), 296.
7. Karl Marx, *Capital Volume 1*, trans. Ben Fowkes (New York: Penguin Books, [1867] 1990), 388, 389. Marx twice uses the term "House of Terror" to refer to the poor house (quotation marks his).
8. As Engels wrote in *The Condition of the Working-Class in England*, however, the advent of the Poor Law in fact stoked more revolutionary sentiment than it quelled: "the workhouses have intensified, more than any other measure of the party in power, the hatred of the working-class against the property-holders, who very generally admire the New Poor Law." Friedrich Engels, *The Condition of the Working-Class in England in 1844* (New York: Cosimo, [1845] 2008), 292.
9. See Jennifer Klein, *For All These Rights: Business, Labor, and the Shaping of America's Public-Private Welfare State* (Princeton: Princeton University Press, 2003), entire, but in particular chapter 1.
10. Several contemporary theorists of biopolitics, in dialogue with and expanding upon Foucault's insights into the eighteenth-century articulation of the biological sciences and political economy, have traced the twentieth-century entanglement of the life sciences and capitalist accumulation. Melinda Cooper's work on biotechnology and neoliberalism is of particular note here (Melinda Cooper, *Life as Surplus: Biotechnology and Capitalism in the Neoliberal Era*, Seattle: University of Washington Press, 2008), as is Michael Dillon and Julian Reid's book *The Liberal Way of War: Killing to Make Live* (London: Routledge, 2009), which examines the biopolitical, and by extension necropolitical, logic of liberal rule and liberal

warfare—focusing on but historicizing the moment of the War on Terror and the place of the "biohuman" therein.

11. In a recent echo of the Sputnik moment, in 2012 a Council of Foreign Relations task force, led by former Secretary of State Condoleeza Rice and former Chancellor of New York City Public Schools Joel Klein, published a report entitled *US Education Reform and National Security*, which claims that declining educational standards and results present a profound threat to U.S. national security. Unlike its Cold War predecessors, however, *US Education Reform and National Security* calls not for a renewed political and economic investment in public education but for the accelerated privatization of the U.S. education system.

12. Michel Foucault, *The Birth of Biopolitics: Lectures at the Collège de France, 1978–1979*, trans. Graham Burchell (New York: Palgrave Macmillan, 2008), 243.

13. Ibid., 273.

14. See Friedrich A. Hayek, *The Constitution of Liberty* (Chicago: University of Chicago Press, 1960), 148.

15. David Harvey, *The New Imperialism* (Oxford: Oxford University Press, 2003), 151, 181.

16. On a related note (one that recalls the Social Security moment), the "National Security Strategy for Homeland Security" of 2002 included a subsection on maximizing the market potential of terror insurance: "*Enhance market capacity for terrorism insurance.* The need for insurance coverage for terrorist events has increased dramatically. Federal support is clearly critical to a properly functioning market for terrorism insurance; nonetheless, state regulation will play an integral role in ensuring the adequate provision of terrorism insurance. To establish a regulatory approach which enables American businesses to spread and pool risk efficiently, states should work together and with the federal government to find a mutually acceptable approach to enhance market capacity to cover terrorist risk." See "National Strategy for Homeland Security 2002," www.ncs.gov/library/policy_docs/nat_strat_hls.pdf. Accessed March 17, 2010.

17. Naomi Klein, *The Shock Doctrine* (New York: Metropolitan Books, 2007), 12, 301.

18. In *The New Imperialism* (2004), David Harvey argues that imperialism's territorial and capitalist logics are rarely in perfect agreement. The convergence of neoconservatism and neoliberalism in the moment of the War on Terror is no exception. While Iraq may be a more market-friendly country in the aftermath of the U.S. occupation, the war has had seriously negative consequences for U.S. capital—notably exacerbating the severity of the 2008 financial crisis.

19. In *Afflicted Powers* (New York: Verso, 2006, 14), the Retort group argues that imperial power in the moment of the War on Terror is characterized by a "deep and perplexing doubleness," the concurrence of the atavistic and the newfangled.

20. See Enzo Traverso, *The Origins of Nazi Violence* (New York: The New Press, 2003), 110.

21. See Michel Foucault, "*Society Must Be Defended*": *Lectures at the Collège de France, 1975–1976*, trans. David Macey (New York: Picador, 2003), 60.

22. David Theo Goldberg, *The Racial State* (Oxford: Blackwell, 2002), 40.

23. Linda Gordon, *Pitied but Not Entitled* (Cambridge, MA: Harvard University Press, 1995), 5.

24. Gwendolyn Mink, *Wages of Motherhood: Inequality and the Welfare State, 1917–1942* (Ithaca, NY: Cornell University Press, 1996), 126.

25. Ibid.

26. David Campbell, *Writing Security: United States Foreign Policy and the Politics of Identity* (Minneapolis: University of Minnesota Press, 1992), 164.

27. Ibid., 159.

28. Thomas Borstelmann, *The Cold War and the Color Line: American Race Relations in the Global Arena* (Cambridge, MA: Harvard University Press, 2003), 29.

29. See Mary Dudziak, *Cold War Civil Rights: Race and the Image of American Democracy* (Princeton: Princeton University Press, 2002), and Carol Anderson, *Eyes off the Prize: The United Nations and African American Struggle for Human Rights, 1944–1955* (Cambridge: Cambridge University Press, 2003).

30. Michael Hardt and Antonio Negri, *Empire* (Cambridge, MA: Harvard University Press, 2001), 195.

31. This is a point I elaborate in a close reading of Hardt and Negri in chapter 3.

32. Hardt and Negri, *Empire*, 195.

33. "Blanco Demands Apology," *The Times-Picayune*, September 1, 2005.

34. Aspects of this post-Katrina dynamic were echoed by the aftermath of Hurricane Maria, in Puerto Rico especially, in 2017. Four weeks after the storm, close to 80 percent of the island's residents were still without power—a blackout that would persist for many for months. The Trump administration's anemic response, meanwhile, called attention to the longer history of U.S. federal neglect—or exploitation—of the island and its people. Though formally citizens of the United States, the people of Puerto Rico do not have a voting representative in Congress; and this qualified political status has long made it more difficult for Puerto Ricans to access federal resources and support services—from programs such as Medicaid to the more immediate protections of emergency relief funds. In the years leading up to the storm, moreover, the austerity program imposed upon the island by its U.S.-based creditors, and by a federal oversight board, had catastrophic consequences for Puerto Rico's infrastructure, and disabled its hurricane preparedness. Like the citizens of New Orleans in the context of Hurricane Katrina, the people of Puerto Rico were both abandoned by the federal government and subject to its punitive control.

35. Neocleous, *Critique of Security*, 13–24.

36. Ibid.

37. Locke, *Two Treatises of Government*, 137.

38. James Fitzjames Stephen, cited in W. W. Hunter, *Life of the Earl of Mayo*, vol. 2 (London, 1875), 168–69. Cited in Nasser Hussain, *The Jurisprudence of Emergency: Colonialism and the Rule of Law* (Ann Arbor: University of Michigan Press, 2003), 4.

39. Hussain, *The Jurisprudence of Emergency*, 6.

40. Achille Mbembe, "Necropolitcs," *Public Culture* 15.1 (2003): 24.

41. Ibid.

42. In his *"Society Must Be Defended"* (2003, 203) lectures, Michel Foucault insists that "while colonization... obviously transported European models to other continents, it also had a considerable boomerang effect on the mechanisms of power in the West." This is an observation made elsewhere by Hannah Arendt, Sven Lindqvist, Enzo Traverso, and others. See "Part Two: Imperialism" in Arendt's *The Origins of Totalitarianism* (New York: Schocken Books, 1951); Lindqvist's *"Exterminate All the Brutes"* (New York: The New Press, 1996); and Travero's *The Origins of Nazi Violence* (New York: The New Press, 2003). The latter writers primarily focus on how technologies of racial violence—e.g., the concentration camp, instruments of industrial and bureaucratic extermination—were born in a colonial setting and first practiced upon colonized people, before their re-actuation in the Holocaust and other instances of intra-European violence in the twentieth century. The procedural question of "emergency" is only peripherally included in these genealogies, but it serves as a uniquely revealing lens through which to observe the routes of affiliation between European conquest abroad and forms of governance internal to Western political orders.

43. Martial law was imposed by General Andrew Jackson upon the city of New Orleans during the War of 1812, and by President Lincoln, with congressional authorization, in 1863 in the midst of the Civil War (Lincoln proclaimed the suspension of habeus corpus throughout the country, a declaration essentially identical in its consequence to the declaration of martial law).

44. For example, martial law was imposed in 1892 by the governor of Idaho, in response to a mineworkers' strike; in 1912 by the Governor of West Virginia, again in response to a mineworkers' strike; in 1914 by President Wilson, in response to the Coal Field Wars in Colorado; and in 1934 by the Governor of California, upon the city of San Francisco, in response to a dockworkers' strike.

45. See Neocleous, *Critique of Security*, 39–75 (in particular 52–59), for a lucid account of the expansion of emergency powers into the economic realm. Neocleous explores three examples from the interwar period—the Weimar Republic, the New Deal, and the Third Reich—to demonstrate the importance of "emergency" discourse and policy to the management of labor relations and economic order more broadly.

46. The emergency declared by President Truman in 1950 lasted until 1978. Emergencies ongoing today include the emergency declared in 1979 by President Carter, in response to the Iran hostage crisis; the emergency declared by President Clinton in 1995, also regarding Iran; and the emergency declared by President Bush in 2001, in the aftermath of the September 11 attacks. The National Emergencies Act of 1976 set a two-year limit on federally declared states of emergency, but the president retains the power to renew the emergency indefinitely.

47. The expansion of executive powers in the twentieth century was the consequence, most profoundly, of a series of great political and economic crises—notably,

of course, World War I, the Great Depression, World War II, and the Cold War—and it has been enabled as well by the related ascent of "emergency" politics. Provoked in part by the arrogation of powers to the executive in the aftermath of September 11, 2001, and in the aftermath of the 2008 financial crisis, several recent studies trace the growth of executive power over the past century and call attention to the relationship between the "permanence" of crisis/emergency and expansion/normalization of prerogative power. See, for example, Eric A. Posner and Adrian Vermeule, *The Executive Unbound: After the Madisonian Republic* (New York: Oxford University Press, 2010), and Peter M. Shane, *Madison's Nightmare: How Executive Power Threatens American Democracy* (Chicago: University of Chicago Press, 2009). Posner and Vermeule consider the expansion of executive powers inevitable and necessary to the functioning of government, while Shane—as the title of his volume indicates—maintains a more critical perspective.

48. See Michael Hogan, *A Cross of Iron: Harry S. Truman and the Origins of the National Security State, 1945–1954* (Cambridge: Cambridge University Press, 1998), in particular chapter 2, "Magna Charta"; also see Michael Sherry, *In the Shadow of War: The United States Since the 1930s* (New Haven: Yale University Press, 1995).

49. See Andrew Bacevich, "Tailors to the Emperor," *New Left Review* 69 (May–June 2011): 101–24, for a discussion of the Wohlstetter School, the foreign policy tradition, based on the imperative of an anticipatory self-defense, that emerged in the early stages of the Cold War and is a clear ancestor of the Bush Doctrine of military preemption. Also see John Gaddis, *Surprise, Security, and the American Experience* (Cambridge, MA: Harvard University Press, 2004), for an argument that traces, in an affirmative register, the doctrine of preemption (inspired by the specter of the "surprise attack") to the moment of the Republic's founding and to the space of the frontier.

50. See Neocleous, *Critique of Security*, 108–22.

51. Karl Polanyi, *The Great Transformation* (Boston: Beacon Press, 1944), 71–81, 136–41.

52. *The Nation* online, http://www.thenation.com/video/160041/how-michigans-financial-emergency-law-abuse-power and http://www.thenation.com/article/159452/noted. Accessed July 10, 2010.

53. Dillon and Reid, *The Liberal Way of War*, 86.

54. In *The Wretched of the Earth* (trans. Constance Farrington, New York: Grove Press, [1961] 1963, 38), Frantz Fanon observed that violence is inherent to and ubiquitous within capitalist order. The universality of capitalist violence, Fanon argued, is revealed in space of the colony, where processes of exploitation and expropriation unfold in the naked light of day, without the social institutions and "middle class" that disguise capital's contradictions in the metropole.

55. See Neocleous, *Critique of Security*, 41–42.

56. As Walter Benjamin wrote, "The tradition of the oppressed teaches us that the 'emergency situation' within which we live is the rule." Walter Benjamin, "Theses on the Philosophy of History," in *Illuminations*, ed. Hannah Arendt, trans. Harry Zohn (New York: Schocken Books, [1955] 2007), Thesis VIII, 257.

CHAPTER TWO. "A GENERAL PRINCIPLE OF DEMOCRACY"

1. Karl Marx, *Capital: A Critique of Political Economy, Volume 1* (Meniola, NY: Dover Publications, 2011; a reprint of the 1906 Modern Library Edition), 744, 794.
2. Immanuel Kant, *Critique of Judgment*, trans. James Creed Meredith (Oxford: Oxford University Press, [1790] 2007), 78.
3. See Christine Battersby, *The Sublime, Terror and Human Difference* (New York: Routledge, 2007), 33, 45–67.
4. Edmund Burke, *A Philosophical Enquiry into the Origin of Our Ideas of the Sublime and Beautiful* (New York: Oxford University Press, [1757] 2015), 33.
5. See Luke Gibbons, *Edmund Burke and Ireland: Aesthetics, Politics, and the Colonial Sublime* (Cambridge: Cambridge University Press, 2003), 21–38 and 147–65.
6. See Sara Suleri Goodyear, *The Rhetoric of English India* (Chicago: University of Chicago Press, 1992), 24–48.
7. Gene Ray—summoning Marx and Lukács—uses the terms "first nature" and "second nature" to distinguish these two moments in the history of the sublime. "First nature," Ray writes, signifies "raw nature beyond the human," while "second nature" describes "self-made" expressions of human violence. See Gene Ray, "History, Sublime, Terror: Notes on the Politics of Fear," in *The Sublime Now*, eds. Luke White and Claire Pajaczkowska (Newcastle: Cambridge Scholars Publishing, 2009), 135. This secondary iteration of the sublime carries the word "nature" to indicate the reified aspect of latter-day forms of sublime power, the ways in which social phenomena appear *natural* and fixed rather than historically produced and mutable.
8. Brian Larkin, *Signal and Noise: Media, Infrastructure, and Urban Culture in Nigeria* (Durham, NC: Duke University Press, 2008), 36–37.
9. Larkin, *Signal and Noise*, 37–38.
10. Cited in Sven Lindqvist, *A History of Bombing*, trans. Linda Haverty Rugg (New York: The New Press, 2003), 33.
11. See ibid., 23, 46.
12. Alex Tickell, "Excavating Histories of Terror: Thugs, Sovereignty, and the Colonial Sublime," in *Terror and the Postcolonial*, eds. Ellecke Boehmer and Stephen Morton (West Sussex, UK: Wiley-Blackwell, 2009), 194–95.
13. September 11 also evoked the disaster fantasies of contemporary films such as *Independence Day* (1996), in which an alien race, morally and intellectually inferior but possessed of immense technological power, invades Earth (specifically, the imperial capital of Washington, D.C.).
14. Retort, "Afflicted Powers: The State, the Spectacle, and September 11" (2004), http://newleftreview.org/II/27/retort-afflicted-powers. Accessed August 18, 2014.
15. For Hegel, the abstraction of terror enables the concreteness of freedom.
16. Arno Mayer, *The Furies: Violence and Terror in the French and Russian Revolutions* (Princeton: Princeton University Press, 2000), 94.

17. Ibid.

18. See ibid., 112–14.

19. The history and contemporary articulation of the violence at the core of the liberal state has been generatively explored by many scholars. Particularly notable in relation to my own account: Nikhil Pal Singh, in *Race and America's Long War* (Okland: University of California Press, 2017), examines how settler-colonial ways of thinking about and acting upon difference continue to guide U.S. statecraft in the moment of Trumpism at home and the War on Terror abroad; Lisa Lowe, in *The Intimacies of Four Continents* (Durham, NC: Duke University Press, 2015), demonstrates how liberal narratives of "freedom" and the "human"—and the universalisms they imply—have long enabled processes of colonial expansion and technologies of racial domination; Chandan Reddy, in *Freedom with Violence: Race, Sexuality, and the US State* (Durham, NC: Duke University Press, 2011), illuminates how the promise of the liberal state to protect its citizens from violence is dependent upon the systematic enactment of violence against a multitude of others deemed unfit for belonging in the "rational" political community. Reddy's argument that the modern liberal state is conceived as a "counterviolence" to the specter of racial difference accords with my own consideration of the ways in which the innate "terror" of the state of nature—and the beings that reside therein—is a pretext for the advent and imperial expression of the security project.

20. G. W. F. Hegel, *The Philosophy of History*, trans. J. Sibree (Mineola, NY: Dover Publications, [1899] 2004), 446.

21. Mayer, *The Furies*, 94.

22. Cited in C. L. R. James, *The Black Jacobins* (New York: Random House, [1938] 1963), 47.

23. Marx, *Capital Volume 1*, 874–875, 915, 918.

24. Ibid., 744, 794.

25. Hannah Arendt, *Origins of Totalitarianism* (New York: Meridian Books, 1958 [1951]), 148.

26. Rosa Luxemburg, *The Accumulation of Capital*, trans. Agnes Schwarzschild (New York: Routledge Classics, [1913] 2003), 446.

27. Rudolf Hilferding, *Finance Capital: The Latest Stage of Capitalist Development* (1910), 406, cited in Arendt, *Origins*, 149.

28. Ibid.

29. Incidentally, the false naturalism of the market was something about which many of the original *neo*liberals, in contrast to their classical forebears, were perfectly candid. As Foucault observed in the 1970s, the ordoliberals that guided Germany's postwar reconstruction understood market competition as "absolutely not a given of nature." Michel Foucault, *The Birth of Biopolitics: Lectures at the Collège de France, 1978–1979*, trans. Graham Burchell (New York: Palgrave Macmillan, 2008), 120.

30. An interesting analogy can be drawn between the economic idea of "laissez-faire" and the political concept of the "exception." "Laissez-faire" is meant to denote the absence of government intervention but is in fact its product. The

"state of exception" signifies the suspension of the law but in fact represents its super-articulation.

31. Idelbar Avelar, *The Letter of Violence: Essays on Narrative, Ethics, and Politics* (New York: Palgrave Macmillian, 2004), 7–8.

32. Aimé Césaire, *Discourse on Colonialism*, trans. Joan Pinkham (New York: Monthly Review Press, [1955] 2000), 70.

33. Greg Grandin, *Empire's Workshop: Latin America, the United States, and Rise of the New Imperialism* (New York: Holt, 2007), 96.

34. Cited in Grandin, *Empire's Workshop*, 96.

35. In November 1973, Congress passed into law the War Powers Resolution, which stipulates that the president can only commit and activate military forces abroad following a declaration of war by Congress.

36. My cursory account of the history of political Islam and Islamist terror is heavily indebted to Mahmood Mamdani. See in particular "Afghanistan: The High Point of the Cold War," in Mamdani's *Good Muslim, Bad Muslim: America, the Cold War, and the Roots of Terror* (New York: Harmony, 2004), 119–77.

37. Ibid., 131.

38. For a sustained treatment of how, in the context of the War on Terror, counterterrorism produces more terrorists, and how counterinsurgency produces more insurgents, see Mark Danner, *Spiral: Trapped in the Forever War* (New York: Simon Schuster, 2016).

39. David Harvey, *A Brief History of Neoliberalism* (Oxford: Oxford University Press, 2005), 162.

40. Frantz Fanon, *The Wretched of the Earth*, trans. Constance Farrington (New York: Grove Press, [1961] 2004).

41. Henri Lefebvre, *Critique of Everyday Life*, trans. John Moore (London: Verso, [1958] 2014), 26.

42. Bat-Ami Bar On, "From Hegelian Terror to Everyday Courage," in *Global Feminist Ethics*, eds. Rebecca Whisnant and Peggy DesAutels (Washington, D.C.: Rowman and Littlefield, 2007), 203.

43. Ibid.

44. James, *Black Jacobins*, 11.

45. See David Scott, *Conscripts of Modernity* (Durham, NC: Duke University Press, 2004), especially the "Prologue" and the third chapter, "Conscripts of Modernity."

46. James, *Black Jacobins*, 392.

47. Nick Nesbitt, *Caribbean Critique: Antillean Critical Theory from Toussaint to Glissant* (Liverpool: Liverpool University Press, 2013), 170.

48. James, *Black Jacobins*, 88.

49. Ibid., 299–300.

50. Ibid., 300.

51. Nesbitt, *Caribbean Critique*, 171–72.

52. Ibid.

53. Fanon, *The Wretched of the Earth*, 5–6.

54. Ibid., 50.

55. Walter Benjamin, *Reflections: Essays, Aphorisms, and Autobiographical Writings*, ed. Peter Demetz, trans. Edmund Jephcott (New York: Schocken, [1978] 1986), 297.

56. Benjamin, *Reflections*, 292.

57. Susan Buck-Morss, *Thinking Past Terror: Islamism and Critical Theory on the Left* (London: Verso, 2003), 100

58. Ibid., 100. The precepts of Western modernity denounced by Shariati, as by Sayyid Qutb and other Islamist thinkers, Buck-Morss contends, were the same foundational principles critiqued by the Frankfurt School: "the Western modernity that Qutb and others attacked was in fact the impoverished tradition of instrumental reason, possessive individualism, and lack of social consciousness that the members of the Frankfurt School ... were criticizing from within" (98–99). In drawing the analogy between Islamism and the Frankfurt School, Buck-Morss is offering a necessary corrective to Western political thinking that defines Islam as premodern, antimodern, or peripherally modern. Yet in laboring to incorporate Islamism within the Western critical tradition of the Frankfurt School, Buck-Morss re-delineates the West-East divide that privileges the epistemic categories and critical location of the former over the latter. The critique of Western modernity articulated by Islamist intellectuals is, in Buck-Morss's account, only intelligible when it conforms to the Frankfurt School model; the moment it steps outside of this paradigm, the critical and political efficacy of Islamism is denied.

59. Mamdani, *Good Muslim, Bad Muslim*, 170.

60. Historically, it is often those who are treated as pure means—the slave, the colonized—who enact a divine violence of pure means.

61. Avelar, *The Letter of Violence*, 95.

62. Slavoj Žižek, "Robespierre or the 'Divine Violence' of Terror" (2006), http://www.lacan.com/zizrobes.htm. Accessed September 3, 2014.

63. Slavoj Žižek, "Shoplifters of the World Unite," *London Review of Books* (online), August 19, 2011, http://www.lrb.co.uk/2011/08/19/slavoj-zizek/shoplifters-of-the-world-unite. Accessed September 14, 2014.

64. Ibid.

65. Ibid.

66. See James Martel, *Divine Violence: Walter Benjamin and the Eschatology of Sovereignty* (New York: Routledge, 2012), 17–66.

67. Ibid.

68. As Nigel Gibson has summarized the Fanonian position: "The point is that one can't know beforehand, so one has to be continually open to the world and its breaths, as Césaire puts it, and at the same time always self-critical, always questioning, always connecting." Nigel Gibson, "Fanon, Spontaneity, and the English Riots," September 6, 2011, https://libcom.org/library/fanon-spontaneity-english-insurrections. Accessed September 3, 2014.

69. Avelar, *The Letter of Violence*, 97.

70. Bat-Ami Bar On, "From Hegelian Terror to Everyday Courage," 203.

71. Walter Benjamin, *Illuminations: Essays and Reflections*, ed. Hannah Arendt, trans. Harry Zohn (New York: Schocken, [1955] 2007), 257, 262, 261.

CHAPTER THREE. "CHOC EN RETOUR"

1. Marc Redfield, *The Rhetoric of Terror: Reflections on 9/11 and the War on Terror* (New York: Fordham University Press, 2009), 84.
2. Davis Simpson, *9/11: The Culture of Commemoration* (Chicago: University of Chicago Press, 2006), 122–23.
3. Simpson, *9/11*, 122; see also Redfield, *Rhetoric of Terror*, 73, for a discussion of the bourgeois hatred of democracy.
4. Gene Ray, *Terror and the Sublime in Art and Critical Theory* (New York: Palgrave Macmillan, 2005), 30–31.
5. Retort, *Afflicted Powers: Capital and Spectacle in a New Age of War* (London: Verso, 2004), 20.
6. Slavoj Žižek, *Violence: Six Sideways Reflections* (New York: Picador, 2008), 1.
7. Ibid., 192.
8. Jean Baudrillard, *The Spirit of Terrorism: Requiem for the Twin Towers*, trans. Chris Turner (London: Verso, 2002), 27.
9. Ibid., 27.
10. Ibid., 28.
11. Ibid.
12. Baudrillard, *Spirit of Terrorism*, 4.
13. See W. T. J. Mitchell, "The Spectacle Today: A Response to RETORT," *Public Culture* 20.3 (2008): 577.
14. Guy Debord, *Society of the Spectacle*, trans. Donald Nicholson-Smith (Detroit: Black and Red, [1967] 1977), ch. 34.
15. Retort, *Afflicted Powers*, 27.
16. Ibid., 34.
17. Ibid.
18. Ibid., 31.
19. Ibid., 100.
20. Ibid., 101.
21. Ibid., 97.
22. Ibid., 188.
23. Giorgio Agamben, *Homo Sacer: Sovereign Power and Bare Life*, trans. Daniel Heller-Roazen (Stanford: Stanford University Press, 1998), 166–80.
24. Ibid., 166.
25. Giorgio Agamben, *State of Exception*, trans. Kevin Attell (Chicago: University of Chicago Press, 2004), 4.
26. Ibid.
27. Ivan Hannaford, *Race: The History of an Idea in the West* (Baltimore: Johns Hopkins University Press, 1996), 230.
28. Michel Foucault, *"Society Must Be Defended": Lectures at the Collège de France, 1975–1976*, trans. David Macey (New York: Picador, 2003), 255.
29. Agamben, *Homo Sacer*, 4.
30. Ibid., 35.

31. Ibid., 37.
32. Ibid., 37.
33. Ibid., 83.
34. Giorgio Agamben, *State of Exception*, trans. Kevin Attell (Chicago: University of Chicago Press, 2005), 87.
35. Agamben, *Homo Sacer*, 166.
36. Giorgio Agamben, *Means without End: Notes on Politics*, trans. Vincenzo Binetti and Cesare Casarino (Minneapolis: University of Minnesota Press, 2000), 38.
37. Enzo Traverso, *The Origin of Nazi Violence* (New York: The New Press, 2003), 19.
38. The genealogical connections between European empire and the Holocaust were also observed by Hannah Arendt, in her *Origins of Totalitarianism* (1951). In her writings on Nazism, which she termed "race imperialism," Arendt discerned that European fascism reproduced racial ideologies and genocidal techniques conceived and practiced in the colonies.
39. Ibid., 24.
40. Michael Rothberg, *Multidirectional Memory: Remembering the Holocaust in the Age of Decolonization* (Stanford: Stanford University Press, 2009), 63.
41. Giorgio Agamben, *Remnants of Auschwitz: The Witness and the Archive*, trans. Daniel Heller-Roazen (Cambridge, MA: Zone Books, 1999), 52.
42. Judith Butler, *Precarious Life: The Power of Mourning and Violence* (New York: Verso, 2004), 67.
43. Ibid., 54.
44. Ibid., 71.
45. Ibid., 67.
46. Ibid., 39.
47. Ibid., 30.
48. Judith Butler, *Undoing Gender* (London: Routledge, 2004), 2.
49. Judith Butler, *Frames of War: When Is Life Grievable?* (New York: Verso, 2009), 77.
50. Ibid.
51. Ibid.
52. Butler, *Precarious Life*, 150.
53. Ibid., 144.
54. Butler, *Frames of War*, 93.
55. Ibid.
56. Ibid.
57. Saidiya Hartman, *Scenes of Subjection: Terror, Slavery, and Self-Making in Nineteenth-Century America* (New York: Oxford University Press, 1997), 10–11.
58. Butler, *Frames of War*, 62. The creative resistance of Guantánamo detainees has been engaged with especially powerful effect by the artist Aaron Hughes, an American veteran of the recent war in Iraq. Hughes's *TEA* project is inspired by Guantánamo inmates who, in the absence of paper to draw on, etched flowers and

other designs onto Styrofoam teacups (which were then seized by military intelligence officials for analysis). Hughes's mobile installation includes hundreds of porcelain cups (initially 779, to represent the number of people held in extra-legal detention at Guantánamo since 2001), and is accompanied by stories, and by dialogue with the audience, that reckon with the War on Terror and the resistance to which it has given and might give rise. The cups themselves are cast by the artist Amber Ginsburg.

59. Judith Butler, "Precarity, Performativity and Sexual Politics," Lecture given at Universidad Complutense de Madrid, June 8, 2009, http://www.aibr.org/antropologia/04v03/criticos/040301b.pdf, x.

60. Ibid.

61. Mbembe, "Necropolitics," 23.

62. Agamben, *Homo Sacer*, 12.

63. Michael Hardt and Antonio Negri, *Empire* (Cambridge, MA: Harvard University Press, 2000), 11.

64. The concept of "diffusionism" that I invoke herein is developed by J. M. Blaut in *The Colonizer's Model of the World: Geographical Diffusionism and Eurocentric History* (New York: Guilford Press, 1993).

65. Hardt and Negri, *Empire*, 189.

66. G. W. F. Hegel, *Lectures on the Philosophy of World History*, trans. H. B. Nisbet (Cambridge: Cambridge University Press, [1830] 1975), 170–71.

67. See Jean Comaroff and John L. Comaroff, *Theory from the South: Or, How Euro-America Is Evolving Toward Africa* (Boulder: Paradigm Publishers, 2012), 13–14.

68. Hardt and Negri, *Empire*, 189.

69. Michael Hardt and Antonio Negri, *Multitude* (New York: Penguin, 2004), 3.

70. Ibid., 18.

71. Ibid., 4.

72. Ibid., 14.

73. Ibid., 20.

74. Ibid., 21.

75. Ibid.

76. Hardt and Negri, *Empire*, 182.

77. Ibid.

78. Ibid., 195.

79. Ibid., 195, 194.

80. Ibid., 25.

81. Ibid.

82. Ibid.

83. Hardt and Negri, *Multitude*, 109.

84. Hardt and Negri, *Empire*, 29.

85. Hardt and Negri, *Multitude*, 108.

86. Ibid., 99, 100.

87. Hardt and Negri, *Empire*, 115. Hardt and Negri's privileging of the biopolitical is related to their understanding of Empire as containing a progressive

dimension, a certain radical potentiality (in the same way that Marx derived a sense of political possibility from the bourgeois ethos of perpetual expansion and advent of the world market). The productive logic and effect of the biopolitical, in other words, mirrors the generative possibilities of Empire itself.

88. Ibid., 234.
89. Luxemburg, *Accumulation of Capital*, 257.
90. Ibid.
91. Michael Hardt and Antonio Negri, *Commonwealth* (Cambridge, MA: The Belknap Press of Harvard University Press, 2009), 230.
92. Hardt and Negri, *Empire*, 146.
93. Karl Marx, *Capital Volume 1*, trans. Ben Fowkes (New York: Penguin, [1867] 1990), 152.
94. Stuart Hall, "The Problem of Ideology—Marxism without Guarantees," *Journal of Communication Inquiry* 10.2 (1986), 43.
95. Hardt and Negri, *Empire*, xv.

CHAPTER FOUR. "VANISHING POINTS"

1. Simon Gikandi, *Maps of Englishness: Writing Identity in the Culture of Colonialism* (New York: Columbia University Press), 14.
2. Ibid., 17.
3. Amritjit Singh and Peter Schmidt, eds., *Postcolonial Theory and the United States: Race, Ethnicity, and Literature* (Oxford, MS: University Press of Mississippi, 2000), 5.
4. Lawrence Buell, "Postcolonial Anxiety in Classic U.S. Literature," in *Postcolonial Theory and the United States*, eds. Singh and Schmidt, 213.
5. See Laura Donaldson, "Son of the Forest, Child of God: William Apess and the Scene of Postcolonial Nativity," in *Postcolonial America*, ed. C. Richard King (Urbana: University of Illinois Press, 2000), 201–22.
6. Du Bois's "postslavery" insights into doubleness, ambivalence, and hybridity, Mostern contends, are echoed in the postcolonial theorizations of writers such as Homi Bhabha. Mostern also notes that Du Bois was "the *first* Marxian theorist of anti-imperialism." See Kenneth Mostern, "Postcolonialism after W. E. B. Du Bois," *Rethinking Marxism* 12.2 (2000): 61–80.
7. The imperial thrust of the young republic did receive attention in the work of another African American intellectual and one of Du Bois's contemporaries; Anna J. Cooper's *A Voice from the South* (1892) articulated the racial logic of "manifest destiny" on the North American continent with the longer history of European civilization's imperial march across the planet in the name of civilizational progress. Cooper's text also anticipates aspects of postcolonial thinking in highlighting the United States' essentially transnational, profoundly multicultural, history and composition. See Anna J. Cooper, *A Voice from the South* (Xenia, OH: The Aldine Printing House, 1892), 51–52. For a discussion of Cooper's anti-

imperialist critique, see Hazel Carby, *Reconstructing Womanhood: The Emergence of the Afro-American Woman Novelist* (New York: Oxford University Press, 1987), 95–120.

8. Teju Cole, *Open City* (New York: Random House, 2011), 52.
9. Ibid., 58–59.
10. Ibid., 59.
11. Ibid., 58.
12. Slavoj Žižek, *Welcome to the Desert of the Real* (London: Verso, 2002), 13.
13. Cole, *Open City*, 220.
14. Ibid., 221–22.
15. Ibid., 7.
16. Ibid., 70.
17. For a reading of Julius's self-detachment, see Claire Messud's "The Secret Sharer," *New York Review of Books* 58.12 (2011).
18. Cole, *Open City*, 96.
19. Ibid., 107.
20. Ibid., 100.
21. Paul Gilroy, *After Empire* (London: Routledge, 2004), 108–9.
22. Cole, *Open City*, 209.
23. In one demonstration of his liberal cosmopolitanism, Julius gives to Farouq a copy of Kwame Anthony Appiah's book *Cosmopolitanism: Ethics in a World of Strangers* (2007).
24. Cole, *Open City*, 107.
25. Ibid., 129.
26. Ibid., 79.
27. Ibid., 80.
28. Ibid., 244.
29. Ibid., 16–17.
30. Ibid., 253.
31. Ibid., 251–52.
32. Ibid., 238.
33. Ibid., 239.
34. Ibid., 71.
35. Retort, *Afflicted Powers: Capital and Spectacle in a New Age of War* (London: Verso, 2004), jacket.
36. Ibid., 14.
37. See Rob Eshelman, "Lit Interview: Retort," *SF Bay Guardian*, http://www.sfbg.com/39/50/x_lit_retort.html. Accessed June 10, 2011.
38. Leerom Medovi, "'Terminal Crisis?': From the Worlding of American Literature to World-System Literature," *American Literary History* 23.3 (Fall 2003): 646, 654.
39. Mohsin Hamid, *The Reluctant Fundamentalist* (New York: Harcourt, 2007), 34.
40. Ibid., 66.
41. Ibid., 96–97.

42. Ibid., 116.
43. Ibid., 151.
44. Ibid., 152.
45. Ibid., 156.
46. Ibid., 178.
47. Amina Yaqin, "Mohsin Hamid in Conversation," *Wasifiri* 23.2 (2008): 44–49.
48. Hamid, *The Reluctant Fundamentalist*, 31.
49. Ibid., 45.
50. Brian Whitaker, "'Its best use is as a doorstop'," *The Guardian*, May 24, 2004, https://www.theguardian.com/world/2004/may/24/worlddispatch.usa. Accessed August 1, 2011.
51. Hamid, *The Reluctant Fundamentalist*, 115.
52. Ibid., 157.
53. Ibid., 74.
54. Ibid., 168.
55. Ibid., 82, 86.
56. Ibid., 113.
57. Ibid., 71.
58. Ibid., 34.
59. Ibid., 168.
60. Ibid., 174.
61. Junot Díaz, *The Brief Wondrous Life of Oscar Wao* (New York: Riverhead, 2007), 1.
62. Ibid.
63. "Junot Díaz by Edwidge Danticat," *Bomb*, October 1, 2007, http://bombsite.com/issues/101/articles/2948. Accessed July 1, 2011. For the citation in its original context, see Édouard Glissant, *Caribbean Discourse: Selected Essays*, trans. J. Michael Dash (Charlottesville: University of Virginia Press, 1989), 63.
64. Monica Hanna, "'Reassembling the Fragments': Battling Historiographies, Caribbean Discourse, and Nerd Genres in Junot Díaz's *The Brief Wondrous Life of Oscar Wao*," *Callaloo* 33.2 (Spring 2010): 498–99.
65. Derek Walcott, "A Letter to Chamoiseau," *New York Review of Books* 44.13 (1997).
66. Díaz, *Oscar Wao*, 1.
67. Gikandi, *Maps of Englishness*, 17.
68. Díaz, *Oscar Wao*, 90, 110, 120, 151, 212, 244.
69. Ibid., 110, 120, 212, 244.
70. Yunior's history lessons are addressed to "you," the reader, whose ignorance is assumed. The rhetorical object of the novel's footnotes is an American with little knowledge of the U.S. occupations of the Dominican Republic and Haiti or the violent history of U.S. power in the world more broadly. The didactic tone and its object echo in certain ways the form of Changez's monologue in *The Reluctant Fundamentalist*.

71. Díaz, *Oscar Wao*, 5.
72. Ibid., 243.
73. Ibid.
74. Ibid., 246.
75. Ibid.
76. Gregg Barrios, "Guest Interview: Junot Díaz," *La Bloga*, October 21, 2007," http://labloga.blogspot.com/2007/10/guest-interview-junot-daz.html. Accessed June 23, 2011.
77. Díaz, *Oscar Wao*, 6.
78. Ibid., 91.
79. Ibid., 94.
80. Ibid., 80.
81. Ibid., 77.
82. Ibid., 50, 53.
83. Ibid., 168, 61.
84. I am borrowing here from Derek Walcott's poem "The Star-Apple Kingdom": "the Caribbean was borne like an elliptical basin/in the hands of acolytes, and a people were absolved/of a history which they did not commit." Walcott, *Collected Poems, 1948–1984* (New York: Farrar, Straus and Giroux, 1986), 387.
85. Díaz, *Oscar Wao*, 31.
86. Ibid., 333.
87. Ibid., 245.
88. Ibid., 246.
89. Ibid., 132.
90. Hanna, "'Reassembling the Fragments,'" 505, 507–9.
91. Díaz, *Oscar Wao*, 326.
92. Ibid., 330.
93. "Junot Díaz by Edwidge Danticat," Bomb, October 1, 2007."
94. Díaz, *Oscar Wao*, 331.
95. These thoughts about the allusion to *Beloved*'s last line and its meaning owes a great deal to Amy Hungerford's lecture on *Oscar Wao* in her course "The American Novel since 1945," Yale University, Spring 2011.
96. Glissant's words and sentiment recall William Faulkner's oft-cited lines from *Requiem for a Nun*: "The past is never dead. It's not even past." And Glissant, of course, was keenly interested in—if also critical of—Faulkner's work, an interest that inspired his book *Faulkner, Mississippi* (1999).
97. Díaz, *Oscar Wao*, 4.
98. Ibid., 236–37.
99. Ibid., 19.
100. Salman Rushdie, "Imaginary Homelands," in *Imaginary Homelands* (London: Penguin, 1991), 9–22.
101. Trevor Paglen, *The Blank Spots on the Map* (New York: Dutton, 2009).
102. See Derek Gregory, "Vanishing Points: Law, Violence, and Exception in the Global War Prison," in *Terror and the Postcolonial*, eds. Boehmer and Morton, 55–98.

103. Gregory is concerned in particular with the contemporary war prison as a site wherein "sovereign power and bio-power coincide," revealing the coloniality of the War on Terror. See Gregory, "Vanishing Points," 57.

104. W. E. B. Du Bois, "The Negro and the Warsaw Ghetto," *Jewish Life* 6 (April 1952).

CHAPTER FIVE. "THIS IS OUR THRENODY"

1. The entrenchment of neoliberal orthodoxy throughout Latin America in particular was made possible, in the latter decades of the century, by the terror tactics of official and paramilitary "security forces." For one thorough account of this history, which focuses on El Salvador and Nicaragua in particular, see Greg Grandin, *Empire's Workshop: Latin America, the United States, and the Rise of the New Imperialism* (New York: Holt, 2007).

2. Jean Franco, *The Decline and Fall of the Lettered City: Latin American in the Cold War* (Cambridge, MA: Harvard University Press, 2002), 12.

3. Rory O'Bryen, "Memory, Melancholia, and Political Transition in *Amuleto* and *Nocturno de Chile* by Roberto Bolaño," *Bulletin of Latin American Research* 30.4 (October 11): 475.

4. Roberto Bolaño, *Amulet*, trans. Chris Andrews (New York: New Directions, 2006), 23.

5. Ibid., 26–27.

6. Ibid., 56, 32.

7. Ibid., 37.

8. Ibid., 75, 77.

9. Ibid., 77.

10. Carmen Boullosa, "Bolaño in Mexico," *The Nation*, April 5, 2007, http://www.thenation.com/article/bolantildeo-mexico. Accessed November 4, 2011.

11. Bolaño, *Amulet*, 77–78.

12. Boullosa, "Bolaño in Mexico," 2007.

13. Roberto Bolaño, *The Savage Detectives*, trans. Natasha Wimmer (New York: Picador, 2007), 7.

14. Philip Derbyshire, "Los Detectives Salvajes: Line, Loss and the Political," *Journal of Latin American Cultural Studies* 18.2–3 (December 2009): 170.

15. Bolaño, *Savage Detectives*, 591.

16. Ibid., 644.

17. As Sergio Villalobos-Ruminott has written, "[*2666*] focuses on the shared horizon of both European and Latin American history as if the old trick of the difference were exhausted." Villalobos-Ruminott, "A Kind of Hell: Roberto Bolaño and the Return of World Literature," *Journal of Latin American Cultural Studies* 18.2–3 (December 2009): 202.

18. Roberto Bolaño, *2666*, trans. Natasha Wimmer (New York: Farrar, Straus and Giroux, 2008), 29.

19. Hermann Herlinghaus, "Placebo Intellectuals in the Face of Cosmopolitanism: A 'Pharmacological' Approach to Roberto Bolaño's Novel *2666*," *The Global South* 5.1 (Spring 2011): 109.

20. Bolaño, *2666*, 114.

21. Ibid.

22. Idelber Avelar, *The Letter of Violence: Essays on Narrative, Ethics, and Politics* (New York: Palgrave Macmillan, 2004), 7.

23. Bolaño, *2666*, 117.

24. Ibid., 189.

25. Brett Levinson, "Case Closed: Madness and Dissociation in *2666*," *Journal of Latin American Cultural Studies* 18.2–3 (December 2009): 182.

26. Bolaño, *2666*, 206.

27. Ibid., 295.

28. Ibid., 348.

29. http://moreintelligentlife.com/story/Bolaño-2666-masterpiece. Accessed October 20, 2011.

30. Bolaño, *2666*, 266–67.

31. Ibid., 267.

32. Hannah Arendt, *The Origins of Totalitarianism* (New York: Harcourt Brace Jovanovich, [1951] 1973), 297–300.

33. There is a connection here to Paul Gilroy's critique of the absence of race in Arendt's theorization of rightlessness and abstract humanity, and in particular to his insight that the "abstract nakedness of being human" is an inherently raced ontological category. See Paul Gilroy, *Darker Than Blue: On the Moral Economies of Black Atlantic Culture* (London: The Belknap Press of Harvard University Press, 2010), 82.

34. Bolaño, *2666*, 741.

35. Ibid.

36. Roberto Bolaño, *Between Parentheses: Essays, Articles, and Speeches, 1998–2003*, ed. Ignacio Echevarría, trans. Natasha Wimmer (New York: New Directions, 2011), 53.

37. Jean Franco, "Questions for Bolaño," *Journal of Latin American Cultural Studies* 18.2–3 (December 2009): 213; For a brief discussion of "extraterritoriality" in Bolaño's fiction, see Patrick Dove, "The Night of the Senses: Literary (Dis)orders in *Nocturno de Chile*," *Journal of Latin American Cultural Studies* 18.2–3 (December 2009): 149.

38. Angel Rama, *The Lettered City*, trans. John Charles Chasteen (Durham, NC: Duke University Press, 1996), 82.

39. Ibid.

40. See, for example, Bolaño, *Between Parentheses*, 160.

41. Rama, *The Lettered City*, 74.

42. Roberto Bolaño, *Distant Star*, trans. Chris Andrews (New York: New Directions, 2004), 3.

43. Ibid., 25–28.

44. Ibid., 80–82.
45. Roberto Bolaño, *By Night in Chile*, trans. Chris Andrews (New York: New Directions, 2003), 1.
46. Ibid., 25.
47. Ibid., 98.
48. Ibid., 95.
49. Ibid., 116.
50. Ibid., 122.
51. Villalobos-Ruminott, "A Kind of Hell: Roberto Bolaño and the Return of World Literature," 198.
52. Dove, "Night of the Senses," 150.
53. Bolaño, *By Night in Chile*, 1.
54. Dove, "Night of the Senses," 150.
55. Bolaño, *By Night in Chile*, 126.
56. Ibid., 127.
57. Enzo Traverso, *The Origins of Nazi Violence* (New York: The New Press, 2003), 15.
58. Ibid., 17.

EPILOGUE

1. Cited in George Packer, *The Assassins' Gate: America in Iraq* (New York: Farrar, Strauss and Giroux, 2006), 41. For an insightful reflection on the political utility of the trope of rupture in the context of the War on Terror, see Anne McClintock, "Imperial Ghosting and National Tragedy: Revenants from Hiroshima and Indian Country in the War on Terror," *PMLA* 129.4 (2014): 819–29. McClintock, in accord with my own account, examines the ways in which "the administration of forgetting"—"the calculated and often brutal amnesia by which a state concocts to erase its own atrocities"—enables the repetition of imperialist militarism (McClintock, "Imperial Ghosting," 820). She is especially concerned to highlight those traces of the past that remain animate, that continue to resonate in the present in uncanny ways, despite their systematic forgetting.
2. Bolaño, *2666*, 206.
3. The "sense of an ending" to the War on Terror provided by the election of Barack Obama was complicated but not entirely contradicted by the ascension of Obama's successor, Donald Trump. Trump campaigned on a promise to "smash ISIS," reintroduce torture, and ban Muslims from entering the United States—rhetoric that seemed to herald the eager resumption of the more bellicose prosecution of the War on Terror under George W. Bush. And indeed, once in office Trump signaled a reversion to the "shock and awe" tactics of the early War on Terror; in April 2017, Trump celebrated the detonation of the Mother of All Bombs (MOAB) on an ISIL affiliate in Afghanistan's Nangarhar Province. But Trump also made a point of repudiating aspects of the War on Terror, stating in August 2016, "Our

current strategy of nation building and regime change is a proven absolute failure." See Janet Hook and Beth Reinhard, "Donald Trump Calls for a New War on Terror," *Wall Street Journal*, August 15, 2016," http://www.wsj.com/articles/donald-trump-calls-for-ideological-test-for-entry-into-u-s-1471291339. Accessed December 21, 2016.

4. Even beyond the role of torture in the apprehension of key intelligence, this version of how bin Laden was located is contested. Notably, the investigative journalist Seymour Hersh argued in the *London Review of Books* that bin Laden's coordinates were given up by a Pakistani intelligence officer, who revealed that bin Laden had been detained/protected by the Pakistani government for five years. See Seymour M. Hersh, "The Killing of Osama bin Laden," *London Review of Books* 37.10 (May 2015): 3–12.

5. For the Bigelow quote, see Kathryn Bigelow, "Kathryn Bigelow addresses 'Zero Dark Thirty' torture Criticism," January 15, 2013, http://articles.latimes.com/2013/jan/15/entertainment/la-et-mn-0116-bigelow-zero-dark-thirty-20130116. Accessed December 23, 2016.

6. Early War on Terror films such as Oliver Stone's *World Trade Center* (2006) and Paul Greengrass's *United 93* (2006) were also affixed, by producers and critics alike, with the "human story" tag. When invoked in relation to such films, the "human" acts as an antonym of the political and as a synonym of the universal. The "human story" unfolds on the plain of the universal, above political fractures or contradictions. In practice, though, the "human story" rendered by texts such as *United 93* or *American Sniper* refuses historical or geographic context; it corresponds to the collapsing of space and time, rather than their transcendence. And it reproduces rather than resists the basic distinction between the human and its outside. It is not only, as Judith Butler has put it, that "dehumanization [is] the condition for the production of the human." The inverse is also true. The "human story" delimits the threshold of the human itself; it defines, that is, in which bodies, times, and spaces the human most naturally resides—and, by implication, in which it does not. This fact was evidenced in the lead-up to the War on Terror by popular sites of memorialization such as the *New York Times* "Portraits of Grief" series. Running in the same broadsheet pages that served as a mouthpiece for the Bush administration's lies, each "portrait" of September 11's victims was painted in tribute not simply to the singularity of that individual life but to the shining American virtues of civic generosity and domestic fullness; the series helped to define the markers of what constitutes a grievable human life, and contributed to the legitimation of a war that would be waged on peoples and bodies whose humanity was not universally recognized as such. For a sustained meditation on the "differential allocation of grievability that decides what kind of subject is and must be grieved," see Judith Butler, *Precarious Life: The Powers of Mourning and Violence* (London: Verso, 2006), xiv, 91. And for an illuminating reading of the "Portraits of Grief" series—its discursive form and political effects—see David Simpson, *9/11: The Culture of Commemoration* (Chicago: University of Chicago Press, 2006), 21–54.

7. Barack Obama, "Remarks by the President at the National Defense University," May 23, 2013. https://www.whitehouse.gov/the-press-office/2013/05/23/remarks-president-national-defense-university. Accessed December 23, 2016.

8. The ways in which *American Sniper* dramatizes the interminable nature of the war, through Kyle's multiple deployments, is emphasized by J. Hoberman in his short piece "The Great American Shooter," *NYR Daily*, February 13, 2015, http://www.nybooks.com/blogs/nyrblog/2015/feb/13/great-american-shooter/. Accessed August 20, 2015.

9. Email correspondence of Norma Perez, cited in Christopher Lee, "Official Urged Fewer Diagnoses of PTSD," *Washington Post*, May 16, 2008, http://www.washingtonpost.com/wp-dyn/content/article/2008/05/15/AR2008051503533.html. Accessed August 20, 2013.

10. Ben Fountain, *Billy Lynn's Long Halftime Walk* (New York: Ecco, 2012), 28.

11. Ibid., 197.

12. Every day, 22 veterans commit suicide. The suicide rate of male veterans under the age of thirty is three times that of their civilian counterparts. See http://www.mentalhealth.va.gov/docs/suicide_data_report_update_january_2014.pdf. Accessed October 2, 2015.

13. Atticus Lish, *Preparation for the Next Life* (New York: Tyrant Books, 2014), 50.

14. Ibid., 118–19.

SELECTED BIBLIOGRAPHY

Agamben, Giorgio. *Homo Sacer: Sovereign Power and Bare Life.* Translated by Daniel Heller-Roazen. Stanford: Stanford University Press, 1998.
———. *Remnants of Auschwitz: The Witness and the Archive.* Translated by Daniel Heller-Roazen. Cambridge, MA: Zone Books, 1999.
———. *Means without End: Notes on Politics.* Translated by Vincenzo Binetti and Cesare Casarino. Minneapolis: University of Minnesota Press, 2000.
———. *State of Exception.* Translated by Kevin Attell. Chicago: University of Chicago Press, 2004.
Anderson, Carol. *Eyes off the Prize: The United Nations and African American Struggle for Human Rights, 1944–1955.* Cambridge: Cambridge University Press, 2003.
Arendt, Hannah. *Origins of Totalitarianism.* New York: Meridian Books, [1951] 1958.
Avelar, Idelbar. *The Letter of Violence: Essays on Narrative, Ethics, and Politics.* New York: Palgrave Macmillian, 2004.
Battersby, Christine. *The Sublime, Terror and Human Difference.* New York: Routledge, 2007.
Baudrillard, Jean. *The Spirit of Terrorism.* Translated by Chris Turner. London: Verso, 2003.
Benjamin, Walter. *Illuminations: Essays and Reflections.* Edited by Hannah Arendt. Translated by Harry Zohn. New York: Schocken Books, [1955] 2007.
———. *Reflections: Essays, Aphorisms, and Autobiographical Writings.* Edited by Peter Demetz. Translated by Edmund Jephcott. New York: Schocken, [1978] 1986.
Blaut, J. M. *The Colonizer's Model of the World: Geographical Diffusionism and Eurocentric History.* New York: Guilford Press, 1993.
Boehmer, Ellecke, and Stephen Morton, eds. *Terror and the Postcolonial.* West Sussex, UK: Wiley-Blackwell, 2009.
Bolaño, Roberto. *By Night in Chile.* Translated by Chris Andrews. New York: New Directions, 2003.

———. *Distant Star*. Translated by Chris Andrews. New York: New Directions, 2004.

———. *Amulet*. Translated by Chris Andrews. New York: New Directions, 2006.

———. *The Savage Detectives*. Translated by Natasha Wimmer. New York: Picador, 2007.

———. *2666*. Translated by Natasha Wimmer. New York: Farrar, Straus and Giroux, 2008.

———. *Between Parentheses: Essays, Articles, and Speeches, 1998–2003*. Edited by Ignacio Echevarría. Translated by Natasha Wimmer. New York: New Directions, 2011.

Borstelmann, Thomas. *The Cold War and the Color Line: American Race Relations in the Global Arena*. Cambridge, MA: Harvard University Press, 2003.

Buck-Morss, Susan. *Thinking Past Terror: Islamism and Critical Theory on the Left*. London: Verso, 2003.

Burke, Edmund. *A Philosophical Enquiry into the Origin of Our Ideas of the Sublime and Beautiful*. New York: Oxford University Press, [1757] 2015.

Butler, Judith. *Precarious Life: The Power of Mourning and Violence*. New York: Verso, 2004.

———. *Undoing Gender*. London: Routledge, 2004.

———. *Frames of War: When Is Life Grievable?* New York: Verso, 2009.

Campbell, David. *Writing Security: United States Foreign Policy and the Politics of Identity*. Minneapolis: University of Minnesota Press, 1992.

Carby, Hazel. *Reconstructing Womanhood: The Emergence of the Afro-American Woman Novelist*. New York: Oxford University Press, 1987.

Césaire, Aimé. *Discourse on Colonialism*. Translated by Joan Pinkham. New York: Monthly Review Press, [1955] 2000.

Cole, Teju. *Open City*. New York: Random House, 2011.

Comaroff, Jean, and John L. Comaroff. *Theory from the South: Or, How Euro-America Is Evolving toward Africa*. Boulder: Paradigm Publishers, 2012.

Cooper, Anna J. *A Voice from the South*. Xenia, OH: The Aldine Printing House, 1892.

Cooper, Melinda. *Life as Surplus: Biotechnology and Capitalism in the Neoliberal Era*. Seattle: University of Washington Press, 2008.

Debord, Guy. *Society of the Spectacle*. Translated by Donald Nicholson-Smith. Detroit: Black and Red, [1967] 1977.

Díaz, Junot. *The Brief Wondrous Life of Oscar Wao*. New York: Riverhead, 2007.

Dillon, Michael, and Julian Reid. *The Liberal Way of War: Killing to Make Live*. London: Routledge, 2009.

Dudziak, Mary. *Cold War Civil Rights: Race and the Image of American Democracy*. Princeton: Princeton University Press, 2002.

Engels, Friedrich. *The Condition of the Working-Class in England in 1844*. New York: Cosimo, [1845] 2008.

Fanon, Frantz. *The Wretched of the Earth*. Translated by Constance Farrington. New York: Grove Press, [1961] 1963.

Foucault, Michel. *"Society Must Be Defended": Lectures at the Collège de France, 1975–1976*. Translated by David Macey. New York: Picador, 2003.
———. *The Birth of Biopolitics: Lectures at the Collège de France, 1978–1979*. Translated by Graham Burchell. New York: Palgrave Macmillan, 2008.
Fountain, Ben. *Billy Lynn's Long Halftime Walk*. New York: Ecco, 2012.
Franco, Jean. *The Decline and Fall of the Lettered City: Latin American in the Cold War*. Cambridge, MA: Harvard University Press, 2002.
Gibbons, Luke. *Edmund Burke and Ireland: Aesthetics, Politics, and the Colonial Sublime*. Cambridge: Cambridge University Press, 2003.
Gikandi, Simon. *Maps of Englishness: Writing Identity in the Culture of Colonialism*. New York: Columbia University Press, 1996.
Gilroy, Paul. *After Empire*. London: Routledge, 2004.
———. *Darker Than Blue: On the Moral Economies of Black Atlantic Culture*. London: The Belknap Press of Harvard University Press, 2010.
Glissant, Édouard. *Caribbean Discourse: Selected Essays*. Translated by J. Michael Dash. Charlottesville: University of Virginia Press, 1989.
Goldberg, David Theo. *The Racial State*. Malden, MA: Blackwell, 2002.
Goodyear, Sara Suleri. *The Rhetoric of English India*. Chicago: The University of Chicago Press, 1992.
Gordon, Linda. *Pitied but Not Entitled*. Cambridge, MA: Harvard University Press, 1995.
Grandin, Greg. *Empire's Workshop: Latin America, the United States, and the Rise of the New Imperialism*. New York: Holt, 2007.
Hamid, Mohsin. *The Reluctant Fundamentalist*. New York: Harcourt, 2007.
Hannaford, Ivan. *Race: The History of an Idea in the West*. Baltimore: Johns Hopkins University Press, 1996.
Hardt, Michael, and Antonio Negri. *Empire*. Cambridge, MA: Harvard University Press, 2001.
———. *Multitude*. New York: Penguin, 2004.
———. *Commonwealth*. Cambridge, MA: The Belknap Press of Harvard University Press, 2009.
Hartman, Saidiya. *Scenes of Subjection: Terror, Slavery, and Self-Making in Nineteenth-Century America*. New York: Oxford University Press, 1997.
Harvey, David. *The New Imperialism*. Oxford: Oxford University Press, 2003.
———. *A Brief History of Neoliberalism*. Oxford: Oxford University Press, 2005.
Hegel, G. W. F. *Lectures on the Philosophy of World History*. Translated by H. B. Nisbet. Cambridge: Cambridge University Press, [1830] 1975.
———. *The Philosophy of History*. Translated by J. Sibree. Mineola, NY: Dover Publications, [1899] 2004.
Hobbes, Thomas. *Leviathan*. Peterborough, ON: Broadview Press, [1651] 2010.
Hogan, Michael. *A Cross of Iron: Harry S. Truman and the Origins of the National Security State, 1945–1954*. Cambridge: Cambridge University Press, 1998.
Hussain, Nasser. *The Jurisprudence of Emergency: Colonialism and the Rule of Law*. Ann Arbor: University of Michigan Press, 2003.

James, C. L. R. *The Black Jacobins*. New York: Random House, 1963.
Jameson, Fredric. *Valences of the Dialectic*. London: Verso, 2009.
Kant, Immanuel. *Critique of Judgment*. Translated by James Creed Meredith. Oxford: Oxford University Press, [1790] 2007.
King, C. Richard, ed. *Postcolonial America*. Urbana: University of Illinois Press, 2000.
Klein, Jennifer. *For All These Rights: Business, Labor, and the Shaping of America's Public-Private Welfare State*. Princeton: Princeton University Press, 2003.
Klein, Naomi. *The Shock Doctrine*. New York: Metropolitan Books, 2007.
Larkin, Brian. *Signal and Noise: Media, Infrastructure, and Urban Culture in Nigeria*. Durham, NC: Duke University Press, 2008.
Lefebvre, Henri. *Critique of Everyday Life*. Translated by John Moore. London: Verso, [1958] 2014.
Lindqvist, Sven. *A History of Bombing*. Translated by Linda Haverty Rugg. New York: The New Press, 2003.
Lish, Atticus. *Preparation for the Next Life*. New York: Tyrant Books, 2014.
Locke, John. *Two Treatises of Government*. New York: Hafner, [1689] 1947.
Lowe, Lisa. *The Intimacies of Four Continents*. Durham, NC: Duke University Press, 2015.
Luxemburg, Rosa. *The Accumulation of Capital*. Translated by Agnes Schwazrschild. New York: Routledge Classics, [1913] 2003.
Mamdani, Mahmood. *Good Muslim, Bad Muslim: America, the Cold War, and the Roots of Terror*. New York: Harmony, 2004.
Marx, Karl. *Capital: A Critique of Political Economy, Volume 1*. Translated by Ben Fowkes. New York: Penguin Books, [1867] 1990.
Mayer, Arno. *The Furies: Violence and Terror in the French and Russian Revolutions*. Princeton: Princeton University Press, 2000.
Mink, Gwendolyn. *Wages of Motherhood: Inequality and the Welfare State, 1917–1942*. Ithaca, NY: Cornell University Press, 1996.
Neocleous, Mark. *Critique of Security*. Montreal: McGill–Queen's University Press, 2008.
Nesbitt, Nick. *Caribbean Critique: Antillean Critical Theory from Toussaint to Glissant*. Liverpool: Liverpool University Press, 2013.
Packer, George. *The Assassins' Gate: America in Iraq*. New York: Farrar, Straus and Giroux, 2006.
Paglen, Trevor. *The Blank Spots on the Map*. New York: Dutton, 2009.
Polanyi, Karl. *The Great Transformation*. Boston: Beacon Press, 1944.
Rama, Angel. *The Lettered City*. Translated by John Charles Chasteen. Durham, NC: Duke University Press, 1996.
Ray, Gene. *Terror and the Sublime in Art and Critical Theory*. New York: Palgrave Macmillan, 2005.
Reddy, Chandan. *Freedom with Violence: Race, Sexuality, and the US State*. Durham, NC: Duke University Press, 2011.

Redfield, Marc. *The Rhetoric of Terror: Reflections on 9/11 and the War on Terror.* New York: Fordham University Press, 2009.
Retort. *Afflicted Powers: Capital and Spectacle in a New Age of War.* London: Verso, 2005.
Rothberg, Michael. *Multidirectional Memory: Remembering the Holocaust in the Age of Decolonization.* Stanford: Stanford University Press, 2009.
Rushdie, Salman. *Imaginary Homelands.* London: Penguin, 1991.
Scott, David. *Conscripts of Modernity.* Durham, NC: Duke University Press, 2004.
Sherry, Michael. *In the Shadow of War: The United States since the 1930s.* New Haven: Yale University Press, 1995.
Simpson, David. *9/11: The Culture of Commemoration.* Chicago: University of Chicago Press, 2006.
Singh, Amritjit, and Peter Schmidt, eds. *Postcolonial Theory and the United States: Race, Ethnicity and Literature.* Oxford, MS: University Press of Mississippi, 2000.
Singh, Nikhil Pal. *Race and America's Long War.* Oakland: University of California Press, 2017.
Traverso, Enzo. *The Origins of Nazi Violence.* New York: The New Press, 2003.
Žižek, Slavoj. *Welcome to the Desert of the Real.* London: Verso, 2002.
———. *Violence: Six Sideways Reflections.* New York: Picador, 2008.

INDEX

2666 (Bolaño), 182n28, 198n17; genealogical imagination of, 17, 148; "The Part About Amalfitano" section of, 149–50, 168; "The Part About Archimboldi" section of, 153–55; "The Part About the Crimes" section of, 151–53; "The Part About the Critics" section of, 148–49; "The Part About Fate" section of, 150–51; the problem of representing totality and difference, 147–55
9/11: The Culture of Commemoration (Simpson), 201n6

Abu Ghraib, 42, 123, 138; photographs of abuse at, 80–81, 90–91
Adorno, Theodor, 76
aerial bombing, 50–51, 167, 200–201n3; the drone war, 52, 169, 172. *See also* Hiroshima, atomic bombing of; Nagasaki, atomic bombing of
Afflicted Powers (Retort group), 78–79, 102, 183n19
Afghanistan: Soviet invasion of, 59: U.S. Cold War involvement in, 59–60; U.S. War in, 12, 17, 18, 29, 89, 96, 121, 122, 123, 169, 170, 171, 173
Africa, 30, 53, 57, 127; the colonial imagination of, 44; European imperialism in, 15, 19, 138, 180n19; postcolonialism and, 106, 145; *See also* North Africa; Southern Africa
Agamben, Giorgio, 10, 42, 76; on "bare life," 84–85; colonialism and, 85–86;
on the concentration camp, 10, 83; on the ethics of witness, 86; on Guantánamo Bay detention camp, 10–11, 82–83; on the history of the concentration camp, 85; on the history of the "state of exception," 86, 87–88; on the *homo sacer*, 82–83; *Homo Sacer*, 10, 83, 84, 85, 93; on Nazism, 85–86; race and, 84–85; *Remnants of Auschwitz*, 87; *State of Exception*, 84
Ahmed, Mahmud, 1, 167
Algeria, 67
Allende, Salvador, 16, 58, 158
American Sniper (film), 171–72, 201n6
Amulet (Bolaño), 147, 150; overlapping temporalities, 16, 142–44
Anderson, Carol, 33
anticolonialism, 7, 44–45, 56, 63–64, 66–69, 71, 73, 92, 99, 108. *See also* anti-imperialism
anti-imperialism, 33, 44, 108, 194n6
Antilles. *See* Caribbean
anti-Semitism, W.E.B Du Bois on, 139
Apess, William, 107
Apocalypse Now (film), 173
Arab Mind, The (Patai), 123
Arab Spring, 17–18, 169–70
Arendt, Hannah, 7, 9; on capitalist accumulation, 3, 55; *Origins of Totalitarianism*, 185n42, 192n38; on "race imperialism," 192n38; on the rightlessness of displaced peoples

Arendt, Hannah *(continued)*
   post–World War II, 152, 199n33; on terror and the modern state, 45, 52
Armitage, Richard, 1, 2, 163, 167
Avelar, Idelbar, 69

Bacevich, Andrew, 182n49
barbarism, 5, 7, 44; civilization and, 17, 42, 64, 149, 150, 155–60, 161
"bare life," 11, 76, 152; exception and the politics of, 82–93
Baudrillard, Jean, 10, 76, 103, 166; *The Spirit of Terrorism*, 78–79
Beloved (Morrison), 135, 197n95
Ben Ali, Zine El Abidine, 169
Benjamin, Walter, 11, 42, 67–68, 93, 160; the Angel of History, 144–45, 168; "Critique of Violence," 67; *Jetztzeit*, 145; "Theses on the Philosophy of History," 11, 73, 186n56
Berg, Peter, 170
Bigelow, Kathryn, 18, 171
Billy Lynn's Long Halftime Walk (Fountain), 18, 174–75
bin Laden, Osama, 51; death of, 18 170–71, 201n4
biopower/biopolitics, 86, 138, 182–83n10, 193–94n86; biopolitical production, 11, 94, 98, 99, 100, 166; empire and, 96, 98; the "multitude" and, 99; race and, 83–84, 98; security and, 83, 96, 98; Social Security and, 23–24. *See also* Foucault, Michel
Black Jacobins, The (James), 63–66; "The Property" chapter of, 64
Blanco, Kathleen, 35–36
Blank Spots on the Map (Paglen), 137–38
Blaut, J.M., 193n64
Blowback series (Johnson), 8
Bobbitt, Philip, 8
Bolaño, Roberto, 73, 104, 140, 167–68; *2666*, 17, 147–55, 168; *Amulet*, 16, 142–44, 147, 150; *By Night in Chile*, 17, 155, 157–60, 181n28; *Distant Star*, 17, 155–57; the "infrarealist" movement, 142, 147; political formation of, 141–42; *The Savage Detectives*, 16–17, 142, 144–47

Bolshevism, 52, 160–61
Borstelmann, Thomas, 33
Bouazizi, Mohamed, 169
Bremer, L. Paul, 28
Bretton Woods system, 25, 26
Brief Wondrous Life of Oscar Wao, The (Díaz), 14, 15, 104, 106, 109, 138, 139, 167; the body as archive, 131–33; the fable and the rumor as a mode of historical witness, 129–31; the problem of historical witness, 127–29, 135–37; reading and writing as modes of historical witness, 133–35
Buck-Morss, Susan, 69, 190n58
Bullosa, Carmen, 143
Burke, Edmund, 76; the colonial sublime and, 46–49; on the French Revolution, 9, 74
Bush, George H.W., 12
Bush, George W., 105, 185n46, 200n3; administration of, 1, 12, 17, 28, 88, 163, 169, 180n18, 186n49, 209n6; the Bush Doctrine of preemptive war, 8, 39
Butler, Judith, 10, 76, 83, 166, 192–93n57; on the Abu Ghraib photographs, 90–91; on "bare life," 88–89, 91–92; *Frames of War*, 87, 91; on humanization and dehumanization, 90, 201n6; on the "new war prison," 87; on the normalization of exception, 87–88; *Precarious Life*, 10, 87, 88–91
By Night in Chile (Bolaño), 17, 155, 181n28; the complicity of literature and state violence, 157–60

Cambodia, 32
capital, 3, 28, 29, 34, 40, 67, 70, 73; finance capital, 15, 29, 119, 121, 138, 165; historical erasure and, 17, 141, 164; historiography of, 6–7, 45, 53–55, 127, 160, 167; imperial or global form of, 11, 55, 78, 93–101, 164, 166; "non-capitalist" strata, 55, 60, 61, 62, 100; real and formal subsumption of labor under, 98, 100–101; resistance to the violence of, 45, 71; security and, 21–29, 72; as spectacle, 76–77. *See also* capitalism; neoliberalism; primitive accumulation

Capital (Marx), 23, 102; theorization of primitive accumulation in, 53–55
capitalism, 3, 20, 26, 27, 32, 57, 68, 77, 80, 98, 102, 177; crises of, 29, 38–41, 165; "disaster capitalism," 150; "double movement" of, 40; laissez-faire, 55–56; limits of, 60–61; Social Security and, 23–24. *See also* capital; neoliberalism; primitive accumulation
Carby, Hazel, 194–95n7
Caribbean, 106, 137, 197n84; the advent of the New World in, 128, 131; imperialism in 107, 180n19
Casas, Bartolomé de las, 4
Central America, 57
Césaire, Aimé, 68, 75–76; *Discourse on Colonialism*, 9, 57
Chamoiseau, Patrick, 128
Chile, 17, 150, 160; military coup of September 11, 1973 in, 141–47; military repression of leftist politics in, 142; neoliberal transformation of, 59. *See also* Allende, Salvador; Bolaño, Roberto; Pinochet, Augusto
"choc en retour," 10, 56, 61, 75–76; of capitalist dispossession, 95, 109; Césaire's theorization of, 9; of colonial histories, 103, 109, 138; of colonial rationality, 104, 166; of emergency/ exception, 76, 85, 89
Churchill, Winston, 5–6, 57
civilization: "clash of civilizations" thesis, 4; the dialectic of civilization and barbarism, 17, 20, 42, 64, 149, 150, 155–60, 161; narrative of and racial thought, 34, 37, 71
Clark, T.J., 79
Cold War, 12, 93, 109; civil rights and, 33–34; counterterror in, 7, 58; emergency governance in, 39; the ideology of "free enterprise" in, 25, 57; Islamism in, 59–60, 68; "low-intensity" warfare in, 57–59; race and, 32–34, 57; U.S. neocolonialism and, 108
Cole, Teju, 73, 139, 140; *Open City*, 2, 14, 15, 104, 106, 109–18, 119, 126, 127, 138, 166, 167
Colombia, 57–58

colonialism, 14, 17; definition of, in relation to "imperialism" and "empire," 180n19; European colonialism, 15, 85, 108; internal and external processes of colonization, 107–8, 139; reification and, 67; U.S. neocolonialism, 108. *See also* anticolonialism; decolonization; postcolonialism; settler-colonialism
colonial modernity, 9–10, 19, 76, 86, 106, 140, 161, 180n19; alternative scholarly use of the term, 179n4; capitalist accumulation and, 3–4; contemporary theory and, 75; the dialectic of security and terror in, 3–8; the "discovery" of the New World and, 3, 19, 166, 177; emergency governance and, 4–5, 42; the "fukú" (curse) of, 136–37; race and, 4, 98; the United States and, 75, 106, 109, 136.
colonial rationality, 16, 68, 104; "choc en retour" of, 9–10, 56, 61, 75–76, 95, 166; decolonization and, 177; globalization of, 101, 165; historical erasure and, 140, 170; terror of, 115; the War on Terror and, 41
Colonizer's Model of the World, The (Blaut), 193n64
Columbus, Christopher, 3, 136, 177
commoditization, 41, 77, 100, 102
Commonwealth (Hardt and Negri), 94, 100–101
communism, U.S. opposition to in the Cold War; 32, 39, 58
concentration camp, 10; the ethics of witness and, 87; history of, 85; normalization of exception in, 83
Condition of the Working-Class in England, The (Engels), 182n8
Cooper, Anna J., 194–95n7
Cooper, James Fenimore, 106
Cooper, Melinda, 182–83n10
Critique of Judgment (Kant), 46
Cuba, 3, 85, 107, 177
Cuban Revolution, 57, 146
Cultures of War (Dower), 8

Daejon, 2, 118, 138
Danner, Mark, 189n38

Darío, Rubén, 154
Das Lied von der Erde (Mahler), 117
Day at the Beach, A (Schulman), 13
Debord, Guy, 10, 78, 80; on the "colonization of everyday life," 62, 76–77, 82; *Society of the Spectacle*, 77
decolonization, 58, 63, 68, 177
Deer Hunter, The (film), 173
dehumanization, 38, 86, 90–91; humanization and, 201n6
DeLillo, Don, 13
democracy: the "end of history" and, 75; "mythic" violence and, 71; the rhetoric of U.S. power in the world and, 33, 57, 94, 96, 174; Robespierre on terror as a "general principle" of, 6, 44–45
Department of Homeland Security (DHS), 28, 112
Derbyshire, Philip, 146
Díaz, Junot, 73, 140, 167; *The Brief Wondrous Life of Oscar Wao*, 14, 15, 104, 106, 109, 127–37, 138, 139, 167
Dieste, Rafael, 168
Dillon, Michael, 41, 182n10
Discourse on Colonialism (Césaire), 9, 57
dispossession, 21, 43, 119, 164; "accumulation by dispossession," 3–4, 95, 101, 165; neoliberalism and, 4, 27, 95, 165; primitive accumulation and, 22, 80. *See also* neoliberalism; primitive accumulation
Distant Star (Bolaño), 17; the complicity of literature and state violence, 155–57
Dominican Republic, U.S. occupations of, 131, 135–36
Dower, John W., 8
Du Bois, W.E.B., 139, 194n6: critique of U.S. imperialism, 107–108; on "double consciousness," 107; "The Negro and the Warsaw Ghetto," 139; *The Souls of Black Folk*, 107
Duchamp, Marcel, 168
Dudziak, Mary, 33

Eagleton, Terry, 74
East India Company, 48
Eastwood, Clint, 171
economic determinism, 102

Egypt, 59, 169
Eisenhower administration, 24
El Salvador, 57, 198n1
emergency: capitalist crises and, 38, 40–41, 165; "choc en retour" of emergency governance, 10, 76; colonial origins of, 36–38, 86, 185n42; executive power and, 36–39, 41, 86, 185–86n47; Hurricane Katrina, 92–93, 184n34; normalization of 11, 42, 73, 82, 87, 88, 93; the "real state of emergency," 73, 94, 103; security and, 36–42; of the state of nature, 4; in U.S. political history, 5, 39, 88; the War on Terror and, 41–42, 62, 72, 93, 96, 165, 167, 169. *See also* "state of exception"
empire, 1, 2, 8, 108, 110, 114, 135, 138, 140, 165, 177; Burke on, 47–48; critique of, 9, 10, 11, 75, 76, 95, 166; Hardt and Negri's theorization of, 93–101, 103, 166, 180n19; as a project of "counterterror," 25; terror of, 53, 81; United States as, 14–15, 25, 97, 105, 121, 122, 123, 126, 136, 181n22; violent resistance to, 68
Empire (Hardt and Negri), 93, 94, 96, 97, 100, 101, 193–94n86
Engels, Friedrich, 182n8
Enlightenment: capitalist rationality and, 21, 25, 149; Haitian Revolution and the radicalization of, 45; imperial expressions of, 5, 35, 44, 47, 97, 108, 160; philosophy of and the French Revolution, 53; race and, 139
Eurocentrism, 3, 74
Europe, 45, 68, 69, 86, 101, 148; "choc en retour" of colonial rationality to, 56, 85; processes of enclosure in, 3, 53, 97; Western Europe, 57, 58
European Central Bank (ECB), 29
European Economic Recovery Program (Marshall Plan), 25
European Union (EU), 29
Executive Unbound, The (Posner and Vermeule), 185–86n47
"Exterminate All the Brutes," 185n42

Falling Man (DeLillo), 13
Fanon, Frantz, 7, 45, 57, 61, 69, 73, 92; on anticolonial violence, 67–68, 70–71; on

decolonization and the creation of a new humanity, 68; *The Wretched of the Earth*, 56, 66, 67, 186n54

fascism, 7, 17, 56; the colonial genealogy of European fascism, 52, 161, 192n7; Italian fascism, 6

fear: bourgeois fear of revolution, 66, 74; the colonial sublime and, 49–50; drone warfare and, 51–52; insecurity and, 61; terror as, 179n8

Federal Aid Highway Act (1956), 25

Federal Reserve, 41

femicide (in Juárez), 150–53

Ferguson, Niall, 8

fetishism, 6, 78, 141, 151; commodity fetishism, 153; of the image, 79

Foucault, Michel, 8, 96, 182n10; on biopower and race, 83–84, 98; on the "boomerang effect" of European colonialism, 185n42; on neoliberalism, 26, 188n29; "*Society Must Be Defended,*" 83

Fountain, Ben, 18, 174

Frames of War (Butler), 87–88, 91, 192–93n57

France, 58. *See also* French Revolution

Frankfurt School, 190n58

freedom: capitalist articulations of, 25, 102; Enlightenment ideal of and the French Revolution, 53; the Haitian Revolution and, 65–66; liberal narratives of, 188n19; rhetoric of and U.S. global power, 32, 33, 39, 75; terror and the realization of, 62, 63, 65–66, 92

Freedom with Violence (Reddy), 188n19

French Revolution: the birth of the liberal state and, 6; foundational terrors of, 44–45, 52, 55; imperial conditions for, 52, 72, 164; theory and, 74–75. *See also* Jacobin Reign of Terror; Thermidorian Reaction

Frost, Laura, 181n23

Gaddis, John, 8

gender: the femicide in Juárez and, 151–53; Social Security and, 31–32;

Germany, 29; Allied bombing of, 116, 166; postwar reconstruction of, 188n29. *See also* Nazism/Third Reich

Gibson, Nigel, 190n68

Gikandi, Simon, 14, 106, 129

Gilroy, Paul, 30, 92, 114, 199n33

Glissant, Édouard, 14, 128, 135, 197n96

globalism, 11, 76, 95, 102, 103, 148

globalization, 11, 75, 78, 99–100, 101, 109; critique of, 93–94; "diffusionist" narratives of, 76, 94, 97, 98, 193n63; neoliberal narrative of, 94, 166; as a process of the global North evolving toward the global South, 62, 95; as the universalization of colonial rationality, 62, 101

global North, 11, 99; capitalist crisis in, 26, 29, 95; "choc en retour" of colonial rationality to, 61, 75–76, 89, 101, 104, 109, 165, 166

global South, 29, 57, 75, 180n13; dispossession in, 95, 101, 165; divide between the global North and the global South, 9, 25; the global North evolving toward the global South, 95; migration from, 36, 109, 165

Goldberg, David Theo, 4, 30

Goldman, Francisco, 143

Good Life, The (McInerney), 13

Gordon, Linda, 31

Gray, Richard, 181n22

Great Depression, 38, 185–86n47

Greengrass, Paul, 201n6

Gregory, Derek, 62, 138, 198n103

Guantánamo Bay (U.S. military prison), 11, 12, 42, 43, 82, 169; history of, 180n18; political subjectivity of those detained at, 83, 89, 91, 93, 192–93n57

Guatemala, 57

Guevara, Che, 69, 146

Gulf War, 81

Haitian Revolution, 7, 45; as represented in James's *The Black Jacobins*, 63–64; theory and terror in, 65–66

Hall, Stuart, 102

Hamid, Moshin, 73, 139, 140; *The Reluctant Fundamentalist*, 14, 15, 104, 106, 109, 119–27, 138, 167

Hanna, Monica, 134

INDEX · 213

Hardt, Michael, 11, 34, 76, 103, 166, 180n19; *Commonwealth*, 94, 100–101; *Empire*, 93, 94, 96, 97, 100, 101, 193–94n86; *Multitude*, 94, 96
Harvey, David, 4, 95, 100, 183n18
Hastings, Warren, 48
Hayek, Friedrich, 26
Hegel, G.W.F., 7, 45; on the French Revolution, 52, 53, 55; *The Phenomenology of Spirit*, 62; on terror and freedom, 62–63
Hersh, Seymour M., 201n4
Hilferding, Rudolf, 55, 56
Hiroshima, atomic bombing of, 57, 81, 136
Hispaniola, 3, 129; "discovery" of and the advent of colonial modernity, 3, 128, 137, 177. *See also* Santo Domingo
historicism, social-democratic, 11
history: the "end of history" thesis, 75, 93; erasure of, 2, 6, 13, 15, 17, 18, 72, 76, 109, 110, 117, 118, 119, 127, 138, 140, 141, 159, 167, 177; literature and the production of, 15–16; presence of, 15, 19, 107, 119, 129, 135, 139; project of bearing witness to, 15, 16, 104, 106, 109, 112, 118, 126, 127, 128, 133, 135–37, 139, 154, 166, 167, 168
Hobbes, Thomas, 30, 36; *Leviathan*, 23; the modern security project and, 3, 20, 97; on property, 23
Holocaust, 160, 185n42, 192n37
Homeland Security, 3, 5, 12, 20, 21, 75, 97, 103, 112, 126, 168, 175, 176, 177; capitalist logics of, 28; emergency governance and, 42, 161; narrative of, 62; racial logics of, 35–36, 124;
Homo Sacer (Agamben), 10, 83, 84, 85, 93
Hosseini, Khaled, 123
Hudson River School, 46–47
Huerta, Efraín, 132
Hughes, Aaron, 192n57
humanism, 87; anticolonial articulations of, 7, 64, 66, 68, 69
Huntington, Samuel, 4
Hurricane Katrina, 29, 81; connections to Hurricane Maria, 184n34; racial dynamics of, 35–36; as a state of emergency, 92–93
Hurricane Maria, 29, 184n34
Hussein, Saddam, 170

"Imaginary Homelands" (Rushdie), 136–37
imperialism, 3, 55, 56, 69, 93, 99, 109, 167; capitalist imperialism, 146; distinction between "imperialism" and "empire," 100–101, 180n19; Euro-American imperialism, 8, 15, 45; European imperialism, 19, 62, 85, 138, 180n19; "race imperialism," 192n37; U.S. imperialism, 107, 170. *See also* colonialism
indefinite detention, 10, 37, 87–88. *See also* "state of exception"
Independence Day (film), 187n13
India, 1, 53, 179n4; Burke on British Empire in, 47–48
individualism, 32, 190n58
infrahumanity, 30, 90
infrarealist movement, 142, 145, 147; manifesto of, 144. *See also* Bolaño, Roberto
International Bank for Reconstruction and Development (IBRD), 25
International Monetary Fund (IMF), 25, 27, 29
Iranian Revolution, 59
Iraq War, 2, 8, 12, 17, 18, 28, 29, 36, 51, 61, 89, 96, 114, 122, 123, 131, 135, 136, 169, 170, 171; narratives of veterans of, 172–77
Islamic State of Iraq and the Levant (ISIL), 68; the terror/counterterror cycle and, 69, 71
Islamism, radical, 69, 190n58; Cold War origins of, 59–60; decolonization and, 68. *See also* Qutb, Sayyid
Israel, 58

Jackson, Andrew, 185n43
Jacobin Reign of Terror, 6, 44
James, C.L.R., 45, 152; *The Black Jacobins*, 63–66
Jameson, Fredric, 21, 34, 102
Japan, 58; atomic bombing of, 81, 136. *See also* Hiroshima, atomic bombing of; Nagasaki, atomic bombing of

Jaures, Jean, 53
Jim Crow, 33, 57
Johnson, Chalmers, 8
Juárez, 150–53
justice: the imperial "state of exception" and, 96; Robespierre on terror as, 6

Kant, Immanuel, 7, 45, 76; the colonial sublime and, 5, 46–49, 51; on the "dynamic" sublime, 46, 77; on the French Revolution, 52, 55
Klein, Jennifer, 24
Klein, Joel, 183n11
Klein, Naomi, 28, 150
Korea, 32, 39, 57. *See also* South Korea
Kyle, Chris, 172, 202n8

laissez-faire economics, 26–27, 55–56, 188–89n30
Latin America, 141, 142, 143, 148, 160; "low-intensity" warfare in, 57; neoliberal transformations in, 17, 198n1
Lefebvre, Henri, 62, 77, 82
"Letter to Chamoiseau" (Walcott), 128
Lettered City, The (Rama), 154
Levinas, Emmanuel, 89–90, 91
Levinson, Brett, 150
liberalism: classical liberalism, 26; embedded liberalism, 26, 40–41; exception and, 36; New Deal liberalism, 27
liberal state: birth of, 6, 74; colonial modernity and, 3; emergency governance in, 36–37, 76, 88; imperial projections of, 88, 164; terror/violence as central to, 45, 52, 86, 188n19
Liberal Way of War, The (Dillon and Reid), 182–83n10
Life as Surplus (M. Cooper), 182–83n10
Lindqvist, Sven, 185n42
Lish, Atticus, 18, 175–77
Llosa, Mario Vargas, 131
Locke, John, 20, 30; "all the world was America," 22, 97, 164; "Of Property," 22–23; on the politics of exception, 36, 37–38; primitive accumulation and, 3, 22; *Second Treatise of Government*, 22
Lone Survivor (film), 170–71, 172

L'Ouverture, Toussaint, 45, 64, 65–66, 74. See also *Black Jacobins, The*
Lowe, Lisa, 188n19
Luxemburg, Rosa: on "non-capitalist strata" and the limits of capitalism, 55, 60–61, 62, 100; on primitive accumulation, 55

Mamdani, Mahmood, 69; on the Cold War origins of Islamism, 59–60; "good Muslim, bad Muslim" thesis, 4
Marshall Plan. *See* European Economic Recovery Program
Marx, Karl, 6–7, 29, 74, 98, 99, 100, 103; *Capital*, 23, 102; on primitive accumulation, 45, 53–55, 80
Matthews, Joseph, 79
Mbembe, Achille, 5, 92; on the colonial state of exception, 37–38, 86
McCarthyism, 32, 33, 39
McClintock, Anne, 200n1
McInerney, Jay, 1–2, 13
Melville, Herman, 106
Mexico, 17, 142, 148, 151, 168; 1968 massacre of student demonstrators in Mexico City, 16, 141, 147. *See also* Juárez
militarism, 18, 60, 126, 138, 175; capitalist militarism, 81; imperial/imperialist militarism, 51, 81, 94, 96, 114, 165, 170, 200n1; Prussian militarism, 149; racialized militarism, 36; of the United States, 57, 58, 102
military sexual trauma (MST), 173. *See also* post-traumatic stress disorder (PTSD)
Mink, Gwendolyn, 31
modernity, 4, 6, 20, 51, 71, 72, 84, 85, 86, 98, 161; capitalist modernity, 54, 177; enlightened modernity, 56, 64, 160; terror and the birth of, 45, 52–53, 86; Western modernity, 190n58. *See also* colonial modernity
modern state, 21, 43, 74, 97; centrality of terror to, 6, 7, 52, 62, 72, 164; the dialectic of security and terror and, 20; normalization of exception within, 5, 38; primitive accumulation and the rise of, 3; state terror and imperial accumulation, 52–56

Morrison, Toni, 135, 197n95
Mostern, Kenneth, 107
Mubarak, Hosni, 169
Multitude (Hardt and Negri), 94, 96
Muslim Brotherhood, 59
Mussolini, Benito, 6, 57

Nagasaki, atomic bombing of, 57, 81, 136
National Defense Education Act (1957), 25
National Emergencies Act (1976), 185n46
National Security, 3, 5, 20, 24, 25, 32, 183n11, 183n16; policy document NSC-68, 39
National Security Strategy of the United States of America (2002), 42
National Strategy for Homeland Security (2001), 42
Nazism/Third Reich, 33, 52, 57, 58, 87, 148, 154, 160; colonial genealogy of, 85–86, 161; as a response to Bolshevism, 160–61
Negri, Antonio, 11, 34, 76, 95, 98, 99, 103, 166, 180n19; *Commonwealth*, 94, 100–101; *Empire*, 93, 94, 96, 97, 100, 101, 193–94n86; *Multitude*, 94, 96
"Negro and the Warsaw Ghetto, The" (Du Bois), 139
Neocleous, Mark, 21–22, 36, 185n45
neoliberalism, 59, 61, 77, 95, 109, 142, 198n1; definition of, 4, 26; emergency governance and, 10, 29, 40–41, 76, 165; militarized neoliberalism, 14, 17, 61, 81, 82; race and, 34, 36; resistance to, 7, 70; security/securitization and, 4, 26–27; terror of, 60–62; the War on Terror and, 18, 28
Nesbitt, Nick, 64, 65, 66
New Deal, 27, 31, 38, 40, 185n45
New Imperialism, The (Harvey), 183n18
New Orleans. *See* Hurricane Katrina
New World, 46, 50, 86, 127, 139; colonial power in, 86; depopulation of, 164; "discovery" of, 3, 135; primitive accumulation in, 45, 53, 164; Santo Domingo as the "Ground Zero" of, 14, 128, 135, 137; settler-colonization of, 3, 15, 20, 43, 138, 177; slavery in, 19, 45, 64
Nicaragua, 17, 145, 198n1
North Africa, 18, 50, 114
Norway, 58

Obama, Barack, 17, 169–70, 172, 200–201n3
"Of Property" (Locke), 22–23
Open City (Cole), 2, 14, 15, 104, 106, 119, 126, 127, 138, 166, 167; contradiction between the form and content of, 15, 110, 117; historical erasure and historical recovery, 109–118; the relationship between the erasure and reproduction of colonial histories, 111, 114, 118; "reverse hallucination," 118
Organization of the Petroleum Exporting Countries (OPEC), 58
Origins of Totalitarianism (Arendt), 185n42, 192n38

Packer, George, 163
Paglen, Trevor, 137–38
Pakistan, 1, 119, 121, 123, 125, 169, 170
Patai, Raphael, 123
patriarchy, 74
Paz, Octavio, 143
Perle, Richard, 163
Phenomenology of Spirit, The (Hegel), 62–63
Philosophical Enquiry into the Origin of Our Ideas of the Sublime and Beautiful, A (Burke), 47–48
Pinochet, Augusto, 16, 141, 150, 156
Pitied but Not Entitled (Gordon), 31
Plural (magazine), 143
Poland, 85
Polanyi, Karl: on capitalism's "double movement," 40–41, 61; on laissez-faire as planned, 27, 56
Poor Law Amendment Act (1834), 23, 24
poor laws, 23–24
Posner, Eric A., 185–86n47
"post-9/11," 10, 43, 101, 161, 177; ahistoricity of the "post-9/11" periodization, 11, 20, 83, 88, 93, 103, 105, 163, 164; literary counterpoints to the "post-9/11" lens, 16, 73, 109, 140, 147, 160. *See also* rupture, trope of
postcolonialism, 67, 68, 101, 147; definition of, 14, 106; postcolonial melancholia, 114; the project of postcolonial witness, 135; the United States and, 14–15, 105–9, 126, 138, 139

post-traumatic stress disorder (PTSD), 173–74. *See also* military sexual trauma (MST)
Precarious Life (Butler), 10, 87, 88–91
Preparation for the Next Life (Lish), 18, 175–77
primitive accumulation, 3, 22, 80, 119, 164; as a condition of the French Revolution, 53, 64; Luxemburg on, 55; Marx on, 53–55; neoliberalism and, 43; securitization and, 28; terror of, 7, 45, 52, 53–55, 72
Project for the New American Century (PNAC), 12
property, 4, 32, 35, 36, 106: security and, 21–23, 41
Puerto Rico, 107, 184n34

al-Qaeda, 60, 68, 69, 114
Qutb, Sayyid, 68, 69, 190n58

race: biopolitics and, 83–85, 98; the birth of the security project and, 30; the Cold War and, 32–34; the colonial state of exception and, 38; Homeland Security and, 35–36; imperial order and, 98, 99; the liberal state and, 188n19; "naturalist" and "historicist" theories of, 4, 30; neoliberalism and, 34; Social Security and, 31–32; the War on Terror and, 4, 89, 90
Race and America's Long War (Singh), 188n19
Rama, Angel, 154
Ray, Gene, 187n7
Rebuilding America's Defenses: Strategy, Forces and Resources for a New Century (PNAC), 12, 13
Reconstructing Womanhood (Carby), 195n7
Reddy, Chandan, 188n19
Reid, Julian, 41, 182–83n10
reification, 6, 71, 77, 78, 152, 164; anti- or de-reification, 63, 64; historical erasure and, 72; literary resistance to, 141
Reluctant Fundamentalist, The (Hamid), 15, 104, 106, 109, 138, 167; the "atavistic and newfangled" nature of contemporary imperial forms, 14, 119–22, 126; the

historical and geographic myopia of the War on Terror, 123–25
Remnants of Auschwitz (Agamben), 87
Retort group, 51, 80–82 , 103, 119, 126; *Afflicted Powers*, 78–79, 102, 181n24
Rice, Condoleeza, 183n11
Rimbaud, Arthur, 146
Robespierre, Maximilien, 74; on terror and justice/virtue, 6, 44–45, 52
"Robespierre or the 'Divine Violence' of Terror" (Žižek), 70
Roosevelt, Franklin D., 5, 38, 39
Rothberg, Michael, 86, 181n22
Rove, Karl, 105, 138
Rumor of War, A (Caputo), 173
rupture, trope of, 72, 164, 177, 200n1; the false endings of the War on Terror and, 18, 170; literary counterpoints to, 16, 17, 18, 73, 109, 140, 147, 160, 172; the postcolonial and, 101, 106; the problem of representation and, 12–19; September 11, 2001, and, 1–2, 6, 12, 13, 18, 72, 75, 93, 101, 140, 163, 170, 181n22; the trope of aberration and, 160–61
Rushdie, Salman, 136–37
Russian Revolution, 58

Santayana, George, 163
Santo Domingo, 130, 131, 139; as "Ground Zero of the New World," 14, 135. *See also* Hispaniola
Savage Detectives, The (Bolaño), 16–17, 142, 144–45; as a counterpoint to the trope of rupture, 147; overlapping temporalities in, 146–47
Schmitt, Carl, 84
"Schooner 'Flight,' The" (Walcott), 137
Schulman, Helen, 13
Schwartz, Lynn Sharon, 13
Scott, David, 64
Second Treatise of Government (Locke), 22
Second World War, 8, 24, 33, 52, 56, 57, 86, 108, 110, 113, 139, 152, 153, 167
securitization, 4, 24, 27–28, 177
security: biopower and, 83, 96; capital/property and, 21–29; colonial modernity and, 3–8; contemporary theorization of, 9, 75; the dialectic of

security *(continued)*
    security and insecurity, 7, 17, 20–21, 24, 29, 40, 61, 140; the dialectic of security and terror, 5–6, 164–165; emergency and, 36–42; as the keyword of contemporary governance, 3; race and, 30–36. *See also* capital; emergency; Homeland Security; National Security; race; Social Security
self-determination, 33, 56, 108
September 11, 2001, 1, 12, 18, 89, 139, 187n13; critique of as a spectacle, 10, 13, 79, 166, 181n22; in film, 201n6; Homeland Security and, 20, 28; image-event of, 78, 79; as imperial nightmare, 51; in literature, 13, 181n22; melancholia and, 114, 124, 167; the narrative of the War on Terror and, 12, 51, 60, 72, 170; the *New York Times* "Portraits of Grief" series, 201n6. *See also* "post-9/11"; rupture, trope of
Sepúlveda, Juan Ginés de, 4
settler-colonialism, 180n19: emergency and, 37; modern racial thinking and, 30; the modern security project and, 3, 43; in the New World, 3, 15, 20, 43, 138, 177; the United States and, 15, 50, 106–108, 126, 188n19
Shariati, Ali, 68–69, 190n58
Sharpe, Jenny, 15
Simpson, David, 201n6
Singh, Nikhil Pal, 188n19
slavery, 19, 110, 112, 129, 152; primitive accumulation and, 3, 53, 54; resistance to, 63–66, 92
Smith, Adam, 54
Snyder, Rick, 41
Social Security, 5, 20, 42; capitalist logics of, 23–24, 27, 183n16; gender and, 31–32; history of, 23–24; National Security and, 24–25; race and, 31–32
Social Security Act (1935), 31
"*Society Must Be Defended*" (Foucault), 83, 184n42
Society of the Spectacle (Debord), 77
Somalia, 51–52, 169
Sorel, Georges, 69

Souls of Black Folk, The (Du Bois), 107
South Africa, 85
South Asia, 1, 46, 138, 167
Southern Africa, 50
Southeast Asia, 57, 58
South Korea, 78
sovereignty, 11, 84, 86, 87–88, 153; imperial sovereignty, 34, 95, 97; modern sovereignty, 4–5, 95; national sovereignty, 93, 94, 96; post-national sovereignty, 95; U.S. sovereignty, 97
Soviet Union, 33, 59
spectacle, 14, 90, 119, 153, 174; of the atomic bomb, 56; "shock and awe," 51; theorization of, 9–10, 76–82, 103, 166
Spiral (Danner), 189n38
Spirit of Terrorism (Baudrillard), 78–79
Spivak, Gayatri, 47
"Star-Apple Kingdom, The" (Walcott), 197n84
"state of exception," 161, 188–89n30; colonial origins of, 37–38; critical theorization of, 10, 76, 82–93; the "post 9/11" trope and, 2, 10; the War on Terror and, 41–42, 43, 72
State of Exception (Agamben), 10–11, 84
state of nature, 20, 23, 84, 97; emergency of, 4; essential terror of, 44, 71, 72, 164, 188n19; race and the imaginary of, 30, 37, 85; as a space of exception, 37–38; the sublime and, 46, 49
Stephen, James Fitzjames, 37
Stone, Oliver, 201n6
sublime, colonial, 46–51. *See also* Burke, Edmund; Kant, Immanuel
Suleri, Sara, 48
Surprise, Security, and the American Experience (Gaddis), 8
Suskind, Ron, 105

Tenet, George, 1
terror: colonial modernity and, 3–4, 44–45, 71–73; conjoined histories of "terror" and "theory," 9, 74; contemporary theorization of, 9, 74–76; definition of, 179n9; the dialectic of

security and terror, 5–6, 164–65; as a form of resistance to imperial power, 7, 62–71; as a method of imperial power, 5–6, 52–62; as a pretext for imperial power, 5, 46–52; terrorism, 60, 68, 88, 122, 169, 183n16. *See also* freedom; modern state; primitive accumulation; War on Terror

Testamento Geométrico (Dieste), 168

Texaco (Chamoiseau), 128–29

Thermidorian Reaction, 6, 44

"Theses on the Philosophy of History" (Benjamin), 11

Thinking Past Terror (Buck-Morss), 198n58

torture, 59, 157–59; the Abu Ghraib photographs, 90; in *Zero Dark Thirty*, 171–72, 201n4

totalitarianism, 32

Traverso, Enzo, 85, 161

Trujillo, Rafael, 130, 131, 132, 133, 135, 166

Truman, Harry S., 33, 185n46; administration of, 24; Truman Doctrine, 39

Trump, Donald, 200–201n3

United 93 (film), 201n6

United States: the "American Century," 56–60; as an empire, 14–15, 25, 97, 105, 121, 122, 123, 126, 136, 181n22; history of emergency governance within, 5, 36–42; the imperial logics of U.S. constitutionalism, 94–97; postcolonialism and, 15, 107–108; settler-colonialism and, 15, 50, 106–108, 126, 188n19. *See also* Homeland Security; National Security; Social Security; War on Terror

USA PATRIOT Act (2001), 39, 42

US Education Reform and National Security (Council of Foreign Relations), 183n11

U.S.-Mexico border, 12, 17, 154, 168

Vermeule, Adrian, 185–86n47

Vietnam, 32

Vietnam War, 57, 58, 59, 90, 109, 135, 136, 139, 173

Villalobos-Ruminott, Sergio, 158, 198n17

violence: anticolonial violence, 66–67; "mythic" and "divine" violence, 67–68; resistance and, 7, 45, 62–71; state violence and capitalist accumulation, 52–62; "subjective" and "objective" violence, 78. *See also* terror

Voice from the South, A (A. Cooper), 194–95n7

Walcott, Derek, 128–29, 130, 134: "The Schooner 'Flight'" (poem), 137; "The Star-Apple Kingdom" (poem), 197n84

War on Terror: Bush administration and, 1, 12, 17, 28, 88, 163, 169, 180n18, 186n49, 209n6; coloniality of, 75, 101, 103, 126, 138; conception of as both boundless and endless, 62, 81, 96, 140; the dialectic of security and terror and, 5–6, 122; false endings of, 17–18, 169–70; hidden geography of, 137–38; narrative of, 2, 6, 12, 60, 72, 105, 163; novels of War on Terror veterans, 173–77; Obama administration and, 17, 169–70, 172, 200–201n; the politics of exception/ emergency and, 5, 41–42, 82–83, 87–92, 93, 96, 97, 165; principal policy documents and laws of, 42; racial logics of, 3, 8, 35, 44, 49, 92–93, 123; representation of in film, 170–72; Trump administration and, 200–201n3; as a "war for the control of appearances," 51, 80, 102. *See also* rupture, trope of; September 11, 2001

Watts, Michael, 79; *Afflicted Powers* (Retort group), 78, 102, 183n19

Weimar Republic, 185n11

Welcome to the Desert of the Real (Žižek), 10, 78, 111, 166

white supremacy, 74

Whitman, Walt, 106

Wohlstetter School, 186n49

Wolfowitz, Paul, 51

World Bank, 25, 27

World Trade Center (film), 201n6

World Trade Organization (WTO), 27

Wretched of the Earth, The (Fanon), 56, 66–68, 186n54
Wright, Richard, 152
Writing on the Wall, The (Schwartz), 13

Yarborough, William, 58
Yemen, 51–52, 169

Yom Kippur War, 58
Young, Robert J.C., 180n19

Zero Dark Thirty (film), 18, 170, 171, 172
Žižek, Slavoj, 13, 70–71, 76: *Welcome to the Desert of the Real*, 10, 78, 111, 166

www.ingramcontent.com/pod-product-compliance
Lightning Source LLC
Chambersburg PA
CBHW020813230426
43666CB00007B/999